AF439069

Even though Michael James is writing about the world of Alzheimer's, where words themselves are erased, he finds the language to tell a remarkable story of love and devotion. We see him navigate this heartbreaking place, at first with Judith and then for Judith. He tells their story with honesty and clarity, educating himself and us along the way. He learns to focus on the moment at hand. Where we might expect to find despair, we find instead a place where empathy and compassion are alive.

– Stuart Kestenbaum, writer and poet, Maine Poet Laureate 2016 – 2020, former director of the Haystack Mountain School of Crafts

In the end, it's all in the details. Also in the beginning. Michael James writes like the artist he is, in the design he's created for telling this involving story, and his accomplished execution, which is mercilessly honest, astonishingly graceful, and always keeps in balance the difference between the beloved and the disease. It is no small feat and the result is quite unforgettable.

– Beth Gutcheon, best-selling author whose novels include
More Than You Know, Leeway Cottage, Gossip, and *The Affliction*

Dear Judy

A Love Story Rewritten by Alzheimer's

MICHAEL F. JAMES

Published by
Pine Eden Press
www.pineedenpress.com
email: admin@pineedenpress.com
6361 Camellia Court
Lincoln, Nebraska USA 68516

Distributed by
Redbrush LLC
1201 Infinity Court
Lincoln, Nebraska 68512
Tel. 855-379-6218 (toll-free)

Rachel Hadas excerpt from "Loneliness" from Strange Relation: A Memoir of
Marriage, Dementia and Poetry, copyright © 2011 by Rachel Hadas, published
by Paul Dry Books, Inc. Reprinted by permission of Paul Dry Books, Inc.
Additional permissions credits are listed beginning on page 268 of this book.

ISBN:
979-8-9876286-0-7 (deluxe softcover)
979-8-9876286-2-1 (trade paperback)
979-8-9876286-1-4 (e-book)

Library of Congress Control Number 2023903719

Printed in the United States of America

First Edition

9 8 7 6 5 4 3 2 1

For Clare and Francesca

*Except for immediate family members and a few close
friends, all individuals and businesses appearing
herein are referred to by pseudonyms, and all
identifying details have been modified.*

*Judy James, photographed in summer 2010, one year
into her younger onset Alzheimer's diagnosis*
(Photo by the author)

1

I was asleep while you were dying.
It's as if you slipped through some rift, a hollow
I make between my slumber and waking.

– Natasha Trethewey, from "Myth" in Native Guard

Dear Judy,

*I'm writing these lines a bit less than a month from what will
be the fifth anniversary of your death. That moment in the first
hour of what would be a predictably hot mid-August day in the
heartland marked the end of before and the beginning of after.
After has turned out to be good, more than good, and I have a lot
to be thankful for. More on that later.*

*You'd been unconscious for three days, and we knew that it
was a matter of hours and not much more than that. I was exhausted that Thursday evening and fell asleep earlier than usual
in the bed alongside yours. For about a week I'd been spending
not just the better part of each day with you, but also nights. I'd
moved your hospital bed as close as I could get it to the one in
which I slept, hoping that I'd hear your breathing, or any other
sound you might make, though I knew that was unlikely. While
your breathing had become much shallower that day, you made
almost no sound. A death rattle wasn't your style.*

*When I did wake suddenly as the air conditioner turned on
a few hours later, the room held blackness, and I stopped myself
before I reached for the nearby lamp, listening. Nothing. I turned
it on after a second or two and looked at your body and saw no*

movement. I reached to touch your face. It was cold. Your mouth was open, your jaw skewed slightly to the right. I put my hand behind your neck, and it was warm there. I moved it down to the center of your back, and that was still very warm. The nurse would tell me later that the heart works hard to hold onto life and that energy takes time to dissipate.

I kissed your forehead, my hand still around your neck. "It's over," I said, "your suffering is over. You have nothing more to lose. It's over." I gently tried but couldn't close your mouth. It was fixed there crookedly, left behind by your final exhalation.

You died around twenty-five minutes or so past midnight that early Friday morning, and I walked to the staff station to let Kristy, the night nurse, know. She and Audra, another on-duty attendant, came in and confirmed this. "We're so sorry," Kristy said. They left to phone the hospice nurse, who'd promised to come whenever you reached the endpoint. They also phoned the sheriff's department, and it wasn't long before a young officer showed up to record your death, the approximate time based on what I told him, and to let me know that I could go ahead and phone the crematory. I'd already arranged for one of their drivers to take your body up to the medical center, where a brain autopsy I'd requested would be carried out later that morning. The deputy seemed only slightly embarrassed as he came into the room, more than likely not because death was something he was uncomfortable with but because he was invading our privacy, this final intimacy, just when it was so palpable and fragile. He stayed only long enough to sign the necessary forms.

When I write about this now, it strikes me as both mundane and undramatic, but at the time it was momentous. Not in any flashy or urgent way because time seemed to have come to a full stop. Everything seemed suspended and unmoving, and space contracted around us in those last hours that we'd be a couple.

You'd come to the end of your life in a morphine-tempered coma, in a private room in a memory care facility where, when you moved in five months earlier, you were the youngest resident. Your self had just evaporated. Simply went. Somewhere? Nowhere?

Your body lay there for the next few hours, but I knew that I was profoundly alone and would be for the indeterminate future.

I played Bach from my smart phone through a set of speakers I'd brought to your room when we first moved you in, the solo cello suites performed by Yo-Yo Ma, and they felt right. You'd loved those too and had, in fact, listened to their entirety over several hours during a Sunday afternoon television broadcast a couple of months earlier, not long after you'd become wheelchair bound. You couldn't hold yourself up very well at that point, and I have a photo I took of you in front of that television set, listing to one side as you listened, just as I was about to leave to run some weekend errands. Listing to the right, the vessel of you slowly sinking, slowly ceding control.

When I returned a couple hours later, you were back in your room, and the staff told me you'd listened to the entire program. I imagine you could lose yourself in Bach, you could float away, you could find the creative core of yourself, even as everything you were was leaving you. You must have known that. To this day I admire your courage, your acceptance. You'd always said, "If I can't control something, I'm not going to worry about it." For most of your Alzheimer's journey, that conviction held.

Couples whose marriages last for many decades become profoundly connected in ways that aren't always apparent even to the parties. Those connections can sometimes be tense and complicated, but they amount to a bedrock so familiar and secure that when a fracture of some sort, however small, unexpectedly intrudes on that bedrock, it's felt vividly, even if it's hard to locate.

About eight years or so before Judy's death I felt a sudden jolt one day, something she said or did, something in the way she said or did it, something subtle but bizarre that was entirely unlike her, entirely off kilter. Though I've tried many times to remember what it was that threw me so, that filled me with such anxiety, I can't retrieve it. Later, as her disease progressed, these glitches would become familiar, and I'd understand them as manifestations of what was happening inside her brain. Words for common objects that she could no longer name, though she could often describe their function. Details she'd recount of some outing or excursion we'd just returned from, confounded with memories of similar experiences in her distant past or that she'd invent on the fly. Fictional information that she'd pull from some corner of her mind to pepper a conversation with a friend who might, or might not, see the fabrication for what it was. Glitches. Hiccups.

Whatever the first of these was, it stopped me in my tracks. In those seconds, as I asked myself what I had just heard or witnessed, she'd already moved past it, and so I chalked it up to a momentary craziness that came out of nowhere and disappeared back into nowhere, something that didn't mean anything. Meaningless things happen, and because four or five months would pass before another glitch upset our domestic equilibrium, I willingly discounted their importance. Two or three of these glitches in that first year of her slow departure were easy to dismiss because they didn't make any sense, and there was no pattern.

She'd always had a terrific memory and could recall numbers with uncanny exactness—an old telephone number, a combination lock code, a credit card number. That kind of mental acuity defined her, and I always felt that her smarts outdistanced mine by miles. It was reassuring that she had that kind of sharpness, that she could take the estimate of any situation and have it figured out before an average person would realize there even was a situation. There was nothing average about her in that respect.

I recall how fast she'd finish crossword puzzles, never looking up a word but sticking resolutely to her own accumulated vocabulary. No one could best her at Scrabble, a fact that caused our son Trevor endless frustration, though he was always willing to try—and fail. I'd given up trying years before; I loved her, but I didn't love a word game I had no hope of winning.

In the year of those early cognitive blips, those little but unnerving jolts that would give me sudden pause, our twin granddaughters were born, and it was logical that the excitement around their births would distract us from those first worrisome but shapeless symptoms. We were both fully engaged with our academic lives, Judy as a visiting lecturer and I as a professor and textiles department chairperson at the University of Nebraska in Lincoln. Career-wise we were both doing well, settled into the rhythms of both our campus community and the broader urban community surrounding it. We'd arrived at the millennium, an auspicious moment to uproot ourselves from our lifelong home and birthplace in southeastern New England and replant ourselves eighteen hundred miles away. Serendipity and timing had played roles in getting us there, and we'd gone with a lot of optimism. "Change is good" was our slogan.

The adjustment to university systems and protocols after years working as self-employed free agents was difficult at times in that first year. We embraced it together and as much for one another as with one another. She supported me over some initial rough patches, and I supported her in turn. Fairly quickly we found that we were living the life we'd hoped we'd find when we ventured westward. Things seemed as if they couldn't get much better.

When we started out more than twenty-five years earlier, we had almost nothing but our love for each other, a baby on the way, and what we'd been able to stuff into her powder blue hand-me-down Ford Mustang. I remember the overcast winter day in early 1972 that we packed it up and left her parents' home in coastal Massachusetts for the long drive to Rochester, New York. I know that we didn't say much to each other during that trip. I think we were both a bit overwhelmed by the future that was our true destination. We were leaving our pasts behind, and the uncertainties ahead scared us. To this day it mystifies me that she was willing to join her future with mine when the tentativeness of it all was so destabilizing. The courage that took, for both of us.

I was starting my second semester of graduate school, studying painting and printmaking. We managed to furnish a small apartment largely with bounty we rescued from street-side discards around our part of town the nights before trash pickups. The rare extravagance of some must-have second-hand store bargain gave us a way to make that street style special. We qualified back then for food stamp assistance, and with the meager revenue from my part-time custodial job on campus, her earnings doing clothing alterations by the piece for a local dress shop, the random ten- or twenty-dollar bills tucked into letters and greeting cards from our parents and other relatives, and the modest student loans I managed to secure, we got by.

Living on a shoestring budget wasn't such a stretch. Being a full day's drive from our families in New England gave us the independence we wanted as we stepped into parenthood and bonded into a functional and efficient family unit. We were fully on our own and liked that. The Whole Earth Catalogue[1] was our go-to resource for finding our way. We gladly, if maybe a bit na-ively, committed our brains and hands to construct the life that our ideals and values pointed us toward.

We were part of that group of people known today as "cre-atives," and making things came naturally to us. She'd learned to sew not long out of kindergarten, and once she was competent enough, her wardrobe always attested to those skills. Like her, in childhood I'd had my own mother's home sewing industri-ousness as a model for making do and making from scratch. We might have grown up poor, but at Easter my siblings and I never looked poor. I taught myself to sew in high school, mostly by looking over her shoulder.

By the time Judy and I moved in together, impressing her with my indifference to traditional gender roles was a well-honed strategy to further endear myself to her. I'd become interested in Americana of all sorts, and particularly patchwork and quilt making. These were undergoing a revival at the time. We'd both been attracted to the ingenious ways that women's creativity had found outlets in quilt patterns and their myriad variations. I knew no better way to learn about them than to make them, and she encouraged me.

Once I'd wrapped up my Master of Fine Arts degree, my enthusiasm for painting was, coincidentally, on the wane. I might have become a respectable painter, but that would have required more ambition and singlemindedness than I felt I could bring to it without difficult sacrifices on the home front. I wanted to be the hands-on parent and partner in the homemaking enterprise that I knew Judy wanted me to be. I aspired to a different marital paradigm, as she did, and creating it was our priority.

It took me only a few months to replace paints, inks, canvas, and brushes with fabric and thread. By any conventional standard she should have wanted me out peddling my art degrees for some teaching position or giving up artistic aspirations altogether for the security of some entry-level salary-with-benefits employment. We discussed those options at the time, and I even applied for some private school art instructor positions. With more wishful thinking than experience, though, I was no potential employer's idea of a promising candidate.

We hung on in Rochester for another year, but my stalled prospects and northwest New York State's relentless winter overcast finally pushed us back to the coast. We knew by then that we wanted our toddler son to grow up in the embrace of his extended family, most of whom were living within a few miles of where we'd both been raised. We settled in Somerset, Massachusetts, her hometown. Sitting on the Taunton River across from Fall River, it was then and remains one of those unremarkable white- and blue-collar bedroom communities with an interesting but largely forgotten history. New England has them in abundance, places where the professional class could feel they'd escaped and where the working class could feel they'd arrived.

What we managed to create for ourselves there over the course of the next quarter century was almost entirely thanks to needle and thread. Common tools and simple techniques could transform fabric into singular expressions of creative vision, and we figured out how to do that. Judy's patience and precision made her an expert tailor and dressmaker, and she knew how to teach those skills to others. She grew a loyal student base in the region that gave her and a business partner the confidence to eventually open their own retail fabric and sewing business. It thrived, as they did, for a full decade. By the time they sold it ahead of our move to the Great Plains, it embodied the notion of real-world accomplishment that Judy had aspired to all those years.

I knew right out of the gate in 1970s America that to be taken seriously as a man who made quilts, those quilts would need to break with tradition. Because I was comfortable with the notion that traditions existed to be challenged, I was game to try. *Stitch like a quilter, think like an artist*, I told myself. Energized by a surplus of self-confidence and ambition, I gradually built a freelance studio career making one-of-a-kind quilts, exhibiting them, writing and speaking about them, and teaching unconventional approaches to quilt design to other textile enthusiasts the world over.

Since our first tentative years together we'd each crafted careers for ourselves and a shared lifestyle compatible with those careers. We'd raised and educated a son who was confident and successful in his own right. We'd traveled a fair amount, and we'd grown a very wide network of friends both at home and abroad. We had no pressing reason to change anything, although, as we neared fifty, our daydreams and casual musings started to bubble up from a kind of vague existential restlessness.

"If you could live anywhere," we'd ask one another, "where would you want to live? If you knew you only had a few years to live, how and where would you want to live them? What have you always wanted to do that you haven't because life got in the way?"

Judy said that she wanted to go back to university to study textile art, to take the skills she'd refined in making clothing from a functional and practical to a more artistic level. I said that my enthusiasm for leading short-term, one-off workshops teaching basic color and design principles was just about exhausted. What a stimulant it would be to teach career-focused students working toward degrees in a college program where I could see them develop over time. What a novelty it would be after years as a self-employed freelancer to be salaried, to have a job with benefits, to have the prospect of building some kind of retirement nest egg.

When I was asked to join an international advisory board for a newly established research center at the University of Nebraska in Lincoln, a door opened. The research focus in question was the history and practice of quilts and quilt making. The gift to the university of a collection of nearly a thousand quilts was the original incentive that prompted the organization of that first board. I guess I'd made enough disruptive noise as a non-traditionalist in the field that my alternative opinions held some value.

By the time I attended their second annual summer meeting, I'd been seriously searching for a full-time art school position for close to a year, with no luck. Like thousands of newly minted MFAs, I was diligent about the pursuit. Problem was, I wasn't newly minted. I had almost no university teaching experience, always a minimum requirement. If I were realistic, teaching semester-long courses as a temporary lecturer was probably the best I could hope for in the crowded East Coast market. Shift my focus to some other part of the country, though, and chances might improve. I pivoted just as the quilt center's academic home at the time, the university's department of textiles, caught on to the alignment of my resumé with an open position in design foundations they had backburnered.

"How do you feel about moving to Nebraska?" I asked Judy while we waited for my luggage at Providence's Green State Airport the evening I returned from that second board meeting. She'd have had every reason to dubiously respond, "Nebraska?

Seriously?" In fact, that's what most of our friends said when, a few months later, we confirmed that I'd signed a contract and we'd be relocating to what the more sports-oriented among them recognized as the home of some of the most fervent football fans on the planet. "Really?" one friend said. "If you'd told me you were moving to London or Paris I wouldn't have been surprised. But Nebraska? Really? Nebraska?"

To Judy's credit, she didn't hesitate. "Let's do it," she said. "I'm ready to sell the business. I want to live somewhere else. Let's just go."

And so, we did.

For the first time in nearly four decades of marriage we were earning enough to cover all our needs and more. We were finally able to begin to save for retirement, one of the attractions of the day job offer that had added to its appeal. The years of running large credit card balances and hoping always that something would come along so that we could pay them off were behind us.

Although I'd achieved a respectable level of success as a visual artist and writer with a couple of books to my credit, and she'd successfully co-launched a retail business that had a faithful clientele and was meeting payroll and paying her bills on time, those years back east were always conditioned by financial stresses. Though proximity to our families and their emotional support and encouragement helped, that could sometimes act as an irritant. I recall my mother-in-law saying within earshot more than once, "Someday when Michael has a real job...," an ego-bruising affirmation that she didn't take artistic enterprise— at least my artistic enterprise—seriously. The irony there was that when the "real" job came along, it turned out to be half a continent away, which meant that our need for financial and career security would ultimately take Judy from her hometown and leave her widowed mother alone. "We'll come back often," she reassured her. We kept that promise, though there was a second irony in our putting such a great distance between us just as Flo entered her eighties: she would outlive her daughter.

When Judy sold her business ahead of our move, she'd already made the decision to enroll in the textile design master's degree program. For her, the opportunity to go to graduate school at that point in life was payback for the many years of long workdays and tight retail margins. The time for serious creative work that had eluded her for so many years was now available, and becoming a graduate teaching assistant in a design program gave her entrée to both visual arts studios and the classroom. She shone in both domains.

I'm not sure I ever told her how much pride I felt watching her grow into both roles she assumed, that of student and that of university teacher. She learned quickly and had a natural gift for generously transferring to others the knowledge and skills she'd acquired. The fact that I was on the faculty in the department in which she was working toward her degree meant that I knew both the territory and the personnel that populated it, and I could see how easily both the faculty and the other students related to her, how comfortable they were around her. Most had no trouble confiding in her because she was a good listener; she gave them her full attention and was never judgmental. Those are good qualities to have in just about any situation, and especially in a small, close-knit academic department.

Once Judy was awarded her degree, she launched straightaway into a disciplined studio practice, and her textile art grew richer and more complex. She'd discovered processes of fabric manipulation and transformation that were a perfect fit for her aesthetic sensibilities, and she quickly turned them to her own expressive purposes. She became a member of a tribe of passionate makers who turned folded, pleated, clamped, stitched, printed, dyed, and over-dyed lengths of fabric into visual art that straddled the borderland between the physical and the immaterial. She'd found a new way to communicate at just that point in her life where she had things to say and the self-confidence and the skills with which to say them.

What we didn't know at the time was that the disease had already left the starting gate, its assault on the neurons in her brain launched, stealthily, imperceptibly. In cases of younger onset Alzheimer's, as we'd learn later, it's typical that the destructive process of the buildup of tau and amyloid proteins in the brain begins years before the first symptoms appear.[2] It's likely that in Judy's case, as she was refining new creative skills and applying them in the studios where she worked and the classrooms where she was teaching, Alzheimer's was already beginning the program of erasure that it would carry out so relentlessly and completely, robbing her of all that new knowledge and of so much more. Her brain was working at cross purposes, and neither she nor I had the slightest idea.

2

Once the realization is accepted that even between
the closest human beings infinite distances continue
to exist, a wonderful living side by side can grow up,
if they succeed in loving the distance between them
which makes it possible for each to see the other
whole against the sky.

— Rainer Maria Rilke, in *Letters*

Dear Judy,

I want to ask you, "Do you remember…" such and such, and then I catch myself. You're not here. You're nowhere. You're gone. Permanently, forever, gone. Since I don't believe in an afterlife, I can't place you in some other dimension of reality or surreality. You live only in my imagination now, and in addressing you, I'm addressing me. But it's comforting, somehow, for you to be entirely in my head, because there, you are. I can believe that you're in on this narrative because for so many years, for more than four decades, you were. It's reassuring somehow, more convincing, to speak to you than about you.

Judy was always pretty good with money—one of us had to be— so I left her to it. My tendency to see wants as needs sometimes ran counter to her very rational and unwavering frugality, but most of the time we avoided conflict. She managed the checkbook, paid the regular flow of household bills, and each year she and her calculator would take a month or so to get everything ready for the annual tax filing. I was content to remain fairly ignorant of the whole process since she did it so well and even seemed to enjoy it. Numbers and calculations were her thing. For close to twenty years before our big relocation westward, she and our accountant, John Silvia, had that annual rendezvous all to themselves. I think I may have joined them once, at most twice. When her skill sets outshone mine, I never hesitated to stand out of her light.

Even after our move, Judy continued that association long distance, the combination of paper mail, email, scans, and phone conferences seemingly easier than finding a new accountant with whom she'd be going back to square one. Not until John died and his firm closed were we forced to enlist the help of a new accountant closer to home.

We'd met Meg through a local nonprofit for which she was serving as volunteer treasurer and were already comfortable around her. She agreed to take us on as clients, and she quickly proved to be as smart and easy to work with as John had been and just as concerned for our interests. "Do you have a financial advisor?" she asked as we were wrapping up our first just-ahead-of-filing meeting at her office. We didn't. "You need one, and here's who you should call." I liked that she saw our need before we did and directed us so matter-of-factly. A week later we were sitting in Roxanne's office.

Roxanne was something of an anomaly. The only woman in a suite of offices populated by about a dozen advisors working for a national firm headquartered in the central US, she was at the time one of only about 15 percent of all financial advisors who are female.[3] That distinction suited us well. We'd come of age as second-wave feminism achieved prominence, and both of us were well past having any doubts that women could and did operate professionally as well as, and often better than, their male counterparts. "I like her," Judy whispered to me after Roxanne stepped out of our first meeting to ask her assistant to copy some documents we'd brought along. I did too.

Roxanne was the opposite of buttoned up. A natural extrovert, she was also something of a comic whose sense of humor and contagious laugh conditioned every meeting we had with her. We always knew we'd be greeted warmly each time we stopped by. The notion she held that her clients were family meant that we were always as comfortable with her as she was with us. It was easy to trust her and to this day, so many years later, I still do.

In hindsight, I know now that those initial getting-to-know-you appointments with Roxanne took place just about the time Judy had settled into the first stage of the disease. By then the rare "glitches" as I called them—jarring moments when her forgetfulness didn't match the everyday variety, instances when she inverted some step-by-step process that she'd done a thousand times and couldn't figure out what step she'd missed—were becoming more frequent, and I was having a harder time rationalizing them to myself and ignoring them. Still, I didn't say anything to her about my concerns. I really didn't want to admit that I had concerns. If she did, she must have felt the same way. "I just forget things" she'd say. "Everyone forgets things." And so, we'd let it go.

That was a particularly busy and stressful time for both of us, but stressful in a good way because we were both enjoying the work we were doing. She was teaching several courses on an ongoing basis as a visiting lecturer, and those required a fair amount of preparation that competed with the studio work she needed to create for the exhibition commitments she'd made. I was chair of the department in which Judy was doing some of her teaching, so my workload was heavy too, and like her, I had numerous exhibition commitments to fulfill. So, while we were energized about the work we were doing, the intense pace required that things run smoothly. There wasn't much leeway for increasingly noticeable "hiccups."

In fall 2007, I made a weeklong trip to Japan to participate as a jury member in the selection process for an international textile art competition. I'd been to Japan on business-related trips numerous times, and Judy had come along at least twice. We both loved the country, its people, its cuisine, its side-by-side contrasts of cutting-edge modernity and steeped-in-tradition customs and values. It was the third trip to Asia that I made that particular year aboard my usual air carrier, and when I arrived at Narita airport for my return flight, I learned that my frequent flyer status had moved up a category. Thanks to that, I'd be making this trans-Pacific leg in first class, a welcome and unexpected loyalty perk. I phoned to touch base with Judy from the first-class lounge, excited both about the upgrade and that I'd soon be home to resume our normal day-to-day life. After nearly three decades as a regular business traveler, the sense of relief and well-being that wrapped around those unfailingly sweet homecomings never diminished.

Among the amenities of the first-class cabin on that flight was a generous individual selection of DVDs. Technology advances seem to come at such lighting speed now that we easily forget how things like movies were delivered on flights even a decade or two past. In that first-class seat, the traveler inserted the disc into a player and watched it on a small screen built into the compartment. Flipping through the offerings, I stopped on a copy of the film *Away from Her*, which had been released a year or so earlier. Judy and I had wanted to see that film when it was screened at the campus cinema, but we couldn't carve out the time. Figuring it was a film she would like, I wondered if I should pass on it and wait for an opportunity when we could see it together, but I was curious. I'd read reviews of the film and knew that it centered on a long-married couple dealing with the wife's struggle with Alzheimer's disease. I may have had a hunch, I don't know, but something told me to take advantage of the relative solitude I found myself in and watch it.

Based on Canadian writer Alice Munro's short story "The Bear Came Over the Mountain," the film stars Julie Christie, an actor whose career we'd followed since her "Dr. Zhivago" success in the mid-1960s. We'd loved her performance in Robert Altman's film "McCabe & Mrs. Miller" that we saw together when we were first dating in the early 1970s, and since then we usually made the effort to see whatever new film came along in which she was featured. That she played a professor's wife in this new film added to my interest, though I wouldn't realize for some time the extent to which we'd eventually share in this fictional couple's experience.

With the cabin lights darkened so passengers could more comfortably sleep, I settled into the recline of the lay-flat seat to watch the film. Ten or fifteen minutes into it, I suddenly found myself in tears, moved by the characters' obvious closeness and sobered by the sense of the familiar in their interactions. The disbelief, anxiety, and sorrow on the husband's face as he quietly witnesses his wife place a freshly washed frying pan in the freezer was particularly affecting. Although the lapse represented by her misplacing the pan was more dramatic than anything I'd witnessed in Judy's behavior to that point, I fully understood his reaction to it. I stopped the film and ejected the DVD, grateful for the cover of darkness as I wiped my eyes. It would be another year or so before I'd watch the film through. By then I'd know it was our forecast.

When, at another of our periodic meetings with Roxanne a few months later, she asked if we'd be interested in considering long-term care insurance as we planned for our future, I said yes almost too quickly. Although I'd not yet said anything to Judy about my growing concerns, I realized that my suspicions weren't too far below the surface. That I was feeling a certain urgency even at that early stage should have told me that we needed to see a medical professional. If we could get signed on for long-term care insurance, though, we'd have something in place if ever it came to that. The notion was reassuring.

With the application completed, we each waited for a phone interview from a representative of the insurance carrier. The calls came one afternoon a week or two later, each of us taking our own on our respective phones in different parts of the house. Roxanne had given us a general idea of what to expect when we spoke with the agent. We'd go over personal and health information in the application, followed by a series of questions that, I'd later learn, constituted a mini-mental status exam. "They'll just want to make sure that your minds are intact," Roxanne had said with the disarmingly hearty laugh that was her trademark. "You're both in great shape, you exercise, no pre-existing conditions. You'll nail it." I was optimistic.

When Judy and I compared notes afterward, I concluded that the questions we'd been asked were pretty much identical. Prefaced by a warning not to write anything down, the voice on the phone began. "What is today's date?" "What year is this?" "What season is it?" "What city do you live in?" "Who is the governor of your state?" and so on. "Now I'm going to give you three words that I want you to remember. We'll come back to them later. Apple. Penny. Table. Repeat them." *Apple. Penny. Table.* When, after having me count backwards from 100 by sevens, make up a sentence using the word *elephant* and one using the phrase "like clockwork," and answer one or two other questions, she asked me to recall the three words she'd asked me to repeat. Apple. Penny. Table. Easy peasy.

A couple days later I got a call from the insurance underwriter. "We'd like to send a nurse to your home to conduct a more in-depth interview with your wife, Mr. James," she said. "It's routine; we find that some folks do better face-to-face than over the phone." Judy didn't seem surprised nor dubious. "Whatever," she said, "that's fine." I guess I was less surprised than concerned. My already elevated anxiety rose a little bit more.

The follow-up interview lasted about an hour. Judy sat with the nurse in the living room, and I didn't hear much at all from the remove of my downstairs office. "It was fine," she said afterward. "She was nice. Asked a lot of the same questions."

"How do you think you did?" I asked.

"Oh, fine, it went fine." And that was it. As far as I know, she didn't think about it again.

At least until the formal determination letters came about a month later, after medical records had been forwarded and other assorted documentation provided. I was approved for coverage. Judy was denied. "Failure to meet minimum cognitive standards" the letter said.

"We have got to find out what's going on," I said. "If you're denied coverage like this because of cognitive problems, then something's going on." She didn't seem concerned in the moment and reassured me that she was fine. "But this isn't fine," I protested. "I've been seeing these glitches in your thinking and your behavior now for almost two years, and we can't go on ignoring them. This is a huge red flag!" I sensed that she wasn't nearly as alarmed as I was, that she didn't want to pursue it, that she just wanted to let it go, but as she shrugged, "I feel fine," I saw that she'd at least humor me. "Go ahead, make an appointment for me if you want to," she said. "But I'm not the one who's calling the doctor."

Cognitive problems of the type Judy was experiencing can have lots of causes. We realized this much from the outset. Years before, she'd been thoroughly examined and tested when, one morning, she'd awakened realizing that something felt different in her relationship to the space around her. She couldn't pinpoint what it was, and only a few hours later, in the middle of a yoga class, did she realize what was wrong. She had no hearing in her right ear. She'd gone to bed the night before hearing in both ears. She woke deaf in one. This led to appointments with specialists over several months' time, all leading to inconclusive results. They were certain she didn't have a tumor, there was no evidence of a stroke, but they couldn't rule that out completely. Judy's father had suffered severe hearing loss over the course of his adulthood, and they agreed that there was a small chance hers could be connected to his, though his had developed very gradually, not overnight. In the end, though, they couldn't really explain it. By that point she'd adapted, and it became something she lived with, that she rarely mentioned. She liked to tease me that being deaf in that ear was really an advantage. "When you snore, I just roll over so my deaf ear is up," she'd say. That was classic Judy, turning a deaf ear to things over which she had no control.

Aging is another culprit we think of when, on either side of sixty, we realize we're misplacing our keys or mobile phone or eyeglasses or whatever it is more frequently. It becomes a bigger challenge to walk ourselves backward through half a day's actions and activities trying to remember where along the way we put them down or slid them out of sight. Judy was just fifty-nine when I'd started noticing those first alarming symptoms, and Alzheimer's wasn't a word that rolled easily off our tongues, certainly not at that point.

A year or so before the insurance denial she'd come off menopause-related hormone replacement therapy. "Could it be that?" we asked ourselves. In her late forties she'd had a hysterectomy after years of recurring endometriosis, and over the next decade the hormone therapy had helped to relieve her of several menopausal side effects. At the health maintenance organization where our medical care was centered during those years, her longtime gynecologist had served as her primary care physician. When we relocated from the East Coast, she again sought out a gynecologist who continued monitoring her hormone therapy. They eventually agreed that Judy could stop that therapy, recommending that, going forward, she find herself a primary care physician, an internist or family practitioner.

True to form, she procrastinated, so it wasn't until that insurance denial that she finally acted. I was satisfied at the time with my own physician, and his office was willing to give Judy an appointment, so she agreed to see him. Two weeks later we found ourselves in Dr. Breyer's examining room.

Physically Judy was in great shape. Blood pressure normal, cholesterol levels good, weight on the low end of what was considered a good range for a woman her age and height. She exercised regularly as she had for decades—yoga, Pilates, and workout classes at the gym, a fair amount of walking, some cycling. She was disciplined with her food intake, and our daily diet aligned closely with the so-called "Mediterranean diet" widely touted as a key to longevity. Even the act of eating for her was always considered and deliberate. She ate smaller portions slowly and harangued me that I ate too much and too fast. She'd be pleased to know that these numerous years later I still make her breakfast granola recipe and have learned to enjoy it with low-fat unflavored yogurt. She leaned on me about that. I came around.

As far as taking preventive measures to avoid the host of illnesses associated with aging, she was doing everything right.

Dr. Breyer listened patiently as I explained about the long-term care insurance denial that had landed us in his examining room. "Okay, I'm going to ask you some questions now," he said, and Judy's third mini mental status exam began. At that point she was answering most of the standard questions correctly. She could still count backward from a hundred by sevens accurately, if a bit slower than she would have a few years before. She could still sketch a decent clock face representation of ten o'clock, could write a simple subject-verb-object sentence, and she knew what a hammer was used for. She couldn't recall three words he'd asked her to remember five minutes earlier. She didn't recall that he'd even asked her to remember those three words.

"I think we'll schedule you for an MRI," he concluded.

Less than a week later we had the results. "No tumor, no sign of stroke," Dr. Breyer said as he handed her the hospital's exam result form. "The scan shows some mild generalized cerebral atrophy, and this isn't uncommon in people your age. There's some evidence of small vessel ischemic disease, but again, in someone your age that isn't unusual." I'm sure we asked him to elaborate on those conditions since at that point our understanding of the brain's pathology was rudimentary at best.

"There are a number of neurologists here in town, and I think it's worth seeing one of them," he said when the exam was over. "I'd like you to have a specialist's opinion, and any one of them is likely to be more up to date on possible treatment options than we are here. And if there's anything we missed, they may spot it." Judy said nothing, but I could read the unease in her posture. "We'll set up an appointment for you with a doctor that several of my patients have been happy with. His name is Morrison," Dr. Breyer continued. "My office will get back to you in a day or two." If he suspected Alzheimer's disease, he wasn't saying.

For us Friday evenings had always been the payback for a full and demanding work week, and we especially looked forward to those first few hours of weekend down time. Whether we were alone together or with friends, it was an opportunity to debrief, to sort the weekend's "to-do" list, and to relax knowing that no immediate deadline was pending. We enjoyed a lake view from the back porch of the home we'd purchased at the time of our move, and on Fridays during the milder months we'd nearly always enjoy a glass of wine there before heading out to dinner. Small pleasures like that shared across four decades had gone a long way to keeping our marriage on an even keel.

Like several university colleagues and some members of the city's art scene, we were faithful patrons of Caffè Milano and that was our Friday dinner destination at least two or three times a month. Besides serving the best espresso in the entire region, their Friday evening family-style meal had developed a devoted following. The husband-and-wife team at the helm of the operation fine-tuned old family recipes and rotated them in succession over several months, one fixed-price option a week usually served with a salad and a selection of good Italian wines. We both liked that we weren't having to make many choices after days of work-related decision making. A meal was put in front of us, a lasagna with béchamel sauce this week, a chicken with penne the next, and everyone in the restaurant partook. It was simple and convivial, and we felt at home.

Because its relatively small dining room limited seating and its no-reservations policy was inflexible, lines at Caffè Milano's door for Friday dinner were part of the experience. It was a good way to meet new patrons or to catch up with acquaintances equally faithful to the restaurant's formula. Danilo—the owner, maître d', bartender, and cook—kept an eagle eye on his turnover. If you were a couple and there were only four-toppers or six-toppers available, you'd be quickly paired up with table mates you might have seen there before, or not. For most patrons Caffè Milano was one way, with little effort, to expand their circle of friends. In the years that we frequented the place, we did just that numerous times, bonding with some of those guests who remain friends even now, many years after tight margins and staffing challenges forced Danilo to close the enterprise.

I know Judy didn't remember a particular couple we shared a four-topper with once, possibly twice. They'd been introduced to us as Tom and Ruthie Morrison. He was a physician and she a former dancer who now owned a ballet school in town. Like many of these after-school academies, it provided youthful casting for the local performing arts center's annual *Nutcracker*. Where he was quiet and guarded, she was outgoing and personable, the type of person who, unlike her spouse, could talk animatedly with anyone and was entirely comfortable assigned to a restaurant table with a couple of diners she'd never met before. That's how we became acquainted.

Though the Morrisons weren't part of the regular crowd at Caffè Milano, we'd crossed paths with them there and had seen them at the fitness center where, like them, we were members, and a few times at the campus cinema. With her we quickly figured out that no more than two or three degrees of separation linked us through a half-dozen people in our respective social networks; with him, if there were social connections, we'd never discover them. He seemed relaxed enough talking about the food on our plates or the weather that day or the prospects of the university's volleyball team, but where just about any other subject was concerned, he was a closed book. When I asked him what his medical practice focused on, he pretended not to hear the question as he lifted another forkful of pasta to his mouth.

When Dr. Breyer's office called to let us know they'd scheduled Judy's neurological exam, we learned Dr. Morrison's specialty. "Well," I remember telling her, "at least we know he likes Caffè Milano. That's a plus."

As we were ushered into his office a few weeks later, I wondered if he felt as awkward shaking hands with me as I felt once I realized he didn't seem to recognize us at all. "We've met before, at Caffè Milano," I said, figuring that he might not be able to recall just where he'd met us and a prompt would set things right. "We spoke about the volleyball team's recent successes." Nothing. Blank. "And about the flooding along the interstate to Kansas City." Still no response. As he reclaimed his seat on the far side of his desk, he gestured toward the two chairs beside us. "Please." Mildly embarrassed, I understood then that this meeting would be purely business, no pleasantries necessary nor, apparently, welcome.

By now Judy was familiar with the mini mental status drill, and most of his initial questions were standard. She answered the predictable ones correctly or close enough to suggest that her brain was still processing most information normally. She had trouble sketching a pentagon, the first time that challenge had been posed. It would be several years before I'd learn just what such a deficit indicated, but at that point I wasn't thinking in abstractions. I just wanted to know what was happening and why.

Judy seemed neither interested nor disinterested. Each small task extended the interview, and I could see that as we passed the forty-five-minute point her patience was beginning to evaporate. Perhaps Dr. Morrison sensed that too. He wrapped up the examination abruptly, folded his hands together in front of him and, looking at them but not at her, said "Based on the results of your MRI and the exams with Dr. Breyer and here today, I believe you have mild cognitive impairment." Period. *Mild cognitive impairment*, I thought to myself. Okay, that sounds benign.

"What exactly does that mean?" I asked. "Is it the same as the 'mild cerebral atrophy' that was listed among her MRI results?"

"Well," he said, looking past Judy to me, "as we age there are often changes in the brain that manifest themselves with some memory loss, and sometimes aspects of executive function are affected. Your wife has some difficulty with more complex multi-step tasks, but at this point I think it's just something to watch." Turning to a cabinet that stood behind his seat, he opened a drawer and removed a small booklet that he extended across the desk and into Judy's hands. "I'd like you to start a month's trial of this medication; it's called "Aricept"[4]. If there are no negative side effects, we'll put you on a regular dosage. Do you have any questions?"

Judy looked down at the sample packet and then picked up her purse. As we stood, I said, "We'll phone if we have any questions. Thanks." He said nothing else. Pleasantries, we knew by then, were not his forte.

I reached for the door, and we stepped into a narrow corridor that led to the waiting room and from there into the blazing light of that early summer day. The din of nearby traffic seemed amplified after the spare quiet of the examining room. I made small talk as we walked to the car, and Judy said nothing. What was she thinking? I'm not sure either of us knew what to think at that point, but in any event, she wasn't forthcoming. We drove the short distance home in silence.

As we turned into our cul-de-sac, I saw that the much-delayed landscape crew we'd hired to build some retaining walls had started work. The crew's foreman was helping to unload a skid of large cement blocks. "I need to go over a few things with Nick," I told Judy, "but I'll only be a few minutes. We'll talk as soon as I finish with him." I could see in her downcast expression both anxiety and fear. "Just hold on, I'll keep it short, then we'll talk." We pulled into the garage, and she went inside.

When I joined her in the kitchen ten minutes later, she was in tears. In her lap was the opened packet of medication Dr. Morrison had given her. "I have Alzheimer's," she said. And then the floodgates opened. Her sobs were thick, suffocating. They strangled her attempt to get more words out. "It says I have Alzheimer's."

I lifted the packet containing the thirty little yellow pills, a month's supply lined up tidily in individual foil-backed compartments opposite a fine-print pamphlet several pages long. She'd already read through the leading paragraphs addressing "Indications and Usage," peppered throughout with the word *Alzheimer's.* "For use in the treatment of dementia of the Alzheimer's type" and "For patients with mild to moderate Alzheimer's disease." And so on. *Damned asshole doctor*, I said to myself. *Damned idiot*, I thought, *he didn't have the balls to tell us what the actual diagnosis is.* My anger at Dr. Morrison's lack of compassion and transparency surprised me, but I set it aside as I knelt to comfort her. "We'll deal with this," I assured her. "We'll figure it out together. You've got me. You're not alone. It's you and me, kid. We'll make it work."

As I passed her a couple of tissues and she began to wipe her cheeks and nose, I saw us for the first time standing on the edge of another world, a place that had no resemblance to anything we'd ever known. I had no idea how we'd figure this world out, or that we could. What I knew was that we were in it together. Alone neither of us would be.

3

– Mark Strand, from *When the Vacation Is Over for Good*

Dear Judy,

I have an image of you in my mind, going back to undergraduate school, where we first met. You're walking toward a set of steps that will lead you down from the art department's allotment of classrooms and studios toward the building's exit. You're wearing a cardigan sweater and a skirt—something you'd rarely see on a student today, but fifty or so years ago this was one of the fashionable options, even in the art department, on the campus of a small state university in New England. Your light brown hair is very long and very straight, falling over your shoulders and part-way to your waist, and a barrette helps to hold it away from your face. Your expression is neutral, and as I watch you approach from where I'm standing, a cigarette between my fingers leaving my lips as I exhale, I hope you'll make eye contact, but you don't. I saw you pass in the hallway numerous times that semester of my freshman year, always looking serious, never looking in my direction. I managed to convince myself you were quite a snob, a way to mask my insecurity and prepare myself for almost certain rejection if and when we were ever introduced.

Many years later I told you about those early instances of our paths crossing and my first—and entirely erroneous—impressions, and you laughed. "I was just shy!" you protested. "I was as insecure as you were! Plus, I was as private a person then as I am now. I pretty much just kept to myself."

You always were, indeed, a very private person, and over the years that trait was sometimes at odds with my tendency to wear my heart on my sleeve. "You don't need to tell people every detail of your life," you'd insist. "You don't have to be an open book."

It didn't surprise me when, a few weeks after Judy's initial diagnosis, she warned me that she didn't want anyone to know. By then we'd told our son Trevor but beyond that no one, and she wanted things to stay that way. "If I want people to know, I'll tell them," she said. It would be another couple of years before she'd do that.

Over the course of that first post-diagnosis year, I did tell a few close friends and family. It seemed too big a fact of our life to hold it secret, and for me to process an experience it's always been important to talk about it or write it down, ways to wrestle with things I didn't fully understand or was challenged to accept. Others' experiences could help me gauge the significance or insignificance of my own, and it seemed that the burden weighed less once I'd shared it. Like us, though, none of our close friends or family had any experience with Alzheimer's disease. They were as shocked and mystified as we were.

I remember thinking at the time that we'd been lucky over the course of nearly forty years together. We'd raised and educated a loving son, we'd had a close and supportive relationship with our extended family, we'd traveled widely both here and abroad and gathered a diverse circle of friends in the process, and we were still one another's best friend. We both did creative work that we drew much satisfaction from, and that creative work was the basis of our incomes. We liked going to work because it didn't feel like work. Things may have been financially tight in some years more than others, but we always managed to cover our bases. Overall, life moved along more or less smoothly, no major setbacks or tragedies casting troubling shadows or plunging us into darkness. We'd been more than fortunate.

So, I wondered, was some kind of bill now coming due, settling the score for our good life together? Some years before I'd read a collection of stories, memoirs really, called *Whereabouts: Notes on Being a Foreigner* by the Scottish writer Alistair Reid. In one of them, "Digging up Scotland," he tells of crossing paths with a local woman at the outskirts of St. Andrews on what he calls "a heady spring day." He remarks that it is indeed a very fine day, to which she dourly replies, "We'll pay for it, we'll pay for it."[5]

Was this going to be our comeuppance?

Because Judy still seemed asymptomatic much of the time and was still going about her day-to-day activities with little change, it wasn't difficult to mentally file her condition as "on hold" and carry on. Although I had begun reading what would become, over years, a sizable library of books exploring Alzheimer's and related dementias, and especially issues around caring for sufferers, she didn't seem to have the slightest interest in researching and studying her likely condition. If she spent any time searching for more information and answers to questions online, she never mentioned it. She would go on with her life as well as she could for as long as she could, and while I was perhaps a bit less sanguine about it than her, it wasn't difficult then to hope that nothing much would change.

We were in denial, of course, because the changes were already happening. A month or so before Dr. Morrison's diagnosis the semester had ended, not soon enough for Judy. "I'll never have to do that again," she said a few hours after submitting her final set of grades. It had been a difficult semester, the second of two taught back-to-back as a colleague's sabbatical replacement. She'd had a very difficult time with organization, and planning each course's next sessions grew more challenging as her ability to hold on to what had happened in the previous days' and weeks' sessions faltered. I'd see her at her laptop in the evening, staring at a blank screen, trying to will a lesson plan to life. She always managed to have something pulled together when she left for campus, but without the help of a kind and sensitive graduate student, she'd probably not have been able to wrap up that semester's two courses.

None of her students came to me that semester. Some students would have been intimidated to bring a complaint to the department chair, and when difficult situations arose, those more timid types tended to band together and enlist someone who wasn't intimidated to knock on the corner office door. While I hadn't hired Judy—our dean had done that—I was, after all, her husband, and there would have been some awkwardness no matter how it was approached. In hindsight, I'm not sure what I'd have done had any of them brought their concerns to me. I didn't have to cross that bridge.

I did try to help her as I could at home during evenings when she struggled to organize her course content. She and the students managed to get through the fifteen or so weeks, and they kept their dissatisfaction to themselves until their course evaluations came in. Over the years that Judy taught as a visiting lecturer, her evaluations had consistently hovered at or on either side of the department average, fluttering around 4.2 or 4.3 on a 5-point scale. Now they'd dropped to the lowest among the teaching faculty. She was humbled receiving those but relieved they'd be the last.

We'd planned out what I came to think of as the summer of her diagnosis many months in advance, and we agreed we'd stick with the plan. We rented a vacation home for a couple of weeks near the ocean not far from our hometowns. Trevor and our daughter-in-law, Veronica, along with their twin daughters, Clare and Francesca, would join us for part of our time there. Being once again in and near the places that made up what we'd always consider our real home, and with the family and friends who'd populated that previous life, we were able to get some distance from the diagnosis. When we loaded up the car toward the end of June, locked the kitchen door behind us, and backed down our driveway, I felt that we were able to leave the diagnosis there, in a catch-all drawer with some unpaid bills and spare change. By putting eighteen hundred miles between it and us and focusing some of that away time on twin two-year-old granddaughters, we would be able to enjoy a brief summer idyll where the words *Alzheimer's* and *cognitive impairment* lost their currency. For the next six years, long road trips would become a kind of balm, a salve that eased the anxiety and tempered the fear.

After three weeks far from the vast open skies and the blazing Great Plains sun, Judy seemed as content as I was when we turned back into our driveway at full midsummer. That time in the east, sheltered by its deciduous canopies and cooled by ocean breezes, had the restorative effect on each of us that we'd sorely needed. The month that followed our return offered her time to relax and get her bearings in her studio while I resumed my campus routines preparing for the pending fall semester. Before the fall gained its usual relentless momentum, we'd be taking one more trip, this time overseas and mainly business related. Organizing toward that was our immediate agenda, and having done similar gigs numerous times in the preceding years, Judy knew what she needed to do ahead of our departure. Or so I thought.

We'd committed to side-by-side solo exhibitions and related presentations at an annual textile art conference and exposition in France. She'd contracted to teach a day-long workshop in which she'd share her particular techniques with textile enthusiasts and admirers of her work, and I'd be offering a couple of public lectures. Over the course of several days there, we'd greet visitors to our respective exhibitions, we'd network with people in the field—among them some longtime friends and acquaintances and many fresh faces too—and as we could, we'd squeeze in some sightseeing. It would be a busy and stimulating week, and by the time our nonstop flight departed from Chicago, everything seemed to be in place. Judy didn't seem to have any qualms about teaching what was, for her, a basic introductory-level workshop, and I had no second thoughts. She was still working with her familiar techniques in her studio, and I fully expected that she'd have no trouble presenting these to a student group in what would be a relaxed, hands-on session.

The evening before her workshop, though, she was out of sorts. She'd made a list of everything she'd brought that she'd need when she taught, and she'd mapped out a series of demonstrations she'd do and exercises she'd ask her students to attack. While they did that, she'd circulate and offer guidance and feedback. This was nothing new; she'd done it many times and should have felt confident that she was well prepared. It was clear that evening, though, that she felt anything but confident. "Another decent night's sleep will get you on track," I said. We'd been there a couple of days, so any jet lag should have dissipated, and she'd slept well the previous night. "Just relax," I said, "you'll do fine."

In the morning we left the hotel soon after breakfast, and I dropped her off at the workshop site well ahead of its starting time. Céleste, a dear friend and artist colleague based in Dijon, had signed up for the class and was there to greet us, so I left Judy in good hands as I headed to a different venue where I'd be delivering several talks later that day.

Busy with my own obligations, I didn't think again about how she might be doing until late afternoon when I realized it was nearly time to pick her up. The circuitous route from the town center to the former school where she'd been all day was slow going by the time I got on the road, and I arrived a bit after her class time had been scheduled to end.

"How'd it go?" I asked as I came into the room. She was alone, packed up, and ready to leave. She seemed tired, a bit subdued. "I guess it went okay," she said. "We finished up early, so everyone was gone by 3:00 I think."

"Oh," I said, "you think?"

"Well, they said they'd had enough, they knew how to do it," she replied. "I showed them everything I'd planned. It went fine."

It wasn't until some weeks later, well after our return, that word got back to me about her students' dissatisfaction that day. One of the organizers shared that they'd had to refund the participants' fees considering the complaints that followed Judy's session. Apparently, she'd successfully shown them one step-by-step process and they'd completed their own set of samples, giving them the basic skill set they'd need to take it to the next level of complexity. Assembled again to watch her demonstrate a second technique, they were mystified to see her start again from the beginning, as if she'd never demonstrated this to them, though she had, a couple hours earlier. It was as if the morning session hadn't happened. Any plan that she might have had earlier in the day was truant. Once they realized she had nothing else to offer, they slowly collected their belongings and drifted off, a few of them heading straight to the organizing committee's offices.

The organizers quietly and generously refunded the registration fees of her workshop participants and said nothing to Judy, nor to me. In the days following, as the conference unfolded and finally wrapped up, we were innocently ignorant of what was, behind the scenes, an organizational and professional embarrassment, both to them and to Judy. She would eventually learn about this, and I would be the messenger. To this day that haunts me. My intentions were good but my delivery disastrous.

When I first learned about her workshop's demise, though, I decided there was no good reason to tell her. Better to let it rest since it was certain she'd never teach again, under any circumstance. As relieved as she was after she'd completed her spring courses earlier that year, she seemed even more relieved after we returned from France. "I'm just going to work in my studio now," she said. "That's all I want to do."

Through that first summer and into the fall season, the ambiguousness of her diagnosis haunted me. Could it be something else? Though she'd submitted to the proverbial battery of tests, from cognitive exams to enhanced lab work to an MRI, combined they hadn't identified more than mild cognitive impairment. With no family history that we were aware of, could there be an environmental cause? As a textile artist, she'd developed a creative practice that depended on chemical manipulations of fabric. She'd been highly conscientious about wearing the recommended protective respirators, gloves, and aprons when working with dyes and other agents, but could there have been some kind of damaging exposure nonetheless? Could it have something to do with the hormone replacement therapy she'd been treated with?

These and other unanswered questions surfaced each time the many distractions of daily life quieted down, and I couldn't set them aside. Those questions needed answers, and we needed to be reassured that there wasn't something else causing her symptoms.

One day I phoned the only University Medical Center faculty member I knew to ask if she was aware of any work being done there dealing with Alzheimer's sufferers. She listened to my capsule version of our experience to that point and then said simply, "Someone will phone you back shortly." An hour later a receptionist from the Neurological Sciences Center called with a day and time for an appointment with the clinic's lead neurologist. We'd see him in about three weeks. Only later would I realize how in demand the Center's clinicians were and how long the wait usually was for an evaluation. My acquaintance's aegis had shortened that wait by about two months, and I was thankful.

"I don't want to go see another neurologist!" Judy responded sharply when I announced the upcoming appointment. "I'm sick of all those questions; I don't know what they want. You go. I'm not going, I'll stay here." I knew better than to dismiss her frustration with the examinations, but I also knew that she was the one sleeping through the night, outwardly unconcerned. I was the insomniac, awake for hours at a time in the darkness, imagining a grim future and wondering if there was more we could do to get answers now. "We'll get a second opinion," I insisted, "and then I'll let it go. But you'll have to come. We can't get a second opinion without you."

She wasn't a happy camper the afternoon of that appointment. It was the first time that I sensed the divide between her wants and needs and my own. I had to have answers. She wanted neither questions nor answers. She just wanted all this to go away. "I don't see why we have to go up there," she said as the passenger-side door closed behind her. "I'm sick of this. It won't do any good." And that was her refrain for the next thirty or so minutes as we reached the interstate and merged with early afternoon traffic. "I don't know why we have to do this. There's nothing wrong with me! I'm fine!" she repeated, her voice growing louder and angrier. "I'm fine!"

"You're not fine!" I finally shouted, my patience exhausted. "If you don't know that, I do! And other people do! The conference two months ago in France? You remember that, right? Well, did you know that they had to refund the workshop fees to all your students? That your students complained after they left your class, that you had only one basic process to teach them? That you started it over once they'd already worked it through? I'll bet you didn't know that!"

Judy stiffened and quieted, and several seconds passed as she struggled to wrap her mind around this revelation. And then she collapsed. Her sobbing was guttural and desperate, and she bent forward, her head in her hands and her torso convulsing. Her humiliation was epic; she'd been fully exposed, by me and by strangers thousands of miles away, and she was devastated. "I'm sorry," I said quietly, my right hand on her back, the other guiding the steering wheel. "I don't want to hurt you. But you have to understand, we need help. We must know for sure what's going on."

By the time we pulled off the interstate near our destination she'd quieted down, her eyes puffy and red but her body more relaxed. By the time we reached the parking lot her mood had lifted. When we greeted the receptionist, she was smiling and friendly. My sudden revelation, the stick I'd wielded to stun her into accepting her condition, never came up again. I think, I hope, that she forgot it. I never have. If I could take one action back, if I could erase one failure in how I dealt with her illness over all those years, it would be that. It was thoughtless. It was mean. It wasn't necessary. In the end it had little bearing. I think I learned from it though. There began my long and slow apprenticeship in patience and acceptance. It would be a struggle, but I'd get there.

Across space and time, from that other shore, I'd love to know, do you forgive me?

4

Love is bigger than anything in its way.
But it has to be said, there is a lot in its way.

– Bono, from *Surrender, 40 Songs One Story*

Dear Judy,

Dr. Langfeldt's diagnosis confirmed the earlier one, but delivered with unusual empathy and compassion, its effect was comforting and reassuring, feelings we'd always thereafter associate with visits to his clinic. "You have mild cognitive impairment consistent with younger onset Alzheimer's disease," he said looking directly into your eyes, his knees and yours nearly touching in the small examining room. "I know that this isn't what you want to hear, but we're here to help and you can count on that. Since you haven't had any side effects other than the rash when you first started taking it, I think that you should continue with the daily dose of Aricept,[6] and I'll see you again in about six months."

"Dr. Langfeldt, do you think that there might be some clinical trials that we could look into?" I asked. I'd been looking at reports on some of the research into memory diseases like Alzheimer's and wondered if that was a route he'd encourage. You and I had discussed this possibility, and you liked the idea. "If I thought it might help them better understand and treat what I have, that would be fine with me," you'd said.

"In fact, I and a colleague here at the Med Center are involved in a couple of studies right now that you might qualify for, Judith," Langfeldt replied, using your full given name, something

*that I know you liked but that few people—myself included—
used in addressing you. "Let me give you some information to
read over, and if you both think this is something you'd like to
explore, we can start the ball rolling."*

*We left his office with a folder of clinical trial documentation
and a sense of hope and possibility, the first time in months
that we'd felt either of those sentiments. Dr. Langfeldt's warmth
and affability, his sensitivity, and his ability to quickly establish
genuine rapport with you as a patient and with me as a caregiver endeared him to us almost immediately. "I like him a lot," you
said as soon as the elevator doors closed behind us. "And I like
the people here too; they're all really nice."*

*The welcome we'd received had been genuine, and the staff
clearly enjoyed working in that neurodegenerative disorders unit.
Part of the state's public university system, the Med Center's
campus in Omaha is a bustling hive of research, education, and
quality medical care. Like you, I felt comfortable as soon as we
passed through the neurology department's doors. The fact that
it was part of the same system that I was employed by, and that
at the time Dr. Langfeldt was, like me, serving as his department's chairperson, created a sense of familiarity. For me, it was
reassuring.*

*One of Dr. Langfeldt's missions was to create new and useful
knowledge through evidence-based research; one of ours was to
better understand both the nature of your condition and how
to live with it. We felt confident as we returned home that day
that we'd turned a corner, that we were at the cusp of a mutually
beneficial relationship with Dr. Langfeldt and his colleagues.
You'd been genuinely enthusiastic for the first time in months,
and that made me hopeful. Some of the heaviness we'd both been
feeling seemed to lift with that visit, and I was grateful.*

Thinking of myself as Judy's caregiver came about slowly, in stages, and my first inkling of what it would mean struck me when we were in those doctors' offices, and I was helping to frame the background of her condition. As her husband, of course, I'd thought from the beginning of our marriage that taking care of her was part of the deal, and as my wife she took care of me too, and we both took care of our son Trevor through the years that we raised him. Taking care of and caregiving aren't really the same though, are they?

The first comes with a commitment to a loving relationship and the desire to provide for mutual needs and wants, two individuals looking out for the other's well-being and happiness. The second recognizes that one partner has lost or is losing agency of one kind or another. The balance shifts, and an imbalance punctures the relationship. Very slowly, over months and then years, the partner relationship—spouses and lovers and confidantes and best friends—morphs into a strange new parent-child relationship, awkward, unnerving, and depressing.

Having come of age and attended college in the sixties, we were progressively minded products of that convulsed era. By the time we became friends, she was solid in her conviction that women and men are equals. Any relationship she entered into would be guided by that. If I harbored any hint of male entitlement or superiority at the time, she quickly disabused me of it. That wouldn't have been a hard sell in any case.

I'd grown up in an extended working-class family headed by my maternal grandmother, a matriarch if there ever was one. Her four daughters, including my mother, were equally strong. While they all made childrearing the centerpieces of their lives, they never played second fiddle to their husbands. If the men fancied themselves the family "bosses," the women, my aunts, might humor them, but they'd slyly wink at one another and at us kids behind their husbands' backs. Growing up in the thick of it, of course, we offspring internalized those family dynamics. We had no illusions about who the real bosses were. They may have nursed regrets about life choices and circumstances, about ambitions unfulfilled or abandoned, but those women thought for themselves and were never afraid to stand their ground.

The art college in which Judy and I were studying when we first met was on a commuter campus populated largely by first-generation college students from the many down-at-heel textile mill towns spread across that region of New England. A lot of those students, ourselves included, still lived at home. This fact explains why we spent long hours beyond class time working away or hanging out in the college's art and design studios. They were accessible to us sixteen out of every twenty-four hours, and as our circle of friends grew, that's where we knew we'd find them. Semester by semester, those social circles expanded and overlapped, friends and friends' friends connecting and blending, disconnecting and reconnecting in a fluid and dynamic exploration of each other driven as much by carnal desire as by intellectual curiosity and affinity.

Somewhere along the line we found ourselves talking across a smoking lounge banquette and bumming cigarettes from one another. One of Judy's best friends, Kathy Doyle, was a painting major like me. She and I and a large handful of other painters shared most of our classes and campus hanging out time. Her English major boyfriend also became a regular presence in that group, and because Judy had gone to high school with both of them, she was naturally drawn into their expanding social network. I learned soon enough that there was nothing snobbish about her. On the contrary, she was really easy to be with.

When we finally started dating, I'd just graduated with my bachelor's degree, and she'd been out of university for a year. She was working as a high school substitute teacher in Falmouth, on Cape Cod. We hadn't had a lot of contact during my senior year, but friends with whom she remained in contact usually had news when I asked how she was doing. We saw each other at a couple of holiday parties just before I started my final undergrad semester, and we ran into one another unexpectedly that spring at a wedding.

"Would it be okay if I come out to Falmouth to see you?" I finally got the courage to ask her as we finished catching up over a smoke. I felt both relieved and hopeful when she said, "Sure," through a broad smile. She dictated directions and gave me her phone number. At that point I should have asked her to dance—we were at a wedding after all—but in my excitement all I could manage was "Well, I'll see you soon." She smiled again. "Don't forget to call," she said as she walked off. *You betcha*, I thought.

That summer before I left for graduate school, I started driving to the Cape to see her a couple of nights a week, always conditional on being able to borrow the family car. Our shared interests in folk music, art house cinema, and books nurtured a relaxed but frustratingly platonic friendship. While I desperately wanted it not to be platonic, I couldn't gauge just where she stood on the subject and was too timid to ask. I'd been a good Catholic boy after all, raised in the fifties and sixties, educated in a parochial school, and though I'd gradually learned how to think for myself, I wasn't mature or independent-minded enough to be the sexual partner that I think she had in mind. Late that August I kissed her goodbye and headed off to grad school, my virginity intact.

When I returned after the first semester, I knew what and whom I wanted. She'd figured it out too that we should be together. We wasted no time sealing the deal, and sometime during the holiday week she told her parents she'd be leaving with me when I headed back to Rochester. They knew her well enough to get out of the way of her determination, but fortunately they approved of me and never objected. A few days after the New Year we packed up her pale blue Ford Mustang—I'd left my ailing Ford Falcon in Rochester, taking Greyhound back to Massachusetts for the break—and headed together to western New York.

A few months later she told me she thought she was pregnant.

"Now listen to me," she said. "I'm having this baby with or

without you. I want this baby. So, if you're not on board, I'll head back to Massachusetts now."

I had to have been terrified. It was fifty years ago; it's hard to really see those two skinny kids that we were, to put myself back into that slight frame of mine and feel my reaction. I do know, though, that from the moment she told me, I was as clear about it as she was.

"Let's get married," I said. "We'll figure it out. We'll make it work."

"Just know this," she said. "It must be fifty-fifty. Everything. The baby, parenting, the cooking, the cleaning, laundry, making money, making decisions. Fifty-fifty."

Less than two months later we married, nearly penniless but happy, sure of ourselves and sure of this baby we'd made. Like everyone else, in the decades to follow we'd struggle and work hard, we'd love one another, we'd fight, we'd agree and disagree, we'd give our child a secure home and advantages we hadn't had. And it would be a long time before we'd have to come to terms with the full implications of "in sickness and in health."

Once it was staring us in the face, I know the idea of her needing caregiving bothered her as much as it bothered me, maybe even more. The fact we were both in it together was cold comfort. In the first couple of years, while she was still managing most aspects of daily life fairly well, the embarrassment she experienced when the disease threw her a curve ball was especially heartbreaking for both of us. There was still so much normality that the menacing deviations were even more frightening.

She phoned me one afternoon, alarmed and on the verge of tears. I was on campus, in my office. "I can't remember where I was going," she said from her car. "I was going somewhere, some errand I think, but now I can't think of it."

"Where are you?" I asked.

"I pulled into a Target parking lot," she answered.

"Which Target?" I asked, an obvious question given that there were at least four Target stores in town at the time. I asked her what stores were nearby and quickly figured out that she was at the Target closest to our home and campus, which made sense. She still moved automatically along familiar routes and generally made it to her destination and back with no complications, at least as far as I knew.

"Okay," I said, "just go home. Do you know how to get home from where you are? Tell me how you'll do that." By then she'd thought it through, and her planned return route was exactly what she'd driven in the first place, but in reverse.

"That's fine then," I said, "just head home." Fifteen minutes later when I phoned her on our landline she was there, relieved but embarrassed. "Now I remember where I was going," she said. "Gabbie just called. I had a hair appointment. She said she'll squeeze me in tomorrow."

What did she tell Gabbie the next day? At that point she was still adamant that nobody should know what she was going through. Maybe Gabbie had figured it out, or maybe not. By the time I started taking her to those appointments myself, Gabbie knew.

I remember another time that Judy phoned me midday, again from her car, and again I was on campus. "I don't know where I am," she said.

"Do you know where you were heading?" I asked.

"Yeah, I was going to the drugstore to pick up my prescriptions," she answered. That helped because for years we'd used the same pharmacy and it was a straight shot from where we lived. "I was driving along A Street and suddenly it was blocked off and they made us turn. Once I got into this neighborhood, I didn't know which way to go." That she hadn't simply followed the other detouring drivers was mildly irritating to me at the time, though now I understand that what she'd have had no problem figuring out a few months before was by then a serious challenge.

"Can you see any street signs?" I asked, and when she said she was too far from the corner, I directed her to drive to that next intersection.

"Okay, I'm at Ellendale and Piedmont," which was all I needed to locate her on the map I'd brought up on my computer screen. Over the next few minutes, I guided her out of that subdivision and back to the main artery that got her to the pharmacy. Once she'd picked up her prescriptions, she phoned me back as I'd asked her to, and we went over the alternate return route, which she managed fine.

"This stupid city," she said later when I phoned to check on how she'd made out. "They're always doing street work and they never give you any notice." There was some truth to that, I had to admit. The wrinkle was hers, though, not the city's.

In those first Alzheimer's years, Judy did tend to have more misadventures when she was out and about than when she was at home, and I know that my anxiety would surface anytime she said she was heading out on an errand or two. Because I'd read enough by then to know that at some point I'd have to stop her from driving, I didn't want to go there any sooner than we'd have to. She was still getting around safely. Her independence meant the world to her, and I knew it helped me too.

"I'm going to the supermarket," she said one hot and humid summer afternoon. Up against a deadline, I was working from home to avoid the steady distractions that complicated almost any day on campus. "Take the list from the table," I reminded her. We'd written down the things we needed, and remembering to take that list with her was key to avoiding a wasted trip. "I won't be long," she said as she opened the garage door. "Back soon."

I heard the garage door close behind her and figured she'd be forty-five minutes or so. The supermarket was only a couple of miles away and a straight shot, much as the pharmacy was. When the phone rang an hour-and-a-quarter later, I had just begun to wonder what was taking her so long. "I've lost my keys," she said as soon as I answered.

"Where are you now?" I asked.

"I'm in the car, in the parking lot."

"Okay, tell me what happened."

She explained that she'd done the shopping, she'd checked out, and when she got into the car, she realized she no longer had the keys.

"Did you lock the car when you first got there?" I asked. We were faithful about locking our vehicles, so I couldn't imagine she hadn't.

"I'm not sure," she said. "Anyway, I've looked all around the car and on the ground between here and the building, and I went back inside too, and they couldn't find them either."

"Well," I said, "wait where you are, and I'll bring the second set. I'll be there in ten minutes."

When I arrived, the parking space next to hers had just been vacated so I pulled my car in. "Let me look," I said.

Judy stepped out of the driver's seat, and I took her place. I immediately saw the keys on the car's floor where they'd fallen, in plain sight.

"Ughhhh," she groaned, frustrated with herself.

"Well, I'm glad they're not lost. Let's just go home now," I said.

It worried me quite a bit that lapses of judgment and momentary confusion, especially when she was behind the wheel, could spell disaster. Most of the time she navigated without incident. She'd always been an attentive driver though she drove a bit too fast for my liking. She never failed to remind me that I was the one with a record of speeding tickets, not her. Yet the thought that she might be involved in an accident at some point, that if her diagnosis were revealed she'd likely be held responsible whether she was at fault or not, kept me awake often enough that when I finally did take her keys for good, I felt enormous relief.

Enrolling in a clinical trial was the strategy we eventually settled on to try to give her some sense of purpose in coming to terms with this illness that we didn't yet fully understand. Dr. Langfeldt had given us three trial prospectuses, and we talked about these options quite a bit over the next few months. By the time we decided to explore her eligibility the following spring, one of the trials had been discontinued. That simplified things, though it didn't make the final decision easier. She couldn't be in two trials simultaneously, so we'd still have to make a choice.

Both options in front of us required a commitment of about eighteen months, something we both agreed wouldn't be a problem. Both were double blind, placebo controlled, and randomized. One trial product would be delivered orally in pill form, the other as an intravenous infusion. In the intravenous immune globulin trial, a certain number of trial participants would be assigned to one of two different dosage groups, and others would be receiving a placebo. This meant that if Judy didn't end up in the placebo group, there was a chance that she'd be treated with a lower dose than some other participants but an equal chance that she'd receive the full dosage of the drug. With the oral pill product, she'd have a 50 percent chance of getting the actual drug, or not. Both trials would require multiple trips up to the Med Center for periodic evaluation and testing.

"Well," Judy insisted, "even if I don't get the actual drug, they'll be learning something and I'll have helped, regardless which trial we go with. It's better than doing nothing." We agreed that the regular evaluations and follow-up that each trial offered would help us keep a close eye on her overall health, and that seemed like a valuable benefit.

After a new round of testing and examinations that took us past the first anniversary of the original diagnosis, Dr. Langfeldt's colleague at the Med Center's testing site, Dr. Ranee Mehta, let us know that Judy appeared to qualify for both trials. "Which one do you want to go with?" she asked. By then we'd already had answers to a host of questions about each trial and had a good understanding of what they entailed. The biggest inconvenience would be getting up to the Med Center for the first infusions and for periodic study visits that would include cognitive testing, blood work, and brain scans. My schedule was relatively flexible, given that all my teaching responsibilities were carried out online. Hers was "anything goes," so a morning or afternoon's time, weekly and biweekly in the first months, then spreading out to every second or third month, was manageable.

We'd carefully weighed the details of each trial option, a lot of information for which, at first, we didn't have the vocabulary. That came in time. Dr. Mehta's staff answered our questions patiently by phone, and when we were back in her office, we were close to a decision. I had one final question. "If this were your spouse, Dr. Mehta, which trial would you want him in?" I asked.

She hesitated. "Well, the decision really is up to you two," she replied. "I really need to stay neutral here." The examining room was still. I remember thinking that this was something of a coin toss—heads you win, tails you lose—though I realized that either way, we had no control over how either trial would ultimately play out.

I tried a second time. "If this were your spouse…?"

"Then I'd probably go with the IGIV study," she answered. "But it's entirely up to you."

I'd asked her that question because I trusted that she'd want the best possible experience and outcome for her partner as we wanted for Judy.

"Are you willing to go with the Immune Globulin Intravenous infusion?" I asked her. At the time this Phase 3 trial was recruiting 360 participants who, over a term of about eighteen months, would be infused twice a month with the IGIV product. Although it was considered an investigational drug for the treatment of persons with mild to moderate Alzheimer's disease, it had a long history in the treatment of patients with a variety of immune deficiency and autoimmune diseases. The investigation would try to determine if it could provide benefit in treating Alzheimer's patients.

"I'm fine with that," Judy replied. "Let's go with it."

In the photo I took of her just as her first infusion started, she's grinning broadly, though her lips are slightly pinched. She'd had to fast that morning until we got to the Med Center, so the unwrapped snack bar on her lap was her belated breakfast, and that smile concealed a mouthful. She liked the nurse on hand to do that first infusion from the moment she greeted us and introduced herself, and by the time I shot that picture, Judy looked totally at ease, an open book on her other lap. The decor around her is laboratory clinical, although the red and blue vinyl upholstery of the assorted infusion chairs seems upbeat, even festive. She could be on some amusement park ride, about to be whipped around another curve, excited and entirely pleased with herself.

It felt good to feel that we were doing something positive and useful, something that would give us a point of engagement with her disease that wasn't dark and hopeless. Since I'd first known Judy, being useful was one lens through which she saw herself, and I think it's how many people saw her. She cared, and it mattered to her that she could help the people in her orbit and make a difference in their lives, however small. I think she felt some pride, too, that day when we launched into the trial. It's also there in her smile.

Looking back now, so many years later, those eighteen months that encompassed our clinical trial participation were a kind of calm emotional oasis during which we began to accept, each in our own way, the cards we'd been dealt. I'd learned about the progressive stages of Alzheimer's and calculated that Judy was in the late early stage by the time the twice-monthly infusions became part of her routine. It was always hard to know for sure since a run of good days would inevitably be interrupted by one or two not-so-good ones. While she was in that trial, though, she held her own. I was grateful for that.

After circumstances forced her to stop teaching, I moved quickly to qualify her for Social Security Disability compensation. The voice on the other end of the phone at the local Social Security office seemed both concerned and sincere. "We'll move on this as soon as you complete and submit the application," she said. Within a couple of weeks, it was approved. While the monthly payment was modest, it helped to offset the loss of some of what Judy would have earned had she been able to continue teaching and grow her art making career. Eventually, that disability benefit would help to underwrite part of the expense of companion care. Before that became necessary, though, the trial would run its course.

How easy the early stages of Judy's Alzheimer's disease seem to me now. Her daily routines changed a bit, largely because she was by then spending most of her time at home. Dressing and feeding herself weren't problems at that point, and she was still working in her studio. I could head off to campus feeling comfortable that she, at home, was comfortable too, and safe. In good weather she'd walk outdoors for half an hour or so, along the bike trail that passed by our back door and the paved walkway that took her around the small lake on which we lived.

Every second Tuesday a nurse would come to infuse her, nearly a full morning of companionship that interrupted her solitude. Otherwise, Judy's studio overlooking the lake was her retreat and comfort zone. Surrounded by the materials of her artistic practice, by the things she'd collected that inspired her—beach rocks, sea glass, aerial photos of this region's countryside—she was able to hold on to a certain measure of control. I'm not sure that she realized then how time dated that comfort and control was.

All the technical and conceptual processes that she'd learned to work with during the time when she was a graduate student and that she'd cultivated and deepened in the years immediately after she'd completed her degree were among the first things she'd lose.

Judy finished the last artworks she'd ever create around the start of the clinical trial, and by then I could see that she was quickly forgetting much of what she'd worked so hard to learn over the previous decade. When visitors to her studio saw her work, they tended to ask about her processes. Around that time, I noticed that Judy's explanations were becoming more generalized, much less detailed—quick summaries that left more to the imagination than any amateur could puzzle out. This loss of precision was so unlike her, and I sensed that she was a little embarrassed by it. She found it easier, though, to patch together a vague summary than to bullet point the step-by-step. Five years later, after I'd moved her into full-time memory care, the best she could offer when staff or visitors complimented her on the intriguing textile art hanging in her room was "Yeah, I used to do that." By then, how she'd done it was as much a mystery to herself as to them.

5

The path is uncharted…It's like riding on a train sitting backwards. We can't see where we're headed, only where we've been.

— Pema Chödrön, from *When Things Fall Apart*

Dear Judy,

A few days after your initial diagnosis in June 2009, I stopped by a local bookstore to see what I could find on mild cognitive impairment. The trade paperback edition of Lisa Genova's novel Still Alice *had appeared earlier that year, and a half-dozen crisp and unblemished copies caught my eye. A book jacket blurb touted the story's poignancy, and a quick scan of a few paragraphs told me it was intelligent and readable, so it became the first of many fiction and non-fiction books I'd read on all aspects of Alzheimer's. At the time you weren't interested in reading it, which was probably a good thing. It would have depressed you, and there was enough depression ahead of you that avoiding it for as long as we could was the best tactic. Better for you to stick to the crime fiction and mysteries that you'd always favored.*

Still Alice is the fictional story of a highly successful linguistics researcher and professor who, at the age of fifty, receives a diagnosis of younger onset Alzheimer's. The story explores the impact of the disease on Alice, on her marriage and her career, and on her relationships with her children and theirs with her. Over the course of its three hundred or so pages, "Ali" and her family experience much of the fear, loss, and grief that accompany nearly every Alzheimer's diagnosis and those of several related neurological diseases.

Toward the end of Still Alice, *the title character's husband, John Howland, sympathetic and understanding of his wife's cognitive decline to that point in the story, decides to leave her in the care of their daughters and a nurse. He departs their home in Massachusetts and his faculty position at Harvard to assume a new medical school appointment in New York City. In fairness, that's a commute that many Northeast Corridor professionals make over the course of months or years, successfully settling into long-term careers in which the workweek and the weekend are geographically separated, with Amtrak or the LaGuardia shuttle making some semblance of domestic life possible. While the author is consistent in keeping the spotlight on Alice's experience of her illness, she offers far fewer revealing glimpses into John's interior life. What's he thinking about, awake in the middle of the night, his sleeping and diseased wife beside him? What do his job offer's pros and cons look like? Why does he opt to relocate without Alice?*

That the Howlands had family members willing to take on caregiving duties in their father's absence was fortunate for them, but I wondered how realistic that was. I also wondered if I'd be able to do something like that—to put my career ahead of our marriage and the responsibilities it imposed. I'd made a point of building a career and artistic practice that worked with and around our home life, and you'd essentially done the same. What would it mean, what would it look like, to prioritize ambition and professional status when disease makes an inopportune entrance upstage? Even if we'd had offspring handy who were willing to take over your care with the help of a private nurse, I couldn't imagine handing over the keys and your schedule of medications, then walking out the door and merging onto the interstate to ascend yet one more rung on the ladder of professional fulfillment.

Lisa Genova, a trained neuroscientist and researcher after all, had done her homework and knew the statistics. Studies show that female partners have a higher likelihood of experiencing spousal abandonment in the face of serious life-threatening disease than the other way around.[7] *John Howland's escape to Manhattan didn't imply any intent to renege on his practical and financial commitment to their marriage, but it raised genuine questions about the nature of his emotional commitment.*

In the film adaptation of the book, husband John is played by actor Alec Baldwin. The screenplay doesn't offer much more insight into John's motivations and rationales than does the novel, though it does alter details of the story that make his exit near the end of the film feel much more like an escape. He decides to leave Columbia University behind in favor of the Mayo Clinic in Rochester, Minnesota, a far longer and much less forgiving commute. The average life expectancy of Alzheimer's patients from diagnosis is eight to eleven years.[8] *While the fictional Alice's disease trajectory is tightly condensed in the film, this John clearly doesn't plan to be in the thick of things for the long haul. The thick of things will be twelve hundred miles away.*

I took you with me to see the film at a downtown cineplex the morning following its nationwide release in February 2015. You were by then in the late stage of Alzheimer's, although that calculation didn't seem as evident at the time as it does in hindsight. I was about a month away from placing you in a full-time memory care residence. While I understood I'd be doing that eventually, I didn't realize it was imminent.

I'd been looking forward to seeing the film version from the moment I read that Genova's book had been adapted for the screen and that Julianne Moore would star in the title role. She's a performer whose work both of us admired and appreciated since we'd seen her many years earlier in Robert Altman's film Shortcuts *and Paul Thomas Anderson's films* Magnolia *and* Boogie Nights, *among others. I had every expectation that Moore the actor would reward Alice Howland the character with a sensitive interpretation. I also hoped that her performance would speak to you in some way.*

Moore's sincere and poignant embodiment of Alice earned her a well-deserved Academy Award that year for Best Actress in a Leading Role. Her approach to interpreting the character and the struggles she dealt with as her disease intensified was measured and honest. For the most part, the narrative line and the other characters that populated the film were believable and realistic. If the book and film's compression of what is usually a longer-term degenerative process into a period of about two years didn't quite ring true, that time squeeze can be forgiven for the sake of the story's dramatic impact and the conventions of film making. In the end, Still Alice *the movie provided a sensitive and reasonably accurate picture of one family's experience of the disease.*

As the film's final credits rolled that Saturday morning in the cinema auditorium, I helped you back into your winter outerwear, sliding on your gloves and adjusting your hat and scarf, tasks that, at that point in the progression of your own disease, you could no longer easily manage. Standing at our seats, I noticed that all around us other couples were engaged much the same way, one partner, presumably a caregiver, helping the other to don coat and gloves or mittens. For a weekend morning screening there were a fair number of patrons, and for a film with this topic, it's easy to assume that many if not most of these couples were familiar with or living through some form or another of what they'd just watched play out on the movie screen.

I'd glanced at you several times during the screening, curious to gauge how you were reacting and if those reactions were in sync with what was happening in the story. Even though you were almost six years into your diagnosis, you did chuckle naturally when the film's humor prompted laughter, and your eyes welled up at moments when sensitive developments in the storyline and their accompanying music conspired to raise lumps in the throats of all the audience members.

"So, what did you think of the film?" I asked you as we walked into the cineplex's lobby and the bright glare of a midwinter's early afternoon.

"It was good, I liked it," you answered.

"Did you feel a connection to that main character, Ali? Did

her story seem familiar to you?"

"Oh, no, no, why?" you quickly replied.

Why? Because in so many ways it was close to our own story, and I hoped you'd pick up on that. I was a bit disappointed that you didn't and discouraged to realize that in another hour or two, by the time we'd stopped for lunch and returned home, the film, the whole outing, would be lost to you. And it was.

Judy's detachment from the character of Alice Howland, her inability to relate to her, shouldn't have mattered to me. During her last couple of years anything we saw in a cinema or watched on television blurred almost as soon as we left the theater or turned off the remote control. If there was something on the screen it held her attention. Once the film or broadcast ended, the theater emptied, our living room quieted, what she'd watched wasn't even a memory. Nothing much stuck at that point. She was fully in the moment, but not in the way that some Zen master or meditation guide would encourage her to be. She may have been physically present, but she was bringing less consciousness to whatever the moment was offering her.

I recall one early evening, maybe two years or so before that outing to see *Still Alice*, we watched the evening news as we typically did, then a favorite program, after which I needed to get some advance work completed for a meeting the next day. "Do you want me to leave the tv on?" I asked.

"No, that's fine. I don't know what I'd watch. Shut it off," she said. I did and left her on the sofa, a virgin crossword puzzle in her lap.

"I'll be downstairs for a little while; just call out if you need anything."

As the light faded outdoors, I was quickly absorbed by papers staring back at me from my desk, and thirty minutes or so passed before I heard sounds of Judy moving across the hardwood floors above me. I could tell she was going from room to room, slowly, quietly, but even at that distance I sensed her unease. As I started up the carpeted steps—she didn't hear me coming—I heard her choke back a sob, then release it. When I caught sight of her as I crested the stairway her back was to me, she was sobbing audibly. "Judy," I said softly. She turned, entirely surprised, frightened possibly, and she looked lost.

"Where did everyone go?" she asked me. "I thought everyone had gone." Everyone? The characters in the tv drama? The newscasters? Me?

I think she was experiencing what's called "sundowning," a common symptom of Alzheimer's disease. Her confusion, pacing, and feelings of abandonment were becoming more frequent by the time we'd reached the start of the fourth year from her diagnosis. I knew that evening when I found her in tears, disoriented and fearful, that the days when I could leave her alone at home were ending. It had taken a few years for us to get there, but it was as clear and unequivocal as a traffic light changing from green to yellow to red. Her independence, what little had remained, was exhausted. Now she would be guided through the rest of her life, hour by hour, day by day.

From the start, I never asked myself, "Why us? Why this?" and I don't think that she did either. At least I don't recall ever hearing her question her condition on that basis. If there was a cause, we wanted to know what that was, but we never thought it was punishment for some failing, divine retribution for our unbelief. Fundamentally, we were both pragmatists. We understood that we are mortal and accepted that fact. We knew that our lives are temporary and that each human life has an end as surely as it has a beginning. We'd each been raised as Catholics, Judy much less strictly than I, so we were both acculturated in Christian belief systems that assumed the existence of a God as well as an afterlife. By the time we married we'd both questioned those beliefs and, for ourselves, rejected them. We believed that we could live good lives honestly and morally as nontheists, that personal integrity isn't contingent on belief in a higher being. We accepted whatever came along, dealing with the good as well as the bad as ethically and conscientiously as possible.

Twenty-five or so years into our marriage we joined a Unitarian Universalist congregation, mostly at my urging; Judy was lukewarm to the idea, at least at first. I'd read their minister's periodic columns in the daily paper we subscribed to and saw that his philosophical perspectives were much like our own. I think that the main motivation for me was the promise of connection with a likeminded community of both believers and nonbelievers, and Judy was willing to come along for the ride. For the years that we were members of that congregation, it offered us social and spiritual enrichment that we found satisfying, yet we never needed it to be more than a way to better understand ourselves and our place in the world we were living in.

Neither of us looked at her diagnosis as some test of our moral fibre imposed by some judgmental, unseen being. It was life, it was a disease, we'd learn how to deal with it, and we'd be largely alone in doing that. Sure, we had many caring and supportive family members and friends who made up another family, but none of them could or would take us by the hand and walk us through this new world. We were on our own to map it, to try to understand it, to work to accommodate it. That intimidating reality was, probably for Judy as much as for me, the hardest part. She had a disease for which there was no effective or long-term treatment and for which there was no cure. We had no experience of it from which to try to squeeze even a tentative action plan. We learned that it would take the person she was and, piece by piece, erase that person and nearly everything she ever knew or felt or imagined.

It must have been horrifying for you, especially at the beginning. Sure, you'd think about the diagnosis and shed tears over it, and in the ensuing years you did express your frustration, sometimes anger, often enough. When you were entirely alone with your thoughts, though, what was that like for you? If I use my own thoughts at the time as a gauge, it must have been almost unbearable. From the moment your sentence was pronounced, "You have mild cognitive impairment consistent with younger onset Alzheimer's," I felt that we were launched in a too-small skiff onto some boundless black sea, no hint of shore in any direction, no rudder to steer with, a single oar—our union—to randomly slap at the water's cold and bleak surface. From your seat in that boat, what were you feeling?

We wondered often if this were something Judy had inherited genetically, not unusual with Alzheimer's disease, an unwelcome gift that keeps on taking rather than giving. As for her mother's side, Florence's parents and grandparents had been gone for so long that there really was no way to get at that medical history, and in any case, they'd died young by today's standards.

On Judy's father's side, the evidence was circumstantial, and again, we knew there was no way we'd ever be able to confirm it. We speculated, though, and while it wasn't entirely rational, I think there was an impulse to get an explanation or even to assign blame. More than once she'd said in frustration, "I've probably got my father to thank for this." She and he had always had a close relationship, though, and I don't think she ever really held him responsible.

He was sixty-nine when he died suddenly in 1989, twenty years before Judy's diagnosis. Her mother found him lifeless on their kitchen floor on a bright Sunday morning in autumn. A smoker for the better part of his adult life, he'd finally quit when grandchildren started to animate family gatherings. By then the damage was done, that massive coronary event only a matter of time. His aversion to doctors' offices, shared by many men of his Depression-era generation, probably also contributed to his early demise. Outwardly fit thanks to a work life building or renovating modest three-bedroom homes, he hadn't carried much extra weight around even into retirement. He rarely said anything about how he was feeling, and when he was visibly under the weather, he tended to withdraw and suffer in silence. The only chronic condition he'd ever dealt with was a gradually worsening deafness that, by his last years, had become nearly total.

The more Judy thought about it, the more convinced she became that her father's deafness had masked symptoms of cognitive impairment or dementia that none of us saw. She recalled taking him Christmas shopping at a local mall for gifts for her mother, when he suddenly became alarmed, maybe by the flow of shoppers? The many competing visual distractions? The din of a large commercial center a few days before a holiday? She wasn't sure. With a panicked expression he'd grabbed onto her arm too forcefully, stammering, "It's all spinning around! Let's go! Let's go!" and Judy, confused, had rushed him to the nearest exit.

"My father had a complete meltdown at the mall this afternoon," I remember her saying the first time that happened. By the time she got him home he'd relaxed, and as she told her mother what had happened, he didn't seem to recall any of it and shrugged off her retelling. When it happened a second time a few months later, she swore off any more good Samaritan outings. "He gets totally freaked out at the mall for some reason. I have no idea why," she said. "The next time he needs a gift for my mother I'll get it myself and let him give it to her. It was scary to see him like that."

We'd both noticed that he rarely remembered "to-do's" that came either from Judy's mother or from us unless it was written down and someone reminded him half a dozen times. Our homes, both of which he'd built from the ground up, faced each other across a narrow suburban street. Given his carpenter's skills, between his home and ours, and those of a few regular clients he'd strung along after he'd officially retired, he was rarely without some pending handyman project.

"Russ, look at me," I'd say to him, believing that his lip-reading skills might help him register whatever request I was making. "I picked up that new lock set for the basement door last week. You said you'd take care of that a few days ago. Any chance you can get to it today or tomorrow?"

"Sure, sure," he'd say. Inevitably, I'd find myself repeating the request a day or a week later. Sometimes I'd look him straight in the eye and ask, "Russ, what did I just say? Can you repeat what I just asked you?" He'd look at me blankly or sometimes he'd smile, slightly embarrassed, and reply, "Ugh, why don't you write it down?" Still, writing things down didn't always do the trick. I wasn't sure he got the words themselves or the meaning of those words strung together. We always chalked it up to his deafness.

Though he dropped out of high school to work full time, he'd always been a reader, and I think Judy got her love of reading from him. By his last years, though, he stopped making progress with the things he read. He'd pick up a book from the table by his chair, open at some bookmarked page that never turned. A short time later he'd set it down, the bookmark undisturbed, that part of the story in eternal stop motion, to be replayed the next time he sat down to relax. She'd get to that same place herself as her disease progressed. I'd sometimes glance at her alongside me in bed as we read, a novel by Louise Erdrich or a mystery by P. D. James in her hands, always on the same page, night after night.

I never met Judy's paternal grandmother, Elizabeth. Although growing up she said she hadn't been particularly close to her, her grandmother was a respected presence in the background of her childhood. Born in 1892 in Blackburn, England, she'd emigrated to the Fall River area with her family in the first years of the twentieth century, married Judy's grandfather Joseph Dionne just as the first World War erupted, and raised four sons with him before his death in 1947. We had one photograph of her taken late in life. In the snapshot she's sitting in the foreground, Judy's father and mother both smiling down at her from behind. She's looking toward the camera, but her eyes seem unfocused, somehow distant. The famous sparkle in her eye that family members always mentioned when they spoke of her had extinguished. She's not connecting with whoever's behind the camera. She looks a bit lost, a bit adrift. I eventually became very familiar with that look, both in Judy and in other residents of the memory care residence where she spent her last months.

Back when we studied that photo not long after Judy's diagnosis, we wondered if Elizabeth had dementia of some sort. Typical for working-class New England widows in the fifties and sixties, she'd aged at home, tended by her sons and their wives, who all lived nearby. Being "a little bit senile," if she was, was par for the course. Faithful to her nightly glass of beer and shot of whiskey, she died unexpectedly at the age of seventy-six in the little Quonset hut she'd called home since her husband passed on twenty-one years earlier. Her sons claimed she died content, that evening's empty beer and whiskey glasses set next to the chair where she was found the following morning. If she did suffer from Alzheimer's or some other cognitive impairment, it was never diagnosed.

6

*…all marriages start in ignorance and many from
need; what matters is what you do after you marry.*

– Donald Hall, from *The Best Day the Worst Day*

Dear Judy,

*It was always important to me that you and I be best friends.
Lovers, check; spouses, check; hands-on parents, check; best
friends threading it all together. Through the years that Trevor
was in grade school and high school I traveled a fair amount,
so when I was away the parenting fell more heavily on you.
Nonetheless, we always caught on when his only-child skill sets
tried to extract a "Yes" from one of us after the other had already
said "No." "We make the rules, kiddo, and nothing's unilateral.
We're both saying no."*

*In a sense we were business partners too. Being best friends
just made it all so much easier. I think that's why, once we
accepted your diagnosis and settled into the first years of our
Alzheimer's journey, we decided we'd make the best of it. That
thing about life giving you lemons and making lemonade from
them, even if that wasn't what you were in the mood to drink.
It's possible that living in the great central breadbasket helped,
the land of practicality and solid, traditional values. Droughts,
floods, tornadoes, insects, whatever. People around here are good
at making lemonade when lemons drop in their laps. Maybe it
was just some kind of all-American optimism.*

Judy plateaued through the months that we were in the clinical trial. At least from my vantage point she didn't seem to lose any ground beyond what she'd already lost. Despite some cognitive impairment, she was managing what are usually referred to as the activities of daily living without too much intervention from me. She chose what she'd wear on a particular day, could bathe and dress herself fine, and usually didn't have any problem getting herself breakfast or lunch. She was still driving to and from the gym where she attended yoga and workout classes and to various markets and shops when we needed one thing or another.

Around the time the clinical trial started, I began making reminder lists for her most weekdays when I would be away the better part of a given day. If she had an appointment with anyone, that would go on the list with the time she'd scheduled. Depending on what was in the refrigerator or kitchen cupboards I'd list a couple of lunchtime options, narrowing the choices to keep things simple. If some part of the house needed vacuuming or dusting, that would go on the list too, though typically we'd do cleaning chores on the weekend when we were home together. She'd always been an exacting housekeeper thanks to her perfectionist mother's example, and unlike me, she was never satisfied cleaning around things or just what could be seen. She'd move furniture and the things furniture held to be sure that no unseen dust would be left lurking underfoot. On the evenings when she cooked and I cleaned up afterward, she usually did justice to the familiar recipes that we cycled through in any given week or month. Early on, she'd sometimes drop an ingredient or two, or a step in the recipe process that would result in a facsimile version of the dish, fully edible but maybe lacking its usual interest or depth of flavor. That was no big deal. I was happy that she had enough to occupy her time through the day and that most of the time she seemed content with the situation.

At that early stage, our social life wasn't affected noticeably.

Friends still invited us out or to their places, and we reciprocated as often as we could. While I'd take on more of the food preparation when folks came over for a meal, we were still able to split up the myriad tasks that hosting a brunch or a dinner entailed. When I started noticing that Judy's post-party cleanup wasn't up to her longtime standards, I quickly learned to let that go. Mentioning it only made her defensive or angry. Better to keep her engaged; anything that smacked of criticism was always counterproductive.

I'd told a few colleagues and friends about her diagnosis, which in hindsight I realize meant that by the time she was well into the clinical trial, most of our social network probably knew what was going on. "Judy seemed fine to me tonight," our friend Jo whispered to me as she stepped through the front door after a convivial evening that began around our dining table and wound down by the fireplace. "She seems just as she's always been." "Judy was great at the gallery opening last weekend," a department colleague shared offhandedly a few days after a campus event. "I'd never have guessed that she has Alzheimer's." Trevor usually phoned me after he'd given her a check-in call. "I just got off the phone with Mom," he'd say. "She sounds great!"

Judy did manage to hold on to her graciousness and interest in others through those first few years, though as time passed it became a greater and greater effort. She could conceal that well, but after an evening out or a few hours with a tableful of guests, I could see the toll it took on her. She'd be exhausted, sleep the only remedy. How fortunate we were that her sleep patterns were never interrupted. That tends to be a major problem with many Alzheimer's sufferers, and it takes an enormous toll on their caregivers.

Judy's participation in the IGIV trial ended in early 2012, nearly twenty months after it began. She'd received thirty-six infusions that might have been placebos, half-doses, or full doses of the globulin product. Neither we nor the Medical Center study team had any way to know, and it hadn't really mattered. She and I felt that we were doing something that might help in the long run, even if it didn't help her in the moment. At the exit appointment there was more lab work, cognitive testing, and a final MRI. We felt a mix of nostalgia and regret as we wrapped things up. "I won't miss those MRIs, though," she said, her wit still intact. "They're loud enough to give me Alzheimer's—if I didn't already have it!"

Early in the trial, a state-of-the-art Center for Successful Aging had opened at the Medical Center. While roving nurses came to our home twice a month for her infusions, most of the periodic testing related to the study shifted to "successful aging," as we called it, not entirely without sarcasm. By then we'd recognized the irony, or at least the challenge, in the notion of her aging "successfully" with a terminal illness for which there was neither cure nor effective treatment.

As principal investigator, Dr. Mehta was unfailingly encouraging and supportive from visit to visit, but it was her study coordinator Carole Dixon, a registered nurse originally from Manchester, England, who made each roundtrip to Omaha an outing we looked forward to. We'd never experienced in any other medical facility the degree of warmth and concern that Carole generously offered us. Judy bonded with her quickly, as I did. Relaxed and soft spoken, Carole gave Judy one hundred percent of her attention with the ease and confidence of a professional and the sincerity of a true friend. Her accent, mellowed by many years living and working in the States, nonetheless betrayed its source in England's industrial north. Once we learned that she'd been raised and trained in Lancashire, where Judy's grandmother Elizabeth and my great-grandmother, Teresa Eccles James, were born and raised, our bond with Carole was cemented. "She's the kindest person," Judy said when we left Successful Aging for the last time. "I'll miss seeing her." I felt the same.

Once active participation in the trial was behind us, Judy started an accelerated downhill slide that nothing would slow. It didn't happen overnight, but the gradual increase in short-term memory lapses complicated both her day-to-day activities and our communications, to the degree that my concerns about her safety quickly became a priority. She was still driving, and I worried that she'd be involved in an accident at some point. Typically, she wasn't venturing far, mainly to the gym for yoga sessions or to the market or to get her hair done. Nonetheless, I didn't feel confident that in a crisis she'd be able to manage on her own. Her language skills were starting to slip as aphasia gained more traction.

With anything that involved a series of steps—for example, something as simple as making herself a sandwich or putting a load of clothes in the washer, then drying and folding them—the chances increased that she'd invert those steps somehow or leave one out, with outcomes that often fell short of the original intention. Often, she'd realize something didn't produce the results she anticipated, but she couldn't figure out why. A day's dishes hadn't come out of the dishwasher clean because she'd run the cycle without dish detergent. She thought her breakfast granola tasted weird but didn't register that she'd put sour cream into it instead of yogurt. Higher-order thinking was fast becoming her adversary. To make her way in the world without that capability put her in a very vulnerable place. Frankly, I wasn't always sure what to do about it.

Nonetheless, when I look back on that period, I can see many ways in which we were fortunate, in which I was fortunate. For many caregiving spouses, especially those working for hourly wages, being employed full time means having to be away from home for eight or nine or ten hours every weekday, and inevitably, as the disease advances, that becomes unsustainable. A job or career is easily compromised when the significant distractions of caregiving interfere with expectations placed on the worker. I was salaried, and my work schedule offered plenty of flexibility. My varied responsibilities could be addressed in numerous ways, and it was the rare deadline that didn't come with many weeks' or months' notice. Because I had moved to fully online course delivery early in my years as department chair, nearly all my interactions with students took place in those virtual spaces. I'd occasionally meet with my students face to face in my office, but those instances were exceptions. We inhabited virtual classrooms, so I could be almost anywhere in the world and still have easy access.

On the other hand, most of the meetings that came with the administrative side of my position were face to face, so a certain amount of my time had to be spent on campus. There were some days when those meetings were back-to-back, though infrequently. Often, with the help of my office manager, I could organize them all into a morning or an afternoon, especially those that repeated at regular intervals. This meant that I could block "out of office / work from home" portions of the day. I'd spread and stack files, folders, documents, and assorted correspondence on our dining room table and carry on from there knowing that I was getting the work done and keeping Judy company. At least for a few hours on days like that I could feel reassured that she was safe and less at risk than she'd be whenever I left her alone.

One day I pulled into our driveway after one of those campus mornings of continual meetings, anticipating a late lunch and then a few hours grading graduate seminar papers. I'd checked in with her a couple hours earlier, between meetings. She'd just showered before I called and was having a cup of tea. She seemed fine. "I'm not sure what time I'll get home," I'd said, "but I'll be there the rest of the afternoon."

I hit the remote to close the garage door just as I opened my car door. It took me just a second to figure out that the loud, shrill beeping I was hearing, easily audible over the sound of the lowering garage door, was the kitchen smoke alarm. I opened the kitchen door into a gray haze that filled the space and immediately moved past me into the garage. I looked at the stove but saw no flames. Judy was there, standing in the middle of the kitchen, and then I saw the saucepan in her hand. "What happened?" I asked. "Are you alright?" Tears were running down her cheeks, and she seemed stuck in place. "What did you do?"

"My lunch, it burned."

Classic. Most Alzheimer's caregivers have a similar story, some leftover scooped into a pan to reheat and then forgotten, charred to a blackened mess, a part of the house filled with smoke. That was our version of this unsurprising mini crisis. Version two: a large wooden spoon in a catch-all utensil container dangerously near the pan on the stove catches fire too, igniting the underside of a cupboard above, and the entire kitchen goes up in flames. That could have been our scenario but mercifully wasn't.

"I'm sorry," she said.

"It's fine; you didn't burn yourself, did you?" I asked. That pan's handle must have been seriously hot, but she had a dish towel between her palm and it. She'd thought of that, thank goodness. "Well, no more heating things up. I'll make you a lunch ahead from now on when I'm not going to be here." Little things, from one day to the next, adding up over time to a complete overhaul of how we went about activities that most people don't give a second thought to. The creative adjustments and changes, though, only worked for a while.

In midwinter 2013 I finally stopped her driving. I'd put it off as long as I could, trying over many months to find ways that she could hold on to the sense of independence that driving afforded her and that I knew was important to her. She wasn't going very far anymore, and there were days when her beloved 1995 forest green Saab didn't leave the garage. That was a rugged car and, at about 160,000 miles, was still serving us well. Its doors had a kind of basso heft, reassuringly solid, and it was equipped with airbags, so I felt that she was relatively well protected. I always breathed a bit easier when I knew she'd be staying put, though, since her being out and about always increased my anxiety levels. There were all the other drivers on the road to factor in.

Judy's most recent driver's license renewal notice had come a year or so earlier, and looking it over the day the notice arrived I was reminded that it asks whether, within the last three months, the applicant has suffered from any impairment of memory or memory loss. *Hmm*, I thought to myself, *what's going to happen when we answer yes to that one?*

"Your driver's license renewal came today," I told her after I'd sorted through the mail. "We've got a month or so to deal with it, so when you're ready I'll go over the form with you."

A few days later I turned the corner into our cul-de-sac at the end of an afternoon on campus and Judy was pulling into the driveway just ahead of me. "What have you been up to?" I asked as the garage door closed. "I just went to get my license renewed," she said with a lilt in her voice, evidently proud of her accomplishment. "You what?" I said, more than surprised. "Yeah, I went over to the DMV before I went to the market. They renewed my license, no problem."

And the memory question, I thought to myself, *how'd you answer that?* If she got her renewal, there's only one way she could have answered it. I didn't pursue it. There were still enough good days at that point that I held onto any moments of relative normalcy. *This must be one of those days, and I guess we should profit by it,* I told myself. Yet, I knew these good days were numbered.

"You know, Judy, we really need to start talking seriously about the future and how we should put things in place so that when we need help—and there's going to be a point when we will need outside help—it won't amount to some kind of emergency."

"Why?" she asked.

"Because you have a progressive disease and it's only going to get worse."

"And what disease is that?" she asked flatly.

"Alzheimer's, sweetie. You have Alzheimer's."

Judy looked at me blankly for a moment, as if this was news and she needed to process it. I guess she did. Her blank expression was erased by a knowing smile that lifted the corners of her eyes and brought a smile to my face.

"Well," she chuckled, "I guess I'm going to have to remember that!"

Whenever her sense of humor showed signs of life, it was

like sunshine blazing suddenly from behind densely packed cloud cover. It warmed me, and I chuckled too.

The driving question nagged at me, though. I checked with our auto insurance agent, and she said that we were covered if Judy were involved in an accident, whether she was at fault or not. "But what if it were known that she had a diagnosis of younger onset Alzheimer's?" I asked.

"Can I recommend something?" the agent asked. "You can have your wife's driving evaluated through a couple of agencies here in town, and they'll give you recommendations on what to do. Why don't you try that? It may be the best way for you to figure out next steps." She referred me to a nearby rehabilitation hospital, and after we spoke with one of their examiners, we got our primary care physician's order for the testing and set up the appointment. Judy wasn't pleased. "My driving is fine," she insisted. "You just want to control me! I can't even have a life anymore!"

She was right that her life was changing. Our lives were changing. She was losing agency, something she'd fought hard for as an adolescent, as all teens do. Nearly five decades later, giving it up would be just as complicated, just as contentious, just as messy.

I was becoming less husband and partner and more parent or warden. I hated that role. I think she understood that I needed to protect her, that her security was becoming a focal point in my life not because I wanted to control her but to keep her safe. Nonetheless, the disease and I, like a couple of ill-matched conspirators, were chipping away at her autonomy, and there were days when she wasn't having it.

We pulled her Saab into Gateway Rehabilitation Hospital's parking lot a week later, and she followed the signs to Visitor Parking. "Just do what you've done between home and here and you'll be fine," I said. I wasn't sure how she'd do with a driving simulator, but behind the wheel of her own car her reactions and timing were still good.

The examiner introduced herself as Sylvia. She appeared to be a few years younger than us, her well-practiced professional demeanor courteous but not friendly. "We'll go this way," she said. She led us through a large, open physical therapy area to a small examining room tucked behind a group of treadmill stations. After she dimmed the lights, Sylvia tapped a keyboard, and three darkened monitors slowly came to life.

I think there'd likely be some disconnect using a driving simulator even for someone with unimpaired executive function. Judy's was impaired, and the artificiality of a horizontal cluster of digital screens running software-generated traffic animations in a darkened testing room, with an examiner and a family member lurking on the sidelines, didn't contribute to her performance that afternoon. She clearly wasn't convinced by the virtual world the technology had placed her in, and I could see that her reaction times were slower than what I'd witnessed on our drive to the testing site. Forty-five minutes later the first part of the evaluation was behind her.

"Okay, now we're going to take you out on the road for the final assessment," Sylvia said. "We have our own car for testing, so we'll head this way." We exited the exam room and started toward the front of the building. "Your husband can sit in the back, and I'll be next to you in the passenger seat."

"We can't use her car?" I asked. "It's what she's used to."

"I'm afraid for insurance reasons and testing parameters we'll need to use the hospital's vehicle," she replied. "It's pretty standard, though."

Ah, but not. Her Saab was four on the floor, a manual transmission that we'd always felt was more involving and fun to drive. A hand on the gently vibrating stick shift made a better connection with the car itself and with the roadway, or so Judy had always claimed. Only on rare occasions in recent years had she driven a car with an automatic transmission—her mother's Toyota when she visited her or a rental when we vacationed at some airline destination. "Point and shoot," she called it. "Not like real driving."

The older model Oldsmobile Cutlass that Sylvia pointed to as we reached the parking area had a larger footprint than Judy's Saab and was less well maintained. A few dents marred the side panels, and the finish had clearly not seen paste wax in many years. When I saw the front passenger-side brake pedal, I figured that it was a well-used driver's ed warrior. *Ah, the road test,* I thought. *Every novice driver's bugaboo, and now, senior citizens' too.*

"Where do you usually do your grocery shopping?" Sylvia asked.

"Grocery shopping?" Judy replied, confused. "I guess at Hy-Vee. The one on Main Street."

"Okay," Sylvia said, "why don't we head there? When we get there, I'd like you to drive into their lot and park in an available space. "How does that sound?"

Judy eased out of the hospital parking lot maybe a bit more carefully than usual but used her signal before she turned and moved into the correct lane as we approached the first intersection. Points for her. Neither Sylvia nor I said anything more as she headed north, and she seemed purposeful enough behind the wheel that I began to relax. She registered the "No Turn on Red" sign at the next major intersection and waited for the green arrow before she turned. More points for her. I noticed her acceleration once she moved into the middle lane on Main Street and sensed that she'd relaxed too. A few city blocks later the market appeared on the right, and I anticipated her next lane change, but apparently, she'd decided on some other destination. The market came and went, or we came and went, as Judy continued in her center lane.

"Judith, do you remember where I asked you to go?" Sylvia's neutral tone didn't completely hide her concern.

"Umm, I'm not sure now," Judy replied as we approached the next intersection. "Should I turn here?" Before Sylvia could answer, Judy suddenly hit the brakes, slowing down as she made a quick glance over her shoulder. Without signaling she moved into the right lane just barely ahead of another driver who leaned on his horn as he slowed down to avoid colliding with us. More points docked.

"Just stay in this lane." Sylvia's curt answer betrayed her irritation. "After the light, stay in this lane and then take the following right turn. We'll go around the block and then head back down to the hospital." From that point she directed her along a return route Judy had driven countless times, though she didn't seem to recognize it. Ten minutes later we were back at our starting point. "Let's go back in," Sylvia said as Judy passed her the keys, "and we'll review all your results."

Sylvia seemed sympathetic enough, though administering these types of evaluations multiple times in a day had to challenge both her patience and stress levels. "You were a bit confused with some of the questions in the first part of the exam," Sylvia said, "but that part of your score is in the acceptable range. The fact that you forgot our destination in the actual road test does tell me that your memory is impaired. My recommendation is that going forward, you do not drive alone. A licensed driver should always be with you. We want you to be safe, and with another driver you'll have some help in any unexpected situation. Are you okay with that?"

I watched Judy's reaction as Sylvia delivered her verdict. She was processing what Sylvia was telling her, and her crestfallen expression told me exactly how she was feeling.

"You drive," Judy told me when we returned to her car. "I don't want to. You drive." Tears rolled down her cheeks as she closed the passenger-side door and buckled her seatbelt.

"Judy," I started.

"I just want my life back," she said before I could continue. "I just want my life back."

Nearly a year-and-a-half after the clinical trial ended, Dr. Mehta forwarded the results of the study. I'd forgotten that one day we'd finally hear back, and so finding that envelope in the mail was a surprise. Judy seemed indifferent, but I felt some tension as I sliced along its top fold and thought to myself, *And the winner is...*

The lead project director's letter opened with the sponsors' thanks for our participation in the Gammaglobulin Alzheimer's Partnership Study of Gammagard IGIV, 10% treatment. It then zeroed in on its main finding:

"Unfortunately, this analysis indicated that IGIV treatment did not significantly slow the rate of progression of Alzheimer's disease on a test of thinking ability and a measure of daily function. Additional analysis is being carried out and more results will be reported later this year."

Although disappointing, that outcome interested me less than the next piece of information they shared with us:

"Your treatment group for this study was a high dose of IGIV."

Reading that, I felt that we'd lucked out, and I wasn't inclined to dismiss any possible effect, however small, that the infusions might have had. "You were getting the full dose IGIV product," I said. "It wasn't the placebo or the half-dose. That's really cool."

Through the twenty months of the study Judy had been entirely stable. I'd seen no worsening of her symptoms. Sure, the "jolts" as I sometimes called them, those weird verbal or spatial disconnections, continued sporadically, but with no more frequency than before the trial started. Day to day, she was getting along fine. Her routines worked for both of us, and we felt no need to adjust nor elaborate.

News releases distributed when the results were announced discussed ongoing data analyses suggesting that certain subgroups in the study may have done better than others.[9] If not significant enough to warrant further study, the possibility existed that at least some study subjects benefited from the treatments. I want to believe that Judy was one of those. I admit I don't have anything more to go on than anecdotal evidence. The pace at which things started to head south for her after the infusions ended, though, gave me reason to feel that she had, in fact, held steady because of the treatments. They'd gained us a longer stretch of near normalcy than we likely would have had otherwise. If it wasn't enough, it was something, and I was grateful for it.

7

We shall wish not to be alone
And that love were not dispersed and set free––
Though you defeat me,
And I be heavy upon you.

— Louise Bogan, from *Leave-Taking*

Dear Judy,

The slow but inexorable accumulation of losses strung out over three or four years' time took a real toll on both of us, in different ways. Coping with them was a full-time effort, round the clock, and though your sleep wasn't affected, mine was. Inevitably, at 2:30 or 3:00 or 3:30 I'd wake from one unpleasant dream or another to the darkness around us and to an ever-evolving list of worries and worst-case scenarios that resisted my best efforts to banish them.

More than once I dreamt that I was kneeling alone on an immense black tarmac in some ambiguous, featureless space. I could see a hulking, threatening piece of wheeled steel and iron machinery coming toward me. It grew louder, and its vibrations shook me as it drew relentlessly nearer, and I could do nothing to stop it or to save myself. I couldn't get myself on my feet, I couldn't run, I couldn't make a sound. I'd wake or pull myself from the dream just as the awful vehicle's shadow overtook me. It exhausted me to have that dream, to feel that powerlessness. Then, brought back to consciousness, my near-constant anxieties would unfailingly be waiting for me.

How did you manage to find the courage that you faced it with, when Alzheimer's was bearing down on you just as relentlessly and unstoppably as that contraption on me? You must have felt something like that, dreamt something of the sort. Despite it all, you managed to embrace each new day, often with delight, even optimism. That was courage, and you had so much of it. I admired that in you then, and I still admire it.

Shaken awake in the middle of the night, I'd get up, bring a cup of herbal tea back to bed with me, pick up a book or my e-reader, and hope that I'd doze off again before the windows brightened or my alarm sounded. Once the day was launched, it often felt as if I were running an obstacle course, trying constantly to manage an increasingly challenging home life and a relentlessly demanding work life.

I think that for you, loneliness became the biggest burden in those first years after the diagnosis. We had many good friends who, like us, had busy home lives and careers that they were investing in. Their spare time was already at a premium, and the best they or we might manage were weekend couples' get-togethers, enough to sustain the friendships but not enough to fill the growing void in your daily life. Your diagnosis forced you to retreat just as you'd reached a level of career accomplishment that you'd worked years to achieve. That premature withdrawal from the work world isolated you by cutting you off from the social networks you were part of, that were so important to your self-esteem. You were no longer participating in those conversations, no longer sharing in those concerns. You'd moved to the peripheries of those circles, and you'd continue to move further away as the disease advanced.

"How have you been feeling?" Dr. Breyer asked as he moved the cold metal head of his stethoscope from one part of my back to another. I was in for my annual physical, a bit more than three years into Judy's diagnosis.

"I'm pretty exhausted, actually," I remember saying. I told him about my trouble sleeping through the night, waking to a whirlwind of anxieties that I struggled to dispel, not always successfully. I told him that some nights I envied Judy and her unfailing ability to get to sleep and to stay asleep. True, by then she was on a daily dose of Lexapro, an anti-depressant he'd pre-scribed for her at my request not long after the clinical trial had ended. Her sadness had become persistent. Although she could keep it at bay around other people, when it was just Judy and me it would overwhelm her, the tears coming on suddenly, silent-ly, abundantly. The anti-depressant seemed to take the edge off her sadness. Her mood improved, some of her sense of humor returned, and the weeping episodes lessened both in frequency and intensity. Witnessing her improvement had an equally tonic effect on me, though it hadn't helped my insomnia.

Gently, Dr. Breyer's fingers began checking the lymph nodes in my head and neck, familiar probing that punctuated each annual exam. "For some of my patients in situations similar to yours," he said after a few moments of silence, "prayer offers them comfort and some measure of peace."

Did I just hear that right? I thought to myself. *Are you pre-scribing prayer for my insomnia?* I said nothing as I lay back on the examining table and he began tapping my midsection. Admittedly, the large family practice group in which he was a partner openly displayed its Christian affiliations. It isn't unusual in the heartland to find yourself staring at crucifixes or biblical quotations or other religiously inflected decor in some phy-sicians' offices and waiting rooms. If the care we received was professional and up-to-date, and if our health and well-being seemed as important to our care providers as it was to us, we could get along fine with true belief on condition it made no de-mands of us.

"Look, Dr. Breyer," I finally said, my natural assertiveness rising with what was likely my deepest inhalation of that exam.

"I'm not someone who prays to any god nor to an idea of God. I know many people who do, and that's fine. Their prayer may help them, it almost certainly doesn't hurt them, and it doesn't hurt me. I was raised Catholic, so I've been there and done that. At this point in my life, though, I'm interested in what science can do to help me and to help my wife. For me, prayer isn't going to cut it."

As I was telling Judy about Dr. Breyer's suggestion later that day, I realized that I'd probably overreacted. He was well-intentioned, I knew that. I also knew that I was stressed, that I was juggling a surplus of responsibilities and expectations both at home and at work. Deprived of sleep, I was far from 100 percent at any of the long list of things that needed attention or that waited for solutions. That frustrated me, and that frustration was an incubator of my negativity and impatience, both of which often enough claimed Judy as their first victim.

The anti-anxiety medication he prescribed as we wrapped up that appointment did the trick as far as sleep went, at least for four or five nights out of seven. I was grateful for that. With six-and-a-half or seven hours of sleep, I could manage a long day without dozing off in a meeting or at my office computer; four-and-a-half or five just didn't bring me to a minimum threshold of functionality. Two weekdays each week I'd leave the house a few minutes before five so I could be at the nearby gym when it opened, and that worked best when I'd had a decent night's sleep. Workout, shave, and shower behind me, I'd be back at home before Judy stirred. I'd have breakfast over the day's paper, get a lunch put together for each of us—mine to take with me—and write up any reminders, suggestions, or to-do's she'd need for the time she'd be on her own. I'd wake her sometime between 7:30 and 8:00 and leave for campus as soon as she'd settled into breakfast. And then I'd hope she'd be okay until I returned.

In the first couple years she was. The disease, though, quietly extinguished her early determination to continue with her art making. The kind of critical thinking and processing that serious creative work requires became harder for her to initiate. There were dark moments when she understood this, and it added to her sadness. Most days, though, after showering and dressing, she would settle down in the room she used as her studio and lose herself in curating and organizing the contents of drawers, storage containers large and small, and the surfaces of her worktables.

She'd handle and sort fabrics and arrange them in groups, stacking leftover remnants whose colors or tonalities pleased her. I think that all things tactile grew in importance for her. Feeling those fabrics, folding and re-folding them, sandwiching them in different ways, offered her a measure of comfort and satisfaction that helped to fill some of the solitude she occupied.

She paid similar attention to her various collections. Stones, sea glass, and small shells, a collection of objects given up by various beaches we'd walked and hikes we'd taken in travels over the course of many years, could take her back to those places at least in spirit. From her home sewing days, she'd amassed a large cache of unusual buttons that she'd originally purchased because they promised to serve as singular finishing touches in the clothes she made for herself. She'd sort and re-sort them in plastic containers subdivided by numerous small compartments. Making decisions about which buttons to group together and how to distribute groups of buttons of varying sizes and colors must have helped her feel a sense of control, a sense that she could still manage those things that had, over many years, inspired her.

It was much the same with photographs, artists' exhibition announcement cards, and the other accumulated miscellany that she'd pinned to her studio walls since she'd taken over that space. During many of those long days alone in her workroom she'd sort and rearrange them, matching or mismatching according to the patterns or textures or colors they contained. It became a kind of work in progress with no declared objective and no outward significance other than that it helped the hours pass. At the same time, I imagine there was some creative value for her in bringing odds and ends together, in making decisions about how to arrange them and how to store them. I'd ask what she had in mind when she grouped these things here, those there; what she was thinking when she moved the contents of this drawer to an abutting one; what she wanted to say with a small altar-like display that appeared on this table one day and then on another across the room the next, enlarged and reconfigured. "I just like to do this," she'd reply. "It's what I like to do."

One day I returned from campus to find her collections of scavenged seashells and souvenir rocks laid out purposefully on our bed. She'd transferred them from her studio across the hall.

"So, it looks as if you've been busy this afternoon."

"I just wanted to see all of my rocks and shells, so I moved them here."

She correctly identified the Swiss source of a couple of uniquely striated stones, surprising me that the memory was still with her.

"Do you have any next steps now that all of these are spread out on our bed?"

"Well, it doesn't matter," she replied.

"I think they may be in the way later, when it's time to call it a night. Do you want to help me move them back to your studio?"

"Why?"

"Well, because it won't be very comfortable to have these in bed with us tonight."

"I want them here."

I decided to let the issue rest, and by the time we were ready to turn in a few hours later, Judy's commitment to their new location had softened, and she agreed to help me move them back. That promised to be a bit of a project since she insisted that each had its own place, and we couldn't mix them up.

"How about we just put them in rows on your worktable and tomorrow you can take your time returning each one to its special spot?" I was too tired to contrive any kind of feint to get her to agree and hoped she'd just go along with it.

"I'm going to work with these tomorrow, so leave them where they are."

That was fine with me.

In subsequent months, these transfers of various objects and materials from her studio to our bedroom became more elaborate and complicated, and some days involved not only our bed but a cushioned chair and ottoman alongside it, and our dresser. What had seemed purposeful to me at the outset gradually appeared more and more chaotic and random, a jumble of things whose associations, if she had any intent in that regard, were unknown to me. I managed to convince her that the dresser top was the best place for her to focus her attentions, relieved when she agreed and the task of clearing off the bed late each evening was put behind us.

Spools of thread. The already mentioned stones and seashells. Snapshots of the granddaughters. Lipstick tubes and skin cream. Small gift boxes, each occupied by more stones and shells, by buttons and beads, embroidery floss, rubber bands, pencils and pens, toothpicks and dental floss, eyeglasses, paper clips and Emory boards, folded tissues, an AARP membership card, an expired driver's license, lip gloss, a pin cushion, some postcards, swatches of dyed fabric, a dried gingko leaf, a chopstick. You're wondering how I still recall this scenario. I photographed it. It seemed remarkable somehow.

I'd always been a neatnik, and at one time she'd have known that this kind of mishmash could really test my forbearance. That was the furthest thing from her mind at that point. And how could I complain, given the hours she'd spend standing at that dresser, handling each item, moving it from here to there, shifting the contents of this woven basket to that metal box, stacking and restacking greeting cards and photos and penciled notes, her left-handed jottings from the before times?

Were you trying to locate some semblance of order in that disarray? Stephen Sondheim's character George Seurat opens the musical Sunday in the Park with George *declaring, "White. A blank page or canvas. The challenge: Bring order to the whole."[10] Is that what you were doing? While I was downstairs in my own*

Three months after Judy's driving evaluation, I finally took her
keys. I hadn't planned to do it just then. I knew it was coming at
some point, but limited to driving with someone else alongside
her, she'd reduced her outings behind the wheel to two or three
a week, when I was free to go along. Having a chaperone took
some of the pleasure out of it for her. Cars represent independence, but her feeling of independence was compromised with
me in the passenger seat.

I'd scheduled my car for an oil change at a nearby service
station. On a warmer day I'd have dropped it off and walked the
mile or so back home, but it was January, a cold morning made
colder by a brisk wind out of the north. "Follow me to Kelly's
service station on 66th Street," I said as we each got into our vehicles. "I'll leave my car, and we'll come back in yours."

I backed out of our driveway and then moved forward to
the intersection a few yards ahead, waiting briefly as Judy backed
out behind me. I turned right and started down the gentle slope
toward our subdivision's outlet. In my rearview mirror I could
see our corner clearly, and as I advanced expected to see her car
behind me. Nothing. When I got to the point at which I knew that
intersection would fade from view, I stopped, waiting. No forest
green Saab. Unsure where she was, I backed into a far neighbor's
driveway and returned to the intersection. Her car was where I'd

left it when I turned from our cul-de-sac. I pulled alongside and she lowered her window.

"What's the matter?" I asked.

"It won't move forward," she said, a bit exasperated. "I can't get it to go!"

"Have you got it in first gear?" I asked.

"Yes! Look, I'm telling you, it won't go."

"Okay, put it in neutral and put the parking brake on. I'll get in."

I pulled my car over, turned it off, and went to hers. She stepped out, I sat down, released the parking brake, slid it into first and began to move forward.

"I don't think there's anything wrong with your car. It seems fine. It's running fine. I'm not sure what you were doing, but the car's fine."

I went back to mine, she retook her driver's seat, and we started over. I circled around behind her then passed between her and our driveway, turned the corner, and continued down the hill, my eyes returning to my rearview every couple of seconds. No green Saab followed behind. Reaching the point where I'd lose sight of the top of the slope, I turned around a second time, unsure what was going on.

"I'm telling you! It won't go!" Her exasperation had increased proportional to my growing impatience. I pulled into our driveway, secured my car, and walked the few steps to hers. Looking in, I noticed that the parking brake was engaged.

"Did you release the parking brake? You can't move forward with the parking brake on."

She looked down at the brake's handle, then at me. "Oh, I think I forgot to release the brake," she said, a mixture of relief, embarrassment, and confusion replacing the irritation that her expression revealed seconds before. I should have seen the humor in this and made light of it, but I wasn't amused.

"This is the last time you're going to drive," I said. "Follow me to the service station and that's it. You're done driving."

I wonder what she was thinking as we drove that final mile.

As soon as I realized what was going on, I'd imagined some similar scenario in which a police officer or some other law enforcement person was telling her to move her car, and she was going through the same exercise, unable to get it to move. That wouldn't go over well. Nope, this was it, no more driving.

In the weeks following, each time we'd enter the garage from our kitchen she'd go to her car, and I'd say, "No, Judy, we're going in my car." Sometimes she'd tear up; always a wave of sadness would overtake her. She didn't object aloud, but each time was like the first, another loss, another subtraction, another insult.

I arranged to sell the Saab a month-and-a-half later. One of the technicians at the service station who'd usually done the tune-ups on her car and knew how well it had been cared for agreed to take it off our hands.

"We don't need two cars right now," I explained, "and there's no point in paying extra to insure it. Matt likes working on your car and so we'll sell it to him. With the mileage it has on it, we'll be needing to do some expensive repairs if we keep it. So, this is the best solution for us and the Saab."

I think she understood. She didn't object in any case. Once the car was gone, the funk she'd fall into each time she couldn't get into her own driver's seat disappeared. She didn't completely forget it, but out of sight was out of mind. Though at the time they were relatively few and far between in Nebraska, we'd see the occasional Saab on the road, and she'd say, "I loved my Saab. That was a great car." She was right. It had served her well and kept her safe. I hated taking it from her, and she from it. As she had done with so much else, she accepted what she couldn't do anything about. She didn't lose sleep over it.

The travel we did that summer clued me into an interesting phenomenon. Removed from our everyday surroundings, Judy's illness seemed much less present, much less in the foreground. Irregularities in her behavior, her increasing forgetfulness or confusion, seemed more exaggerated at home. When we traveled, some disorientation or confusion and even forgetfulness aligned better with the dislocation that travel imposes. Sure, I was sometimes filling in gaps in her thinking, but generally those irregularities seemed less extraordinary when we were far from our domestic everyday.

So long road trips became both escape and relief. Almost anything beyond a two- or three-hour drive qualified. It simply had to be enough time to let the mostly flat or gently rolling landscapes of the Plains and their broad expanses of uninterrupted sky decompress and relax us. It didn't matter much whether we were cruising along a major interstate or opting for the more easygoing pace of state or county highways. As each successive mile marker approached and then disappeared, we settled into the moment. Enclosed in a steel cocoon, we were whole, a singular unit contained, isolated, and protected, not just from the physical vagaries of the road but from the psychological aggressions of the disease.

I don't know the degree to which Judy was conscious of this, though it was always plain to me that she appreciated getting away from all the things that kept reminding her of her slowly mounting losses. She was always game when I announced a pending trip and eager especially in the last hours before we'd set off. That was true throughout those six years, even beyond the point at which she couldn't hold on to a particular destination and had to be reminded, again and again.

"Where are we going?" she'd ask an hour or two out of Lincoln.

"We're going to Somerset; we're going to see your mother. It's a long drive. We won't get there until Saturday. Just relax."

"Where did you say we're going?" she'd ask an hour or two later. I learned on the longest trips to substitute the nearest destination, so that I didn't feel that I was repeating myself endlessly. "We're going to Louisville," I'd say, "to visit our friend Neisja," or

"We're going to stop for lunch with my brother and his wife in Columbus," or "We're going to Youngstown, to spend a night with Susan and Bob." While Judy could still write things down, she'd make lists of these destinations to help her remember. It's curious; I found one the other day bookmarking a photo album from a three-week trip we made in the summer of 2010. Her familiar combination of left-handed cursive and block letters recorded the outgoing itinerary:

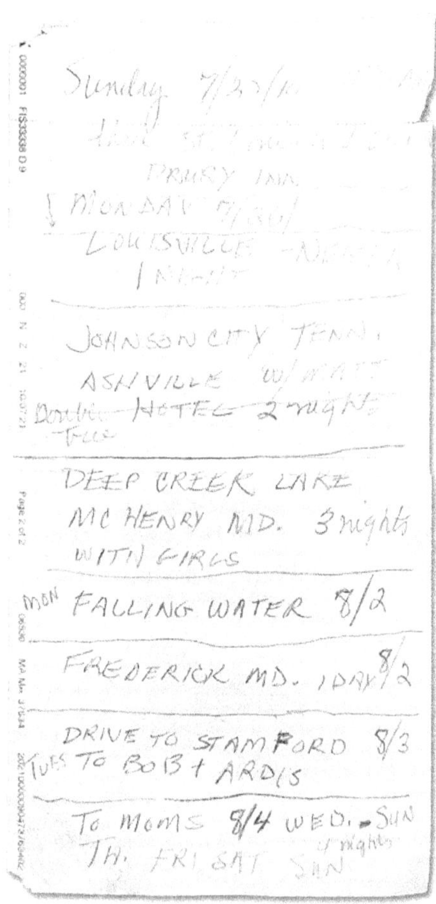

On the back side she'd added the stops along the return trip that had us back in Nebraska a dozen days into August. From repeated handling and frequent reviews her list slowly wore around the edges, her penciled items' smudging contributing to the patina that slip of paper acquired during thirty-six hundred or so miles. I'm glad to have that list; it prompts some very vivid memories these ten years later. As it did for her, then.

Homeward bound by car one Sunday midway through that first diagnosis summer, after a weekend getaway to Central City, Colorado, where we'd enjoyed performances of three operas in two days presented in a restored nineteenth-century opera house, I thought to check for any voice messages as we were approaching the Nebraska border. In the mountains we'd had only spotty phone service, and not long after arriving I'd zipped my phone into my messenger bag's pocket, out of sight, out of mind for the duration.

When the second message sounded, we recognized our friend and university colleague Eva's voice.

"Hi, you two. Don't be alarmed, but the Lincoln police are trying to get in touch with you and want you to phone them. One of your neighbors told them you worked at the university, and that led them to your dean, who didn't have your cell number. She remembered that Tom and I are friends of yours so that's how they tracked us down. It's something about your home being broken into. I won't keep you, just give the police department a call. Okay, talk soon."

The officer I reached within a minute or so was matter of fact.

"Neighbors walking past your home about 9:00 this morning noticed that a large picture window at the front was smashed through, and we've determined that someone entered your home. No idea yet if anything was taken, and we'll need you to confirm that one way or the other. Do you have an idea when you'll arrive back in Lincoln?"

We were still about five hours out, so I gave them an ETA.

"Do you have someone you can enlist to board up the window at some point today? Right now, it's open to the elements."

"Yes, I'll phone our contractor; he lives nearby, and if he can't do it, I'm sure he can find us someone who can."

"That sounds good. Phone us when you arrive back at your home, and we'll send an officer to do a walkthrough with you."

That five-hour drive seemed twice as long as it would have otherwise, and we said little the entire way. Whatever relaxation and recreation benefit the weekend had provided was now supplanted by yet another wave of apprehension and malaise. Had somebody deliberately targeted us, and if so, who and why? Was this totally random? Had we entered on some "when bad things happen to good people" part of our lives?

Standing in our bedroom, its shattered window now backed by a sheet of raw plywood, a lot of "what ifs" raced through my mind. What if we'd been home? What if the intruder or intruders had entered the room just as we roused ourselves? What if they had weapons? What if…

The classic term for how we felt in that moment was *violated*, and seeing stains of blood on our bedcover and on our floor, broken glass strewn over, under, and around our bed, no other word describes the feeling more aptly. The officer who showed up a quarter-hour after we walked through the door was sympathetic, though I sensed that for her this was routine. They figured that at least one person entered our bedroom through the smashed window and in doing so cut himself or herself, hence the numerous drops of blood on the floor and on the duvet. They'd already taken samples to a lab. The blood stopped about five feet into the room, so they guessed the perpetrator had somehow staunched the wound by that point. Since there appeared to be a computer missing from another room, they surmised that the motive was theft.

"Well, actually," I told the officer, "I put my wife's laptop out of sight before we left, and I left mine on campus this past weekend. If hers is where I hid it, then we may not have a theft." The computer was indeed where I'd concealed it, slid between some books on a shelf alongside Judy's white computer table, now blackened by fingerprint powder. Not until later that evening would we discover that the only thing taken in the break-in was a decades-old radio-alarm clock combo resting on a small stack of books that included Judy's e-reader that she'd forgotten to bring along on the weekend trip. The worthless clock likely went because its red electronic digits were the only things the intruders could see in the darkness of our room. They weren't going to leave empty-handed. The $400 e-reader might have brought a few bucks, but its inconspicuousness redeemed it. These folks surely weren't bibliophiles.

A couple days later they'd identified and arrested the perpetrators: two neighborhood brothers, juveniles who'd drunk a bit too much and over several nighttime hours had meandered through numerous backyards, overturning outdoor furniture, smashing ceramic pots, randomly targeting no one in particular—a little Saturday night mayhem to bring some sparkle to their under-stimulated suburban lives.

Unfortunately for us, ours was the only home broken into. Fortunately for us, we weren't home. The older brother had apparently goaded the younger, who'd thrown the stone that destroyed the window and who'd entered, cut himself, and as he bled and began to panic, grabbed the nearest thing he could see, the clock radio, and made a quick exit. We learned another day or two later that neighbors a few houses from us had been awakened by the sound of shattering glass, had seen the teens running away from our home not many seconds later, had presumably scratched their heads, then promptly returned to bed, notifying no one. Thanks, neighbors.

We slept at best fitfully that first night back in our own bed. I couldn't shake the notion that this break-in paralleled that of Alzheimer's four weeks earlier. Our psychological and emotional lives had been upended, and now our sense of domestic privacy and security had been similarly assaulted and compromised. If there was an uncanny symmetry in it, that was cold comfort. Forces beyond predictability and our own ranges of experience were reshaping the lives we'd created for ourselves. We were coming to understand, in that first summer of her slow departing, that while we may have had some control in creating the lives we aspired to, we had little control in holding them together.

8

*Life is enriched by difficulty; love is made more
acute when it requires exertion.*

– Andrew Solomon, from Far from the Tree

Dear Judy,

*Learning to live with Alzheimer's was learning to cope with
everything it brought into our lives and everything it took from
them. It was a struggle for both of us, in almost entirely different
ways. As you moved more and more into the moment, I looked
more and more into the future. I was forced to, by everything
that I was reading and hearing about the disease and what it
had in store for us, from books and videos and podcasts and
support groups—a continuous mix of information sources that
often left me overwhelmed and fearful.*

*When I stopped by the offices of the local chapter of the
Alzheimer's Association for the first time, I was hoping to learn
about any resources they might be able to provide. After intro-
ducing myself to Christie, the friendly receptionist who greeted
me, I explained how and why we'd been prompted to seek your
diagnosis as well as the outcome of having opened that can of
worms. "Did Dr. Morrison's office give you a packet of brochures
and other information about what we offer here?" Christie asked.*

*"Well, no, actually. All we left with after her diagnosis was
the trial packet of Aricept."*

*"Yes, that's what I thought you'd say. We bring them packets
of information regularly, stuff that would be useful to people new*

to Alzheimer's, but up to now no one we've spoken with has been given those packets. We suspect the materials go straight to their recycle bin, but we're persistent. We'll continue to drop stuff off there. It would be nice if their patients received them."

Christie seemed resigned to Dr. Morrison's office's indifference, but it raised my hackles a second time. We could have used some direction, someone to point us toward useful information and support geared to the situations couples like us found ourselves in. If nothing else, it would have saved us valuable time. But in the end, maybe having to track down resources myself helped me get a better sense from the start of the medical, social, and financial hurdles we'd now be facing.

"You and your wife are welcome to join our patients and caregivers support group," Christie said. "Right now, they're meeting on Thursday mornings at a church that's centrally located. There's coffee and water, and usually we have some sort of guest speaker or presenter. Does that interest you?" I replied that it did, and Christie gave me a printed schedule of upcoming presenters. I broached the subject with you later that day.

"I'm not interested in joining any support group," you said, the tone of your voice making your irritation unmistakable. "Why don't you just leave me alone? I don't need more people to tell me I'm crazy!" You were justifiably angry about your diagnosis in that first year and resistant, at least at first, to my efforts to figure out how we'd manage it.

"Look, let's just give it a try," I said. "If we don't like it, we don't have to go back. I just think it's worth getting a sense of what kind of information is out there and what kind of help might be available to us."

"I don't need any help! I just want this to go away!" you yelled. "I just want everybody to leave me alone!"

By then you were in tears and retreating to your studio, your refuge. I followed you.

"Look," I started, "We—" You cut me off.

"I know you just want someone else!" you said through your tears. "Go find someone else! You just want to get rid of me."

What was this? Where did this come from? It had nothing to do with the subject of the moment. It had nothing to do with anything. But of course, it did, didn't it? In those first couple years your fear of abandonment would resurface every now and then, usually whenever we were having a disagreement about something. The disagreement didn't have to have anything to do with our actual relationship. I might show some impatience with you over some garden-variety household issue, and suddenly you'd raise the alarm. "You just want to get rid of me! You just want me out of your life!" I think for you that was a real fear, and it was never too far below the surface. I'd reassure you; I'd calm you down, that fear would go into remission, then weeks later I'd say something in the wrong way, or show some impatience, and you'd explode again. I understood where that was coming from, and I know that you knew that it wasn't going to happen. I was never going to leave you. It broke my heart, really, to see how the disease could make you feel so vulnerable, even desperate.

"Sweetie, I love you," I'd say each time, wrapping my arms around you. "I'm not interested in anyone else. I'm interested in you. I'm here to help you. I just want what's best for you. You're just going to have to trust me on that."

While Judy was resistant at first, my promise to take her out for lunch after the support group meeting eventually swayed her. Those meetings were interesting as far as they went, which wasn't ever far. We tried to be faithful about attending over the course of the four or five months during which we were active participants. I think the basic problem was the frequency of the turnover in the clientele. We'd introduce ourselves around the table at the start of each meeting, which I guess served as some sort of bonding mechanism for the handful of regulars. That small handful, though, was always outnumbered by new folk who might show up for a meeting, disappear for a few weeks, reappear for a meeting or two, then drop away completely. Each couple—and people tended to come in twos, a caregiver and a patient—was at a different stage in the experience, so while in theory we might all be in it together, in practice we were in our own sad little boats, paddling along anxiously if not aimlessly, trying to figure out just how to navigate this strange condition we were adrift in.

"I liked that woman," Judy said as we left one of the meetings at which we'd greeted and spoken with a new face, a person roughly her age with the same diagnosis, whose father had brought her. "She seems very nice. What was her name?"

"Sally," I replied. "She said her name is Sally." I thought she seemed nice too and had learned a bit more about them from her father. He'd lost his wife to Alzheimer's some years before, and now his daughter was, like Judy, in the early stages. I really felt for him and could see in his attentiveness to Sally and in the resigned sadness that his affability barely disguised the weight of responsibility that he willingly shouldered.

"Maybe they'll come again next week," I said as we headed home after the meeting adjourned. "Maybe they'd be interested in going out to have lunch with us afterward."

"That's a nice idea," Judy replied. "I hope they come again. What was her name?"

But they didn't return, at least not when we attended. Paths crossed at these support group get-togethers, but their intersections didn't necessarily lead anywhere. Sure, there was some solace in knowing that other people were dealing with similar challenges, some relief sensing that our own challenges didn't seem as daunting as what others were facing. At least for us, though, making new friends wasn't one of the outcomes of our involvement. That may have been expecting too much from folks who were, most of the time and knowingly or not, emotionally exhausted from grieving their own or their loved one's losses. Hard to become fast friends knowing the friendship is time-limited from the outset.

Bruce and Virginia were the longest-term members of that support group during the months that we were regulars. They were a decade younger than us, and her Alzheimer's onset hadn't come as a surprise. The disease ran in her family. She'd lost her mother and a sister to it and was caring for a second sister when her own symptoms began to accelerate. Now her son and daughter-in-law were helping Bruce to care for her, and all of them were struggling with likelihoods and eventualities. Shoes no one else would want to walk in.

Virginia's lush, dark hair framed a kind and flatteringly well made-up face. Unlike most of the other people who tended to show up at the group in loose-fitting gym-type clothes of the "easy on, easy off" variety, Virginia favored outfits that would have been appropriate in any corporate board room. Judy commented to me after one of the meetings that she thought Virginia dressed very well. I mentioned this to Bruce.

"Well, Virginia managed a bank here in town before the Alzheimer's started, and she always prided herself on looking professional. So, I do my best helping her with her clothes and makeup. I know how much it meant to her."

"So, you help her with her makeup?" I asked.

Bruce chuckled. "It's funny the things you learn to do when something like this hits you. I went over to the cosmetics department at Dillard's with her a year or so ago and had them show me how to 'put on her face' as they say. It's easier doing it myself since she'd reached the point where she'd over-apply it, sometimes to clownish effect. It looked weird and could be a mess to clean up."

I wondered aloud if it mattered that much to her now.

"You know," Bruce said, "at some point she's going to look in the mirror and have no idea who's staring back at her. I want her to see herself the way she always has been, to see the person she knows is herself, looking back at her. So, it's not a big deal. I do it for her. And for me too. I like having a pretty lady on my arm." He laughed again, both amused and bashfully proud.

I appreciated both Bruce's openness and the degree to which he'd stretched himself to help Virginia maintain some semblance of normality. I also admired his acceptance of her illness and their situation. He was clearly in it for the duration.

By the time we met them, her ability to speak, to carry on any kind of conversation, was entirely compromised. "Her aphasia's pretty advanced now," Bruce told me over coffee after one of the guest presenters had wrapped up a session on powers of attorney and updating last wills and testaments. "Whole sentences are a thing of the past now, and she's struggling just finding the word for something like a cup or a piece of toast. I do think she still likes coming to the group, but maybe it's just me who needs the socializing. Anyway, I'm happy to speak for both of us. I was always more the extrovert anyway."

"It must be hard for your son, after losing his grandmother and an aunt to the disease, seeing it happen to his mother," I said.

"Yeah, it's hard on the kids. We have a daughter too, but she lives in Florida, so she doesn't get back here much. My son and daughter-in-law have been great, though, a lot of help. If they had their own kids, they'd probably be too tied up to help. But they don't, and they're not planning to have any. They don't want this thing showing up in the next generation. The family history's not very good as far as dementia goes."

"That's tough," I responded. With three-year-old granddaughters of our own, I understood the grandparenting pleasures they'd be foregoing. I wondered if his son had considered genetic screening as a possible way forward, but I thought to myself, *I don't know this fellow and his family at all well; I don't want to be prying into their affairs.* I let the question go.

Judy couldn't connect with Virginia, though, and I regretted that *disconnection* seemed to be the operative notion for her and the other patients in the group. Most were past making new friends, at least in that kind of weekly roundtable. It was the caregivers, the spouses and children and even parents of the Alzheimer's sufferers, who sought connection, who hoped that solidarity would fill in some of the lonely places the disease had opened in their lives.

"What are you doing?" I asked Judy one evening just before shutting off the light on my nightstand. Our normal routine had us in bed by 9:30 most nights, and we'd read for fifteen or twenty minutes or so, as much time or as little as wakefulness would give us. I could easily get lost in whatever I was reading, and on that night, I was somewhere else, in someone else's life. Judy's movements distracted me, and that distraction irritated. I like disappearing into a book, and sometimes being nudged back to reality seems an unkind intrusion.

"I'm no-ing my blose," she said matter-of-factly as she squeezed tissue against her nostrils.

No-ing your blose, huh? I thought. In those first few years, holes in Judy's vocabulary had slowly become more frequent, and "you know, the thing for eating soup" (spoon?) or "that stuff for my hair" (gel? conditioner?) were workarounds she used to get across to me just what she needed at a particular moment. It could sometimes feel like a game of Jeopardy.

"You know, the thing for cleaning up the floor." What is a vacuum cleaner? Or "that thing for opening the wine." What is a corkscrew?

Inversions of phrases like "blowing my nose" were less frequent and more amusing, probably because she didn't seem to register them. She knew perfectly well what she was doing, and while scrambling it might have sounded comedic or poetic to a listener, in her head she heard it right. There was no poetry or comedy intended.

When Bruce from the support group had mentioned his wife Virginia's advanced aphasia, it seems to me now that was the first time I'd heard the word aphasia in everyday conversation. If someone had asked me then to define *aphasia*, I'd have hesitated, though I'd inferred what he was talking about simply from watching his wife in those meetings. Her verbal communication ability was just about nil.

Judy had been losing a word here or a word there almost from the start of her symptoms—that wasn't news. Learning that it had a clinical diagnosis helped me to begin to take some of the pressure off her to find the right word for whatever it was she wanted or needed or was trying to tell me. It was a lot harder for me to lose patience with her when I understood that she couldn't do a thing about it.

But maybe I can, I thought. One of the positives about how I've always gone through the world is that I've tended to be proactive, to look for solutions before things get beyond me. I suppose that's also one of my negative features because it can look controlling if you're on the receiving end. More than once over the years Judy had cautioned me about some plan in progress, whether I was over-detailing an itinerary for a trip (I can still hear her asking "Can't we just leave a couple of nights open in case we want to detour between Brittany and Paris?") or trying to schedule an outpatient surgery for myself at an optimal moment of least disruption to her and me, to my office staff and students, and to my studio assistants. "Just schedule the damned surgery, for Pete's sake!" she said, seeing much more clearly than me the minimal disruption it would likely cause anyone.

When her aphasia became more pronounced, I fixed on finding ways to postpone what I realized was likely to be an inevitable deterioration. I'd noticed that she'd begun to hesitate whenever she signed her name, as if she were stuck on a certain letter and how to form it. It probably wasn't very important at that point since I was writing all our checks and in the normal course of household business there weren't too many occasions when both our signatures were needed. That simple skill, though, connects so much with our identities and our selves. I hated for her to lose it.

Enter Julia Heller, PhD, and her graduate assistants. I'd asked a colleague who chaired our college's department of speech and communication disorders if any of their faculty were doing work with dementia sufferers. She pointed me in Dr. Heller's direction, and an email exchange led to a first meeting. In hindsight I realize how helpful various colleagues were to us over the years and how networking within the university system had sometimes paid valuable dividends.

"Well, you already know that Alzheimer's is a neurodegenerative disease," Dr. Heller said over coffee in the campus recreation center cafe where we first met. "Your wife's ability to do things like sign her name will most likely fail completely at some point. I think maybe we can delay that a bit by working with her to reinforce or strengthen what she can do now so that maybe she can hold on to those skills longer than she would otherwise."

"That would be great," I said, "and if you can learn anything useful from working with her, that would also be a plus."

"What we can do," Dr. Heller continued, "is meet with Judith weekly from the start of this upcoming semester, and then we can evaluate things and decide if it's worth proceeding. My graduate assistant Kendra Moser will work with me to set up different activities, and she'll record the details of each session and report those to me. I'll be on hand at least part of each session, but I think it's important that Judith build trust with one person, and I'd like that to be my graduate student. How does that sound?"

I was fine with it, and we scheduled Judy's initial interview session a week out. My immediate task was to convince her that this was the good idea that I thought it was.

"Who's this person?" she asked as I began to frame the parameters of this new intervention later that day. "What does she want me to do?"

"Just listen to me for a minute. Julia is a faculty member in our college. She's in speech and communication disorders. One of the client groups she and her grad students work with are people with the kind of cognitive impairment that you have. People with Alzheimer's, like yourself." Although by then Judy had accepted that she was an Alzheimer's sufferer, she never liked being reminded, and I was treading carefully. "I've noticed how it's getting harder for you to sign your name and to recognize words on the page, and I think they might be able to help you hold on to some of those communication skills. That's what they're good at. Communications."

"What will I have to do?" She tended by then to be wary of new situations and new people and resisted my throwing things at her that she wasn't already familiar with.

"You won't have to prepare at all, and I'll be taking you to the sessions, and you'll be working closely with one of Julia's grad students, named Kendra."

"She's a graduate student?" Judy asked a bit dubiously.

"Yes, she's a grad student working with Dr. Heller, with Julia, and she's excited to work with you. You'll be helping them as much as they'll be helping you. A win-win. What do you think?"

"Well, sure, I'll do that. It's on campus, right? Will you be there?"

I reassured her that she'd recognize the location on campus, that I'd be with her, and that she'd have fun with both Julia and Kendra. "Let's try it a few times, and if you really don't like working with them, we won't have to continue. Nothing's binding. Let's just see how it goes."

I was relieved that she didn't resist in the way that she'd opposed other initiatives along the way. The notion of working with a faculty member and a student appealed to her, and the idea that she might help them by spending some time with them mitigated any hesitation or resistance she felt.

"And you'll take me there?" Judy repeated.

"I'll be with you, don't worry about that. It'll be fun for me too."

I'm not so sure that I thought any of it would be fun, but I guessed that it would at least be interesting. And it felt, again, as if we were doing something, not just passively letting all this wash over us.

Julia and Kendra put Judy at ease within minutes of meeting them. They were relaxed, upbeat without being overbearing, and genuinely interested in finding ways to help her. Judy picked up on this right away, and she relaxed too. If it sometimes seemed as if they were quizzing or testing her, she didn't seem to mind or even notice.

With help from me they created a file card–sized ring binder with pictures and factoids about Judy's life and used it to launch conversations and to prompt both her long- and short-term memory. The evening before each appointment I'd quickly put together a one-page outline of our past week's activities—visiting friends for dinner on the weekend, going for a long walk on the bike trail, watching a new episode of a mystery series on public television—and they'd come up with questions to help Judy flesh out as much as she could remember about whatever it was we'd done. Eventually I shifted to noting activities on a monthly planner, and that worked better for Judy. Seeing the weeks and days laid out and identified provided a visual structure less challenging than an entirely verbal one.

Cued by the notes that I had penciled in, Julia or Kendra would prompt Judy to elaborate, discreetly recording each additional piece of information her memory spontaneously provided. Her details were often accurate: she filled out "walked to Akins" with "to get vitamins" and "we took the bike path" and "there were people walking dogs," all pieces of that excursion that she'd silently registered and was able to retrieve. I think their encouragement as they teased her to elaborate, and their congratulations when she was able to, gave her a sense of accomplishment, even if she wasn't always clear about just what she'd said that won their approval. She'd laugh with them, sometimes self-deprecatingly, sometimes conspiratorially, sometimes nervously. While I wasn't always sure she understood the goals of these sessions, the pleasure she took from them seemed genuine, and these contacts, if only an hour a week, helped to give her shrinking social life some interest, maybe even some importance.

Kendra was both patient and persistent in having Judy practice writing her name, though after a few months' effort we could all see that whatever synapse controlled her ability to link the *d* with the *i* in Judith and the *m* with the *e* in James was broken and wasn't going to be fixed. She let that go when it became clear the frustration Judy started to express wasn't worth the efforts that created it. If she started to close up, they pulled back. I admired how well they read her responses and adjusted theirs in turn.

These weekly sessions at the speech and communication disorders center began the same year as our granddaughters were entering kindergarten. We should have both been celebrating the discoveries they'd be making as they learned the alphabet and began to explore letters and words on a page, starting their journey to literacy. Judy should have been reading to them, helping their kid's fingers to form As and Bs, counting numbers or raisins, adding two, subtracting one, doubling four.

Instead, as they were learning these things, she was unlearning them. Alzheimer's reversed her own literacy project, coldly, indifferently. Sentence by sentence. Word by word. Letter by letter.

9

Not long after I ended Judy's driving, I started researching local homecare businesses. I knew that the stage at which she would no longer be able to be left alone was approaching. I thought that segueing into this gradually, while she could still understand why we needed to take this route, would be easier than waiting for some push-comes-to-shove moment, when it might overwhelm her or both of us. I started broaching the idea every now and then, hoping that she might warm to it.

"I don't need anyone to be with me," she insisted each time. "I'm fine by myself. And anyway, Sam's here a lot. If I need anything I can ask her."

Judy had been fine, more or less, up to that point. Because my studio was in our home, my studio assistant Samantha Vaughn spent all or most of the twenty hours a week that she worked for me in that studio. She had a key to the house and usually came four out of five weekdays. Her schedule was flexible, though she liked to stick to regular hours most weeks, on some days splitting them between work on campus and work in the studio. Judy and Sam knew each other well and had been graduate students together when we'd first come to Nebraska, so Judy was comfortable having her at home. Sam was all business, extremely focused and hardworking, and my production needs and exhibition commitments meant that she had no time to waste. Apart from the usual pleasantries, they usually didn't interact much. While they were on different levels of the house and might not even cross paths, I think her presence helped Judy's comfort level, reassuring her when I wasn't there. It certainly helped to reduce some of the stress I was also experiencing. If anything of an emergency nature were to happen, we knew we could count on Sam to help. That was a gift.

Several times I'd raised the possibility of bringing Judy's mother from Massachusetts to live with us permanently. Those discussions failed to get traction. I reasoned that because Judy was no longer able to travel alone, their visits were limited to those Judy and I could do together, so her mother's isolation had been growing, incidental to her daughter's. Admittedly, this notion wasn't among my most well–thought-through ideas. Flo was eighty-eight years old at the time. Her health was stable, and she was still living independently. We knew that at some point she too would need care. Could we mitigate two difficulties, one impending, the other eventual, by moving her in with us? Did I really think I could manage taking care of both of them? On good days I wanted to believe I could. But then there were the not-so-good days.

We ran the idea by Judy's brother Russ and sister-in-law Nancy, who were at the time living just outside the metropolitan Houston area. "It would be a way for the two of them to have some daily companionship," I argued. "Maybe every few months Mother could fly down to Texas to spend time with you," I offered, sensing that this probably wouldn't be practical long term.

"Maybe we could have some kind of trial run, bring her out here and see how she does."

It was serendipitous that Russ's son-in-law Nick, who with our niece Kara lived close to them, was heading to New England in May on business. He arranged to fly back to Texas with their mother in tow. Flo would test the waters, staying six weeks or so with them and then another few weeks with us. We drove down from Nebraska to pick her up in early July.

Her time with us played out uneventfully. I generally felt reassured heading off to campus that they would be safe, that each of them could watch out for the other. They went for short walks in the neighborhood, worked out what they'd share for lunch, sat out on the deck overlooking the lake when temperatures weren't extreme, worked on jigsaw puzzles together, and reminisced. Would this day-to-day be something we could maintain at length? That was the million-dollar question. I hoped it might be.

We drove Flo back to Massachusetts in late July, timing our arrival to coincide with a nephew's wedding. They both handled the trip well, and we enjoyed our time together in transit. Although her mother always claimed that Judy had been a difficult adolescent, and Judy had sometimes felt her patience tested by her mother through her adulthood, by this time in their lives, the bond they shared was tight and their friendship genuine. Flo and I got along well. More alike than Judy and she were, we could push each other's buttons, and occasionally I saw in her some of my own less-than-desirable traits mirrored back at me. Being critical and judgmental were in her mother's DNA, as in mine.

A month or so after our return I had a phone call from Flo as I was on my way home from campus after a busy early Fall semester day. "How's Judy doing?" she opened with.

"She's good, how are you?"

"I've decided what I'm going to do," she said, uncharacteristically foregoing the small talk and getting right to the point. "I'm going to move to Texas to live with Rusty and Nancy."

"Well, okay," I said, taken a bit off guard. "You've discussed all of this in detail with them?" She confirmed their numerous conversations since we'd last seen her.

"Can I ask what made you finally decide to opt for Texas?"

Her reply wasn't what I was expecting. "Well, if Judy dies of the Alzheimer's, you won't have any legal obligation toward me."

I hesitated for a second, surprised and a little angry. "That may be true, Mother," I said, my tone betraying the hurt I felt. "But I'd have a moral obligation!"

"No, it's all right, I'm going to move in with Rusty."

Geez, I thought, *forty years I've been part of your family, and you think at some point I'd treat you as if you were just a passing acquaintance? Really?* I'd always felt that I held her on nearly equal standing with my own mother. No legal obligation? Where did that come from?

"Well, your mother's decided to move to Texas to live with Russ and Nancy," I told Judy not long after walking in the door. "Kind of disappointed me."

"Why are you disappointed?" Judy asked. "It's probably better this way. She'd drive us nuts if she came here." *So,* I thought to myself, *she still gets to you sometimes. Some things haven't changed.*

"You know how she is; she's always complaining about something. And she gets on my nerves, the same stories all the time, and if she gets something in her head, she doesn't let it go."

Interesting, I thought to myself smiling, not too different from how you've been lately. I stifled the impulse to voice that thought, knowing that Judy might miss the humor and irony and take offense. By then I was wise to the fact that throwaway lines could have unintended consequences. Her self-esteem was shot by her diagnosis and had never recovered. Any intimation that I was laughing at her or her condition could easily bring on the floodgates. I wanted her to be on an even keel as much as possible.

"Well, realistically, it would probably be more than I can handle here, taking care of you and your mother too. But all those years after your father died, it was us who looked out for her in Somerset, having her over for meals, going out shopping with her, shoveling her driveway when it snowed, and taking her out to eat. She's your mother. You'd think she'd want to help you out, to help us out, when we could use some help." Increasingly aware of what we'd be facing down the line, I guess I was over-anxious at that point, looking for partial or temporary solutions even when I knew they might add complications that wouldn't help in the long run.

"I'll be fine," Judy said. "I'm fine here. I don't need her or anyone. I can take care of myself."

A couple of months later Flo was packed up and relocated to Taylor Lake Village, Texas, near Galveston Bay. From that point we'd have a more southerly road trip destination, which in the dead of a Nebraska winter wouldn't be such a bad thing.

On Judy's sixtieth birthday I'd remarked, "You sure don't look like you're sixty," and she came back quickly with "Well, this is what sixty looks like!" To the end, she looked ten, sometimes even fifteen years younger than her actual age. Sure, she regularly had her hair color renewed, but it always looked natural, unexaggerated. She'd never carried any extra weight, she was faithful about pampering her skin, she exercised and ate selectively, even sparingly. Whenever we ran across a news or lifestyle article touting the benefits of exercise and a Mediterranean diet in helping to prevent diseases like Alzheimer's, we'd be quick to counter with "Yeah, but…" We could do all those things, watch our diet, stay active, avoid all kinds of overindulgence, and still Alzheimer's could quietly and invisibly launch and advance its destructive excavations.

When I began searching through the websites of local home companion services and care providers, the white-haired, some-times frail-looking clients pictured there brought me up short. It wasn't how I pictured Judy, or us. We were too young for this, too young for Alzheimer's; we didn't match the profile. Of course, while younger onset Alzheimer's is uncommon, it's not rare. Of the roughly 5 million Americans diagnosed with the disease when Judy was, approximately 5 percent, or 12,500, were early onset cases.[11] Those were people who, like us, had jobs and careers to advance, families and homes to maintain, and futures to imagine and plan toward. We weren't ready to be reclassified as "out to pasture." The notion of forfeiting independence was not just frightening, it seemed entirely unnatural.

Yet, we couldn't ignore the eventualities of the neurodegenerative disease that she had. Well, I couldn't ignore them. She could, and did, at least a good part of the time, and maybe that denial was the best way for her to cope. The "if I can't do anything about it" rule that she'd always lived by. Admittedly, after four decades together she knew me well enough to expect that regardless the problem or conundrum, I'd lose sleep trying to figure out a solution. Whether reactive or proactive, I'd take the bull by the horns and suffer the consequences. She'd look on with tolerance or, more likely, skepticism.

"So, there's a business here in town called *A Trusted Friend Homecare*," I dropped into our dinner conversation one evening not long after her mother decided against moving in with us. "They have people who are trained to provide companionship and to help people with diseases like yours cope with all the everyday things that you have to do."

"I don't need anyone to keep me company. I'm fine alone."

"Well," I continued, "you really aren't doing much with your days anymore. You sit in your studio sorting all the stuff on your sewing table, you watch birds at the feeder outside your studio window, you wait for me to get home. That's not such an interesting agenda."

"I don't want anyone I don't know in the house with me. I'm fine the way I am. Why do you always want to control my life?"

That question had been raising its ugly head more often as Judy moved into the middle stage of the disease, and I became more anxious about the wisdom of leaving her to her own devices each weekday. I was worried about her safety and vulnerability and about her peace of mind. I'd seen her become disoriented and confused, wondering where "everyone" had gone when for days there'd been no one at home but her and me. I'd return home after the better part of a day on campus, and there she'd be in her studio, the paraphernalia that resided on her worktable's surface rearranged again and again, her lunch in the refrigerator uneaten.

"Why don't we just give it a try? There's no long-term commitment. If you really don't like having someone visit you, then we can drop it."

I'd already invested a fair amount of time phoning several of the companion care services in town, trying to educate myself on a subject about which I knew very little. General philosophy or mission, rates, terms, and cancellation policies, even the tone of voice of the person who answered at the receiving end of my call—it all factored into which agencies on the list of five or six got crossed off and which remained in consideration. I'd narrowed it to two before agreeing to appointments with personnel managers at the respective businesses.

The outdated dark-paneled walls at the first of the two agencies contributed to the dull, fluorescent-washed blandness of the waiting area. Located in a sixties-era office complex within walking distance of our home, it was at least convenient. The owner ushered me into her office as she repeated the well-memorized description of their mission and modus operandi, almost verbatim what she'd delivered when I'd phoned. I was being greeted by a preprogrammed sales pitch, I realized. Why had I thought this was going to work? She'd sounded upbeat and knowledgeable when we'd first spoken, but now she sounded stale. Friendly but distracted, she put such a positive spin on their companionship program that "too good to be true" began echoing in the recesses of my judgmental self. When she took a phone call in the middle of our appointment, I knew this wouldn't be our provider. I white lied my way out of that office with a promise to get back to them after a couple of additional interviews, though I knew this would be our final contact, and I'd scheduled only one other meeting.

Although *A Trusted Friend Homecare's* offices were in a

semi-industrial complex on the far side of the city, their interiors were well-lit and comfortably, even smartly furnished.

"My wife is very resistant to the idea of having someone come in to spend time with her," I said as soon as I'd introduced myself to Carmen, *A Trusted Friend's* client care coordinator. "She's actually pretty adamant about it," I added, "so I'm not sure this will work out. That said, I know that at some point in the near term I won't be able to leave her alone anymore, so I think it's better to at least get things in place. I need an agency that is willing to get to know her and to work with me and with her to help her hold onto a good quality of life for as long as she can."

"It's not unusual that some of our clients don't like having strangers in their homes with them at first, and we understand that," Carmen responded. "Our care providers are trained to build trust with the families we serve, and we equip them with a host of strategies for befriending their companions and strengthening those friendships. In cases like yours, where the client can move about freely and enjoy activities outside the home, it's even easier for our providers to build real friendships. It takes a little time, but it's very doable."

"What happens if my wife doesn't connect with a particular caregiver?" I asked. "She's always been a very private person, and I guess I'd say she's pretty selective about the kind of person she opens up to."

Carmen explained that the detailed personal profile of Judy that they'd create would help them narrow the field of potential companions. Their roster was extensive, she assured me, and once they'd met Judy and talked with her about herself and her interests, the types of things she liked and didn't like, they'd have a good sense of who might be a good fit.

"Let's meet Judy," Carmen said, "and then we'll be able to make some recommendations. We don't have one set of strategies or activities that we use with all clients," she added. "We know that each of our clients is an individual and we tailor our approach to respect their individuality." This was what I'd hoped to hear.

"I told you I don't want anybody here!" Judy protested after I announced Carmen's pending visit. "I'm not a baby! I know how to take care of myself! Why don't you just leave me alone?"

I knew that little by little I was becoming her warden, her jailer, and sometimes I think she saw me that way. Mostly, she understood that I loved her and cared about her, though at the same time, I'm sure it looked to her as if I was cutting her off from different parts of her life that she'd always controlled.

Judy, you see now that it wasn't me, right? That it was the disease? I felt as handcuffed as you did.

"Look, I'm sorry," I said, "but I think it's important that you meet Carmen and that we set up some companion visits to try it out. She's coming here to meet you in a couple of days. She's very nice, and I'm pretty sure you'll like her. In any case, we're going to try this out, like it or not."

I reminded Judy that my peace of mind was at stake as much as her independence. "I want to be able to go to campus and not be worrying about how you're doing here at home." She'd heard that before and wasn't persuaded.

"I can take care of myself," she repeated. "I don't want anyone in our house!"

You handled the visit with Carmen well, answering her questions about likes and dislikes, what you did each day, and showing her around your studio and the collections of fabrics, buttons, stones, and seashells that you passed the time sorting and rearranging. "Michael thinks I need someone to be with me," I heard you tell Carmen, "but I'm fine on my own. I don't mind being alone. He thinks I'm a baby. He just wants to spend more time with his girlfriend."

That notion that I had another woman in my life had begun to surface earlier that year. When you became overwhelmed with sadness or frustration, or I'd said something to you a little too impatiently or abruptly, your fear of my rejection rose to the occasion. "I know you just want to get rid of me, I know it!" you'd declare. "You've got some other woman who's not crazy like me, who's not losing her mind!" The tears would well in your eyes and flow down your cheeks, I'd comfort and reassure you, the episode would eventually pass. Did you really believe that? I didn't think so at the time. It was the disease and the insecurity it had planted in you, fertilized by the small losses that were accruing and transforming into bigger losses as the months passed. The safeguards and limitations that I felt forced to impose were hurting both of us, you in your loss of autonomy, me in the loss of your trust, something that I'd never risked compromising.

I never betrayed my love for you, but I'll be candid: I came close. If I'm going to be honest with myself, and with you, then yes, I did risk everything we'd put into our relationship. And not just once. Each time, I pulled back and got a grip on myself. The trust we'd built in each other over the years was too valuable to forfeit. But I did put it on the line.

I was on the West Coast one early autumn in the late eighties, teaching workshops over the course of a couple of weeks, moving every few days from one destination to the next. At the time, Judy and I were both putting a lot of effort into our respective careers, maybe more effort than we were putting into our marriage. I was leading two 3-day sessions almost back to back at a conference center overlooking the ocean near Monterey. A Sunday break would give me a short window in which to catch my breath and do a little sightseeing, and I was looking forward to that.

A couple of people had registered for both of my workshop sessions, and by the end of the first one, Martina, a woman from Southern California who was ballpark our age, had offered to drive me over to the aquarium in town on that free day. I knew the Monterey Bay Aquarium's reputation and was happy to get away from the conference center for a few hours in the company of someone who I'd learned by then was thoughtful and had a good sense of humor. As I typically did at these conferences, I'd taken meals with rotating groups of students, Martina among them. I guess I'd say that she and I had hit it off.

On the drive into town, we discussed some of the high points of the previous three days' design problem solving, and I mused on a couple of things that hadn't quite worked out as planned. Second-guessing myself after concluding a design workshop was par for the course. I was rarely fully satisfied, and usually as critical of myself and my group leadership role as I was of my students and their creative output.

"You're an excellent teacher," Martina said. "You've really opened my eyes to the tensions that hold visual designs together and how they act on the viewer. I'd just never thought of those things before. I feel as if you've provided me with tools that give me more purpose as a designer, more control. I really appreciate that."

Tell me more, I thought. When I wasn't so sure about the merits of the strategies I was using in these hands-on engagements, having my ego stroked helped. Having it stroked by someone as smart and interesting as Martina was even more likely to do the trick. It was a good session. I did get through to the students. Martina said as much.

I'd been a little concerned that the aquarium would be packed with Sunday visitors and dismayed to find that it was. After an hour or so of dodging scattershot six-year-olds and slow-moving family groups, I had to bail. "The exhibits are wonderful, but there are too many people here to really enjoy it. Can I buy you lunch?" I asked Martina. "You treated me to the aquarium; I get to treat you to lunch. Let's walk from here and find some place quiet." A few blocks away we landed on a nearly empty café that still had an hour to go on its lunch service.

"Sit wherever you'd like," the waiter said by way of greeting. "I'll bring you menus."

Three hours later lunch was behind us, and Martina and I were well into our second happy hour chardonnays. We'd shared our life stories, or key parts of them anyway. She'd told me about her unhappy marriage, the husband single-mindedly focused on an unrelenting law practice that she felt had destroyed any semblance of meaningful relationships with her and their college-bound daughter. Resigned to the climate at home, she'd poured her energies into art and craft courses at the local community college and the occasional retreat-type workshops that would give her space and distance and contact with stimulating people who shared her interests and encouraged her enthusiasms. Like me. She'd felt so encouraged in the previous days' workshop sessions. I'd shown her new ways to see, to think. She could hardly wait for the next three days to get underway. She was so grateful.

And I was so…what? Enchanted? What was this frisson I was feeling? What was going on here? I knew I was attracted to her, but we cross paths all the time with people that we're attracted to. This was different, and disturbing, but in an exciting way. A bit dangerous because I could see that she was attracted to me. I could feel it. No question. It felt good. *Nothing wrong with that,* I told myself.

On the drive back to the retreat center, as Martina talked about films and music she liked and foods she didn't, I thought of Judy. I couldn't come up with a single reason why I would want to betray the trust we'd built over nearly two decades together, and the idea of doing that horrified me. Judy was a beautiful soul, she was kind, she was solid, she was as good a friend as I could ask for. Yet the bewitching electric charge was still there when Martina parked the car and we headed to the center's lobby. Cued by a sign pointing in the hotel pool's direction, I looked at Martina and asked "They have a saltwater pool here. Feel like a swim?"

"I'll meet you there in ten minutes," she said.

A pool attendant was the only other person around, and he came and went, restocking towels and folding umbrellas, ignoring us. Martina and I floated and paddled and watched the day's light fade above us, not saying very much, staying at opposite sides of the pool. I knew what I was thinking and knew it was playing with fire. I wasn't sure what she was thinking, but I had a hunch and guessed it was accurate.

"I'll be locking up the shower cabana soon," the pool attendant said in our direction at about the same time I realized night had fallen, "so if you folks want to shower here this'll be your last chance." Pulling a large bin overflowing with towels, he left the pool enclosure and disappeared into the darkness.

And then Martina and I were in that shower together, our lathered hands exploring one another's skin, and I realized the frisson was gone, I wasn't excited anymore, I was thinking of Judy and feeling a huge wave of guilt and regret. If she saw me now, I thought to myself. How could I do this? I'd been faithful all these years, it was a point of pride. And now I was betraying that trust?

"Look, Martina, today's been fun, but we can't do this. I can't do this. It isn't right. We're both married, this would open a minefield. I love my wife. You've got unfinished business with your husband, and maybe you can repair that. But we've got three more days of work ahead of us, and this is looking to me like a major mistake. I'm sorry, I need to say goodnight. It's been nice, but we can't go anywhere with this. I'll see you tomorrow."

The next three days we acted like nothing had happened. *And nothing did happen*, I told myself then, with some relief but with wobbly conviction. I finished my work there, professional and polite, headed on to the Bay area and finally to Seattle, and got home to Judy the following weekend. I put it behind me. A close call that I could file if not forget, that I'd never have to mention to her. And never did.

Improbably, a year or so after that close call, Martina turned up on our doorstep. While visiting a friend in Boston, she phoned and asked if she could come down to Somerset to visit my studio, to meet Judy, to have dinner and catch up. It felt awkward to me, and I should have told her the timing wasn't good, but Judy said fine, and we invited her down. There was a vibe—guilt or discomfort on my part, I suspect—that I think Judy picked up on, and it dawned on me that she saw Martina as a threat. She was civil, even cordial at different moments that day, but whatever sixth sense she was tapping into reframed the entire encounter. "Don't ever ask her back here," she said firmly later that evening after Martina had left, and we never discussed it again.

I wonder now whether Judy's insecurity about my faithfulness some twenty years later was rooted in Martina's visit that day. I suspect it may have been. Mea culpa.

A few years later something like my misadventure with Martina happened in France. I was the guest of a provincial arts commission in the country's southwest, invited to do a keynote talk for the launch of an exhibition, then to teach a weeklong design workshop. I'd been in several countries in Europe over the course of nearly a month, and this was my final gig. I was looking forward to being home.

After the first long day of the seminar, I retreated to my hotel for a short rest before heading out to explore the city center. My ramble was interrupted when I crossed paths with one of the arts ministry's associate directors, someone I'd spoken with several times in the previous weekend's rush of events and receptions. Her name was Stéphanie ("Steph, s'il te plaît," she'd insisted an hour later, midway through our first glasses of Chablis), she was striking and poised, and she was tolerant of my moderately fluent but flawed French.

We chatted animatedly as shadows lengthened and the late afternoon rush of townspeople passed around us. Aware that I'd soon be looking for some place to have dinner, I asked her, "Do you have any cafés or bistros you'd recommend in this *quartier*?"

She laughed. "There are wonderful little places every few meters here," she said. "Pick almost any one."

"Well, you pick one and join me for an apéritif."

A few minutes later we were seated in a simple but warm café tucked under a half-timbered antique of a building a few steps down from the pedestrian walkway. The clientele leaned young and a bit bohemian, the atmospheric wood-paneled interior oozed history, and soft lighting wrapped every surface in a gentle luster. If I were designing a set for a romantic rendezvous, I couldn't have improved on that one. Ninety minutes of easy conversation with Steph left me wanting more, both of the room and of her.

We met like that for drinks three of my remaining four days. By the eve of my departure for Paris and my last few days in France, though Stéphanie and I hadn't kissed beyond the traditional greeting "bises" on both cheeks, hadn't really touched, I was imagining canceling the Paris visit and spending the weekend with her.

"There's a train strike starting tomorrow evening," Steph reported, though I'd already heard news of that likelihood, not unusual in France. "Maybe you won't get to Paris. In that case you can stay with me this weekend." She smiled conspiratorially.

I returned her smile as my inner soundtrack convulsed. *What are you doing? What on earth are you thinking? You're happy in your marriage, you love your wife, you're playing with fire here. You barely know this woman! What are you attracted to?* I guess it was that frisson again, that electric charge, my ego and libido wanting, but not needing, to be stroked.

The next afternoon, just as the workshop ended and participants were packing up and saying their goodbyes, the arts center's concierge got my attention from across the room.

"You have a phone call, monsieur" she said, leading me to her small office.

"It's Steph," the voice at the other end said. "I was serious yesterday, stay the weekend if you can. It would be nice."

"I've made plans already, Steph, and I have my train ticket." *And I'm married! And I have a very happy life at home, and I don't have any reason to betray Judy!* I liked the attention coming from her, she was awfully attractive, we'd had some lovely conversations the previous few days. *But I love my wife!*

"We'll see if my train leaves on schedule. If I'm stuck here, I'll let you know."

The train left as scheduled and got to Paris on time. I never spoke with Stéphanie again. That little episode got filed under "embarrassing waves of wishful thinking" and "knowing moments of shaking sense back into myself." Judy and I had a warm reunion a few days later, as usual, and if she thought that I'd ever considered a brief and secret dalliance thirty-five hundred miles away, she never asked, and I never brought it up. And I never came close to crossing that line again.

"Today, Barbara from *A Trusted Friend* is going to be spending the afternoon here," I reminded Judy the morning of the first care companion visit I'd scheduled. Carmen had described Barbara as someone who enjoyed reading and who painted as a hobby, was a little younger than us and an empty nester, had worked for them for going on five years, and had several other weekly clients who had nothing but praise for her kindness and thoughtfulness. "I'll come home for lunch today, so I'll be here when she arrives."

"I don't want anybody here," Judy said again. "I'm fine by myself."

"I'll see you at lunch," I said, and we kissed goodbye.

The front doorbell rang at one o'clock as expected, and Barbara introduced herself. Judy seemed wary but shook her outstretched hand. I quickly showed her around the house and in the kitchen pointed out where she'd find tea and utensils and the few other things she might need if at any point she might want to fix a snack. She was personable if not outgoing, and I figured she might be just as wary of this first meeting as Judy appeared to be.

"I'll be home at about five," I said. "Barbara will stay with you until then. It's a nice day; maybe you can go for a walk." I grabbed my bag and headed to campus.

About three that afternoon my office phone rang. It was Carmen.

"Everything's okay, but we have a bit of a problem," she began. "Barbara phoned me about ten minutes ago. She's outside your home. After going for a walk around your neighborhood, they'd sat at your kitchen table chatting for a half hour or so. Suddenly Judy told her it was time to leave. She went to the front door, opened it, and stepped outside. Barbara followed her out, and Judy told her to go to her car. Before Barbara could react, Judy was back inside and bolted the door. Barbara told Judy through the door that she needed her purse, which Judy retrieved for her from the living room. She opened the door enough to pass her the purse then locked it again before Barbara could reach for the handle. Right now, she's outside, and she's not sure what she should do. Judy won't let her in."

"Well," I said, "I knew she wasn't enthusiastic about having someone in the house with her, but I didn't expect this." I thought for a few seconds.

"Judy's been clear to me about what she wants and doesn't want. Maybe I should have taken her more seriously. I hoped I'd be able to start getting her used to having someone with her a couple of afternoons a week. I guess we'll have to go with this; she seems pretty determined. If she can dig in her heels like this, it's hard to argue with her. Tell Barbara she can take off, I'll pay the full fee for the afternoon, and I'll talk with Judy about it later today. I'm very sorry."

That evening Judy wasn't equivocal. "I didn't like that person," she said, "whatever her name was. She doesn't like me, and I don't like her! I don't want her here again!"

Why argue? I asked myself. At that point I felt she was still reasonably safe at home, though I knew she was often lonely and anxious, and often bored. I taped reminders of various kinds around the house, I printed her a rough schedule of my comings and goings each day, and I phoned her every couple of hours. I wasn't worried that she'd wander. The last time she'd gone for a walk by herself she'd returned after only a few minutes, said she didn't like walking, something didn't feel right, and from that day never left the house without me or someone she was comfortable with.

I decided to let it drop for a while.

A few months later Judy's mother flew up from Texas for another extended visit. "It'll be good for you to have your mother here with you," I said after she'd shared her flight information with us. "My mother drives me up a wall," she replied. "She'll just get on my nerves." That's when it occurred to me that this might be an opportunity to revisit the homecare companion option.

"I think it'll be easier for you, then, if we hire someone from the homecare business to come here in the afternoon and spend time with your mother. That way you won't feel like you need to entertain her."

Judy liked that idea. I spoke again with Carmen at *A Trusted Friend*, and she agreed that it was worth a try. They'd send someone for a three-hour shift twice a week to spend time with Judy's mother. The care provider would be prepped on the ruse and over time would pull Judy into her conversations with her mother and any activities she'd bring for them to do.

It worked better than Carmen or I had anticipated. After Lisa's first visit, Judy and her mother were both enthused. "Lisa's very natural and relaxed," Carmen had said in describing her to me, and from what Judy's mother said, she put them both at ease right away.

"She told us a funny story about losing her cat and how she found it again at the pet rescue place," Judy's mother said, chuckling as she tried to piece together the outlines of that misadventure. "She's a hot ticket!"

Judy agreed. "She was fun, I like her. My mother likes her too. I think she could come again."

10

*You can't be close to the mortality of friends
without being brought to think of your own.*

– Wallace Stegner, from *Crossing to Safety*

Dear Judy,

*Here I've arrived at the chapter that you might have been
inclined to skip over, had you known it was coming.*

*We never had a space nor the time in our shared lives for pop-
ular sports. While I had run for many years, competing in local
footraces during many of those, we didn't think of that as sport so
much as effort invested in staying relatively fit. My cluelessness
about the cultures, rulebooks, and fan behaviors of just about
all team sports came from a complete lack of interest going back
to my childhood, a disinterest that was then and remains now
unapologetic. When Trevor played basketball during a couple of
his high school years, duty had me in the stands for some of those
games, though he was clearly frustrated by my parental faux pas.
"Dad," he scolded me, "don't sit with the other teams' parents, for
Pete's sake!" and "You can't be reading a book while the game's
going on! Jeez, pay attention!" Guilty as charged.*

*As we continued to feel our way into the alien territory of
dementia, though, I began to feel that I needed something that
might be able to transport me out of it, at least for short periods
of time. There were moments when I growled within myself, not
wanting to be the thoughtful partner, the devoted caregiver, not
wanting to be present, not wanting to do the next responsible*

thing. Sometimes I resented the increasing time that your care demanded and how that managed to squeeze out what little time I might have had for myself. I never said as much to you, though once or twice I sensed that you recognized what was going on in this regard, and that may have given you reason to feel a little guilt, though you never expressed that. I didn't blame you. Once in a while, though, I simply wanted some time that I didn't have to share with Alzheimer's.

We were at our friends Eva and Tom's place. It was a Friday evening in early May 2011, three couples at their dining table along with Eva's recently widowed father Bernie, odd man out. Judy was probably in the late early stage at that point. Gauging just where she was in the disease's progression was no easier near the end of the journey than at the beginning, but I played with those calculations over and over. The reality is that it's fluid, the borders constantly changing, the patient seeming to gain on the disease one month, then the disease leaping forward the next. Only in the accumulation of losses could I find some way to measure how close she was to a new threshold or whether she'd already moved beyond it. It seemed to matter less and less to her as it mattered more and more to me.

Anyway, she'd always been comfortable in their home, she especially liked spending time with Eva, and we were enjoying ourselves.

"Hey, Tom, feel like going to hit some balls on Sunday morning?" Bernie asked his son-in-law by way of launching a new conversation thread as we were finishing dessert. Bernie was a lifelong golfer and religious in his devotion to it. Judy and I knew diddly-squat about golf.

"Do you play golf?" Bernie asked me after he, Tom, and the other husband guest, Mark, had agreed that a driving range outing before the weekend was over suited each of them. "No," I answered, and before I could think on it, I added "but I wouldn't be averse to learning."

A month before we'd been to a fundraiser in Omaha, a benefit auction and dinner held at a venerable old country club. Friends had purchased a ten-topper and invited us to join the group they were putting together that included associates from the area arts community and the medical center. While Judy was browsing the auction preview tables with another one of the spouses, I'd wandered off to a set of windows that offered an expansive view of part of the golf course. The sun was setting on what had been a crystal-clear day. Shadows stretched long across the fairway, alternating with glowing solar highlights. It looked seductively verdant and pristine, a vignette of atmospheric and botanical perfection. Golf course as parkland. How had I missed that?

My reverie was interrupted when our host Stuart asked over my shoulder, "Do you play golf?" He was someone we hadn't known very long, a modest yet personable fellow who worked as an upper administrator in the university system. As I admitted that I didn't really know the first thing about golf, I made a mental note that it could be a useful skill set to add to networking strategies that might benefit a department chair's programmatic ambitions and aspirations. "Lynn and I are members here," he added. "If you ever take it up, let me know. You could join me for a round."

So, the seed was planted.

Tom phoned early that Sunday morning. We were still in bed.

"So, do you want to join us at the driving range?"

I smiled as Judy looked at me dubiously. I hadn't really thought they'd follow up, nor had I considered what I'd do in that event.

"Well, I guess I could. I don't see why not. The course by Holmes Lake? What time? And you have clubs I can use?"

As I hung up a minute later, Judy's doubtfulness turned into amusement.

"You're going to do what?"

"I'm going to meet Tom, Bernie, and Mark at the driving range. Why are you laughing?"

"I don't know, it's just kind of funny. I've never pictured you playing any kind of game that involved balls."

Actually, during the summer of 1971 when Judy and I started dating, I was playing a fair amount of tennis, something I'd taken up while an undergraduate, halfheartedly at first but with growing enthusiasm. She and I never played together, and so it wasn't on her radar as it was on mine, at least until I fractured my right ankle on the tennis court a few weeks before driving off to my first semester of graduate school. It would be forty years before I again let any kind of ball come between me and my skeletal integrity.

So, here's what I learned that first time I stood at the top of the Holmes Lake course's driving range. I say top because it's at the head of a long downward slope, offering a prospect of treetops and rooftops unusual for this flattest of topographies. Those treetops conceal the lake that otherwise would be part of that prospect.

I liked the order of it all. The generous spacing of the practice stations with their contoured range ball receptacles flush to the artificial turf pad and a convenient club's length from the tee grip. The logic of a golf bag's partitioning and the taxonomy of irons and woods that partitioning imposes. The arrangement of the distance markers, their incremental disposition at once aspirational and intimidating. The curious choreography of the golf swing, the approach to it, the execution, its capacity to mercilessly deflate the humblest ambition of a novice player. The sharp snap off the metal face of a neighboring golfer's drive shot and his confident pause at the apex of his torso's twist as he follows his ball's ridiculously straight trajectory past the 250-yard panel. Most of all I think I liked the open, green space that surrounded us, so generous and relaxing, and the camaraderie of these men who had joined to patiently, if tentatively, tutor this rank beginner.

I'm not sure why I decided that morning on that driving range to take on the challenge of learning how to hit a golf ball.

My group of eager tutors was encouraging, but each alternately gave me advice that seemed to contradict or downright negate the others. A well-meaning bunch, they could clearly see I might be one of those who falls in the hopeless category, though if they thought that, they kept it to themselves. As determined as my strokes were, they failed to make contact four times out of five, bounced waywardly forward when they did, and never, not once, became airborne.

"So, how was it?" Judy asked when I returned. "Did you have fun?"

Fun was a word that I wouldn't associate with golf for quite a long time. Humbling, yes, but fun seemed a far too unrealistic expectation for someone who'd just survived his first driving range outing but was cowed by the embarrassment it generated.

I'd noticed something, though, by the end of that hour. I hadn't once thought about Judy and me and Alzheimer's and the anxieties, fears, and frustrations of caregiving. While I felt as green as the landscape into which I'd tried to send a few dozen balls, I also felt lighter, fresher, stimulated, even intrigued. This was something I could try to learn to do that would clearly take so much focus that for small bits of time I could be in my own body, my own mind, my own space.

"Well, I could see right away I didn't have any idea what I was doing," I said to Judy, "but I like everything about it. I think maybe I should take some lessons or something."

"You should," she agreed. "You need something for yourself. You never stop. Golf would be good. Take your mind off things."

I appreciated that she recognized not just how much her own life was changing, but mine along with hers. In different ways, we were both trying to make sense of the slow transformation of our partnership. While she could, she was willing to give me much needed space without exacting any tribute in guilt or caregiving overtime.

Looking back, I don't know how I was able to squeeze out that time given how full the day-to-day already was. I always seemed to be bargaining for time—tradeoffs at home, on campus, in the studio, with Judy, with colleagues, with myself. Something left hanging here that I could make up for in a day or two, the needed time recovered in an unexpected meeting cancellation or a lull in the middle of exam week, or a legal holiday overlooked or forgotten. The day job was always more assertive in its time demands, and I usually deferred to it, dutiful type-A striver that I was. With eventual burnout as a likely outcome, I began to understand that I would have to reimagine my relationship to work if caring for Judy and caring for myself truly mattered.

We make time for things that are important to us, not just for the sake of quality of life and variety, but sometimes for sanity's sake. Golf helped me to come up for air when I often felt that I was drowning in to-dos. A quick basket of balls on the driving range of a course under ten minutes from campus now made more sense than a sandwich at my desk scrolling the day's email inbox. A quick 45-minute lesson after I'd dropped Judy off at a yoga class gave me time to pick up a takeout order of fajitas before I met her again at the gym and relieved me of kitchen duty. Somehow it would be doable. I just needed to see time as something that broke down into adaptable, bite-sized pieces.

I thought a night's sleep might temper the enthusiasm I took with me after that driving range initiation, but the next morning, I woke keen to sign up for lessons. Running an internet search, I learned of a nationwide program called "Get Golf Ready," and a couple of clicks later I'd found a local golf course that participated. A bargain-priced week's worth of one-hour evening lessons in small groups with a club pro might help me to summon the chutzpah I'd need to go from the driving range to an actual course. I told myself it was worth trying, and I told Judy this was something I wanted to do and felt I needed to do. She said she was fine with it—not interested herself, but okay with my interest. "I'm fine being at home," she said, and that was still true then. I had misgivings, though, about taking yet more time that wouldn't be shared with her, time during which I wouldn't be adding interest to her life. It seemed selfish, and I felt conflicted, but not enough to pass on the opportunity. I suspected that down the line I would need a lifesaver of some kind, and maybe this would be it.

My driven approach to work and career extended to whatever leisure pursuits I might be interested in at any point in time, and this was true of golf. I committed to it as if my life depended on it. The truth is maybe it did.

By the final session of the Get Golf Ready program, I'd already signed up for a weekly private lesson with Nate, the young golf instructor who'd calmly and patiently led us through the basics of Golf 101. Navigating the club's compact executive course with him for the first time at the program's closing session, I didn't feel remotely close to being golf ready. He agreed that I could probably benefit from continuing guidance.

"You're not what I'd call a natural," he said with a smile, "but if you practice, I think you'll like the results we'll get in a month or two."

"Look," I said, "if you can help me feel some small degree of self-confidence by the end of the summer, I'll be very grateful."

"Well, let's see how it goes," Nate replied, kindly. "I like a good challenge."

Over the course of that summer in 2011 and the fall and winter months that followed, Nate stuck with me as I painstakingly sought my inner golf swing. We scheduled weekly lessons, usually when I could drop Judy off at the fitness center where we had memberships for her workout or yoga classes. I felt reassured that she'd be comfortable and secure around people that she knew, if only casually. If her classes ended before I made it back from my own lessons, I knew I'd find her in the gym's atrium commons area. She never wandered, something I was grateful for then and remain so to this day.

Many caregivers have difficult jobs made even more complicated by demented loved ones who follow the now-you-see-me-now-you-don't script. One minute the twosome is raking and bagging leaves side by side. The next, the caregiver is anxiously scouting the neighborhood or beyond for his suddenly missing charge. The sufferers' vulnerabilities and the unpredictable risks and dangers of the world beyond their doorsteps loom large in the Alzheimer's caregivers' collection of anxieties and fears.

In Judy's case, she seemed to recognize her increasing vulnerability as the months and years passed, and in some ways, she policed herself. One weekend afternoon, when she returned home prematurely from a walk around the lake by our home, surprising me by the quick turnaround, she was matter of fact. "I got down to the bench on the bike trail, by that big tree, and it just didn't feel right. I'm not sure why, but I just decided to come home." She never left the house alone again. She had enough executive function in her to figure out that home equaled safe but not enough to explain to me just what it was that prompted her to cut that solo outing short. It was a relief for me but another disappointing loss for her.

A colleague's wife with whom we had a few years' acquaintance, a German-born librarian named Annaliese, also attended those classes at our fitness center. Once I realized that she crossed paths with Judy there nearly every week, I asked if she'd be willing to email or text me periodically to let me know how Judy was doing. "No problem," she'd said. A kind and empathetic person, she understood and was happy to keep an eye on Judy whenever she was on hand.

I'm sure you'd have accused me of spying on you if you'd known, and you'd have been pissed. The truth is it did feel undercover. Occasional reports from people like Annaliese, though, helped me get a sense of how your social skills were faring and how you were managing when I wasn't around to provide backup. It wasn't much, it didn't demand a lot of Annaliese, but it helped reassure me that you'd be safe, and I'd be better informed.

Going back to our first years together, when our shared interest in all things textile helped to launch our respective careers, Judy knew this about me. Whenever I developed an interest in something, be it gardening, cooking, childrearing, long-distance running, or traveling in the UK and Europe—all impassioned pursuits at one time or another—books on whatever the subject, bought, borrowed, or rescued, would predictably take up residence. I didn't necessarily read every title cover to cover; there was rarely enough time for that. A paragraph here, a chapter there, or a leisurely skim with a highlighter in hand inevitably paid dividends in useful knowledge or insights that the interest itself, whatever it was, hadn't yet revealed. I imagined, too, that I'd absorb something just by having the books around, magical thinking that I realized was irrational but that stays with me still. So it was, eventually, with books about Alzheimer's caregiving. And so it was with books about golf.

When lessons with Nate and driving range practice were finally put on hold by a heavy early-season snowfall and plunging temperatures, I redirected my enthusiasm to golf literature, a genre, like pretty much all sports writing, of which I was entirely ignorant.

Judy had dated a basketball player in high school, and while she wasn't much interested in sports by the time we met, she'd sat in the stands over the course of a few youthful seasons and absorbed some of that culture. I'd attended a small parochial school that didn't offer sports, not that I'd have been interested if they had. To the everlasting dismay of the men in my family, father and uncles in particular, my aversion exceeded their enthusiasm for their seasonal weekend obsessions: basketball, baseball, and football. Once the radio or television was turned on and my family's small flat filled with the announcers' play-by-play, I'd make a purposeful exit—off on my bike, out on the porch with a book, and once I had a driver's license, cruising around in the family car for a couple of hours with a friend or two whose minimal interest in the Boston Red Sox or the Celtics or the Patriots or whichever team happened to be playing matched mine. Disappointing sons to working men who believed that sports were the lingua franca of their gender.

That playing a sport, any sport, could offer soul-satisfying fulfillment along with health benefits wasn't lost on me. I favored sports that I felt offered space for the life of the mind or accommodated it by virtue of their form and practice. Distance running, for example. Fifteen- or eighteen-mile marathon training runs lend themselves to reflection and contemplation. Over the months when I trained for the 1982 Newport, Rhode Island, marathon—my one and only—Judy said that I seemed more relaxed overall, less anxious, happier. A big part of that attitude adjustment was probably more physiological than psycho-emotional, but the kind of solo time that distance running imposes clears space for cleansing mind work. It worked that way for me. Until the finish line. My first strangled words to Judy and Trevor three hours, fifty-four minutes, and four seconds after starting were "That's it. I'll never have to do that again!" They looked dumbfounded that I'd finished at all. And therein lies the problem with solo sports. There's no one with whom to parcel out the embarrassment when results are less than stellar. Still, I learned a lot during those running years, and from brief dalliances with tennis and kayaking, and from a much longer cycling practice. I never needed my body slamming into someone else's to get a mind kick. Going solo or with one equally focused partner, step by step, shot by shot, stroke by stroke suited the introvert that I am at heart.

Which is probably why golf found me, or I found it, when I needed it most.

Nate moved on to manage a course in a small town a hundred miles away before I could enlist him for another season of lessons. Another local club pro, Sven, agreed to take me on as his student, and I marked my first anniversary as a golfer under his tutelage. By the end of that second golf summer, I'd pretty well absorbed the rules of the game, had grown accustomed to the layouts of a handful of local courses, and had secured in our friend Paul a regular golfing partner generously inclined to take my novice playing and hectic schedule in stride.

Because Paul worked for himself and prioritized golf as one of his life's greatest pleasures, he seemed always willing to meet up for a quick round just as the sun was rising or on the spur of the moment if a meeting cancellation freed up a few hours of my time. We started scheduling regular weekend rounds and expanded to foursomes when other golfer friends were available.

Still, I enjoyed solo rounds best. I especially liked getting to a particular executive course near our home, a place called West 9 that has long since been bulldozed, before the sun rose and the lingering mists of spring or fall had cleared. Knowing that Judy was safely asleep and wouldn't rouse until I returned for breakfast with her, I'd walk those quirky nine holes as quickly as my bogey-double bogey game allowed. Occasionally I'd surprise myself with a rare par, though those successful holes remained elusive. The truth was my progress in the game was excruciatingly slow. "One step forward, two steps back" seemed to define my game's trajectory. It didn't matter. Caring for myself started to seem as important as caring for Judy. If I'd do that by chasing small, dimpled balls from flag to flag across dew-soaked fairways, so be it. Medicate me with fresh air and peace and quiet. It became an indispensable part of my weekly routine.

Once we'd reached the point when she couldn't be safely left alone anymore, I started bringing her along for late afternoon or early evening rounds. We'd walk the nine holes, usually at times when other golfers were few and our slow pace wouldn't be too disruptive. Local league season hadn't started yet, or had just ended, so while other folks were having dinner we'd be on the fairways, Judy scavenging for interesting leaves or stones, me scavenging for wayward balls. She loved being outdoors, and the soft, raked light of those times of day pleased both our aesthetic sensibilities. Now and then I'd have to let faster golfers play through. No one ever gave me any indication that a guy zigzagging his way across a long fairway with a nonplaying wife in tow was remarkable. Curious maybe, but not remarkable.

One Christmas I bought Judy a putter, a surprise that she thought amusing and, by the time she had it in her hands, I realized was probably entirely misguided. *Who wouldn't enjoy putting*, I'd thought, *and who couldn't learn to putt, at least passably?* The pleasure in putting comes within the context of the entire game, of course. Standalone and it loses both its raison

d'être and its suspense. She didn't get much out of it, my instructions such as they were meeting up with her inability, by then, to
hold onto a new idea or a new task. "Why am I doing this?" she
repeated, and yes, I asked myself the same question. Trying to
engage her in something we could do side by side, trying to make
tagging along more active for her, less passive. I thought that
was why I'd proposed it. Time we could spend together doing
something we got a kick out of before that too was gone. Except
that getting a kick out of it wasn't in the cards for her. "Why am I
doing this?" she asked each time. I stopped trying to answer. She
was okay with being a walking buddy, but I'd have to find golf
buddies elsewhere.

A year or so before Judy's initial diagnosis, we'd hired a local attorney to draft new wills for us, a task many years overdue. So
much had changed in our lives that the 1979 edition was seriously outdated. Our son was grown and married, their daughters,
our only grandchildren, were growing toddlers, and our physical
and financial assets had likewise grown. We now had retirement
accounts promising a reasonable afterlife once the world of work
and careers was behind us. A growing art collection, of our own
work and that of artists we either knew or admired or both, also
seemed like something that needed to be accounted for sooner
rather than later.

I'd asked around among colleagues and the handful of friends
who, like us, had built modest art collections over the course of
their working lifetimes. Do you have an attorney? Do you know
of an attorney who knows anything about art and collections of
art? Over the course of several months of asking, Edward Reich's
name came up enough times that I finally scheduled an appointment at his offices.

It turned out we'd met his artist wife Annmarie at a museum

exhibition opening a year or two earlier and had seen her work in several gallery shows, often enough to recognize it at a glance. Her renderings of Nebraska's agricultural landscapes and livestock were natural and unfussy, descriptive but not overly literal, unpretentious in the best way. If the emotional sensibilities revealed in her work could hint at what qualities she might have looked for in a life partner, we were optimistic that we'd find him compatible.

We immediately appreciated Ed's mild manner and how relaxed we felt each time we sat down with him. He was unfailingly even keeled, welcoming but not blustery, perceptive but not intrusive, measured and precise with every practical detail of our discussions and the documents that followed from those discussions. We saw qualities in him that we'd seen in his wife's artwork: sureness and competence, integrity, honesty. Heartland values, to be sure, but entirely without sanctimony. Life imitating art imitating life. We knew we were in the right hands.

A year after we'd completed the work on our updated wills with him, Judy got her diagnosis. I knew that we'd need to adjust some of the terms and make provisions for her eventual care and protection in the event I predeceased her and didn't want to delay dealing with that. "We need to see Ed and make sure we've got everything in place to account for your illness and how things might play out," I said.

"Do I have to go?" was her only response. I made the appointment. It would be routine, just a few adjustments.

"Since we last saw you," I said to Ed once we'd settled into one of his office's meeting rooms, "Judy's been diagnosed with Alzheimer's, and I'd like to get things in place so that should something happen to me and I can no longer handle our affairs, or she's widowed, she'll be protected and the resources will be in place to cover the care she'll eventually need." He listened patiently as I detailed how Judy had been turned down for long-term care insurance, how we'd pursued a diagnosis, how out-to-sea we both felt once we'd accepted our new reality, and how important we agreed it was to make sure she'd be protected should anything happen to me first. "I've heard that in cases like this, some people divorce to protect one partner's assets, to protect the caregiver from impoverishment. Is this something we need to consider?"

Ed didn't respond immediately. The pause after I'd run through our questions and concerns fit with his style—careful, measured, unhurried. When he finally cleared his throat and raised his eyes again toward us, something in his tone changed. He started, then lowered his eyes, his voice dropping to almost a whisper. "Annmarie got the same diagnosis as you, also this past summer. You and she are the same age, you're both artists. Not the kind of coincidence we have any interest in celebrating, is it?"

We could never have imagined this kind of alignment. It was so unexpected that the mental pause it prompted seemed to swell in the space we occupied, uncomfortably displacing the room's air, leaving me nearly breathless. "We're really sorry to learn this, Ed," I said. "I don't know what else to say. This is incredible." I know now that it wasn't incredible. It was his, and our, reality. Coincidental, surely, but not incredible. Hundreds, thousands of people get the same diagnosis each day. Why not us? Why not Annmarie and Ed? Still, the revelation stunned us. What were the odds?

Ed and I never became friends, though the common experience that Alzheimer's represented incubated a mutual understanding that conditioned all subsequent meetings. Once in place, the professional relationship seemed—rightly—resistant to change. I invited him to join me for a round of golf once, and out of curiosity about West 9, the course I'd proposed and that he'd never played, he accepted. I'd heard he was a very good golfer, his passion for the game understated but his playing skills far more advanced and surer than mine. I recall the embarrassment I felt as he parred or birdied each hole, though he never revealed the slightest impatience with my double and triple bogeys. Ed would never witness my eventual and long-fought-for improvement. I'd remain well and permanently out of his league.

I started meeting with Ed by myself, mainly because it was easier to get to the point without having to tiptoe around your sensitivities, especially early on when you were still in some degree of denial. Sitting across from one another at a conference room table, he and I walked through various scenarios and hypothetical futures in which you and I might find ourselves. He gave me the information I needed to the extent that he could, recommended external resources when whatever I sought was out of his purview, and remained consistently judicious with any advice he might offer. He usually kept his own personal experience off the table, though when I asked him directly, "How is Annmarie doing?" he'd update me as concisely as he could. Fellow travelers we were, but it was a shared path neither of us wanted to be on.

I worked with Ed to set up a revocable trust that helped to reassure me that our assets and your care would be well managed if I became incapacitated or died before you. Resolving issues like this helped me to sleep a little easier and gave me the sense that I was being both pragmatic and proactive. The disease may have been piloting our future, but dealing with ground-level practicalities provided a semblance of control, and that was enough to temper the sometimes-paralyzing anxiety that gnawed at me. You were typically incurious as I'd report on the outcome of the latest appointment, and that was fine. You were one of the fortunate ones whose caregiver could be trusted to unfailingly put his loved one's interests at the forefront. I was one of the fortunate ones to be able to do that.

11

Love costs anxiety, joy has a price:
the fragile edge and smoky smell of limits.
    Loneliness
lacks any such suggestion of an end.
    It is forever,
and plentiful beyond imagining.

           – Rachel Hadas, from *Loneliness*

In early Spring 2013, just shy of four years into Judy's diagnosis, I set up a regular schedule of caregiver visits with *A Trusted Friend* providers. Though her heart wasn't really in it, she was increasingly anxious about being left alone, anxiety that I'd been feeling too for many months. Although my studio assistant Samantha continued to be a presence in our home a part of most weekdays, Judy didn't always register her comings and goings, and often tended to forget she was there. Out of sight, out of mind. Sam had work to do and deadlines to meet in any case and wasn't there to keep Judy company.

Because she'd quickly grown comfortable with Lisa during her mother's stay with us the year before, and Lisa was still available, we confirmed that she could cover two afternoons a week. Finding regulars for the remaining weekdays took a few weeks to work out, and it amazed me how certain Judy could be that a particular provider was or wasn't a good fit. I'd greet first-timers at the door, all predictably cordial and eager, and four hours later Judy's verdicts would be unequivocal. "I don't want that person again" or "She was okay, she can come back" and in a couple of instances, "I really liked her, she can come anytime." She'd always been measured in her judgments, the Libra in her weighing things at great length before she made decisions, so this directness was something new. Alzheimer's-related disinhibition on a modest scale? If that were the most disinhibited she'd get, I'd be fine with it.

A Trusted Friend worked with us to organize a real team of care providers. While my top priority was to have so many hours a day covered, freeing me to focus on the demands of my day job, theirs was to develop a care plan that would keep Judy engaged and comfortable. A three-ring binder served as a client journal in which each day's activities were recorded, along with Judy's overall mood and demeanor, her likes and dislikes, any food, snacks, or drinks consumed, any outings or excursions they'd planned for her, and her reactions. While the different providers rarely crossed paths, they all had access to these journal entries, and checking the daily comments helped them to maintain some degree of consistency and predictability. I liked knowing how things had gone each visit, and Judy settled into new relationships that filled the void each day had come to represent.

We also started making short daily notes in monthly planners that served as quick reminders for both Judy and me of what we'd done on a given day and the days before that. It filled in the blanks for her care team as well. They'd see what we'd done the evening or the weekend before, where Judy and I had been, what films or exhibitions or performances we might have attended, and this helped them to structure conversations with her. I printed photos I'd taken of some activity we'd shared or event we'd participated in, and these helped her recall at least some of the things she'd seen or done over a week's time. Since her short-term memory was so compromised, I think she was sometimes mystified that we'd done one thing or another about which she couldn't pull up a single detail. That was fine; it was the disease, in the face of which I wanted her to hold on to and enjoy as much life as possible.

Some of Judy's relationships with the *Trusted Friend* team

members ripened gradually into solid friendships, perhaps no more solidly than with Lisa. She was one of Judy's first successful matches, and the two of them were so alike in temperament that I think it was natural for them to bond. They looked enough alike that mistaking them for sisters would have been unremarkable. They settled into the moment—any moment—calmly, patiently, appreciatively. Neither of them put expectations ahead of experience. They were each open to, and accepting of, whatever happened on a given day.

When Lisa brought her guitar along and played and sang for Judy, Judy always mentioned it later, after things had quieted down and it was just her and me. "Lisa sang for me today," she'd say. "She's a good singer. I'm not such a good singer." When Judy was in high school, though, she sang in chorus. I know this because every Christmas she reminded me whenever the local classical music radio station sent choral passages from Messiah into our home or car. She must have really enjoyed her time singing those uplifting "For unto us a Child is born" and "All we like sheep, have gone astray" melodies.

It didn't take very long before she began anticipating her care team members' visits, though there were days and weeks when she struggled to sort out who was who. Each of them seemed to favor certain activities, and they all learned quickly what types of things Judy enjoyed. There tended to be enough variety from day to day and week to week that even if she weren't feeling very upbeat or social, they could usually bring her around. Lisa, Evelyn, and Deborah planned walks outdoors whenever the weather was comfortable enough. Deb often had Judy bring along her point-and-shoot to photograph trees, leaves and berries, ducks and geese, and other natural features glimpsed on those walks. She even printed enough of those digital files for Judy to put together a couple of albums with her help to serve as conversation starters and memory prompts.

Once Deb learned that Judy was an afternoon tea drinker, she programmed a weekly excursion to the Teavana shop in a nearby shopping mall. There, whatever the weather outdoors, they could walk for twenty minutes or so before sitting down to chat over one of the shop's fruited herbal infusions. Judy appreciated Deb's easy camaraderie and her sense of humor. "We were laughing so hard people were looking at us," she told me once after an afternoon outing. "She's just so funny." I never did learn what comic magic Deb devised to amuse Judy so. I was grateful that Deb could almost unfailingly lift her spirits, mood upswings that tended to last hours after she'd finished her shift.

Evelyn had retired from nursing a few years earlier, and she brought that experience to her caregiving practice. She wore her conscientiousness like a treasured brooch and was always dutiful in making sure Judy had eaten a proper lunch. An avid gardener, she could always coax Judy into helping her with weeding our two raised beds, a task in which I couldn't interest her no matter how often I tried or how encouraging I sounded. In snapshots Evelyn shared with me of the two of them sitting side by side in local public gardens, their broad smiles confirmed their compatibility.

Evelyn's twice weekly shifts usually ended late in the afternoon when I returned from campus. Typically, I'd phone Judy to let her know I was on my way. According to Evelyn, after one of these quick calls Judy replaced the receiver, turned to her, and said impishly, "Well, our fun's over!" I chuckled hearing that, grateful for the easy rapport they shared. I knew, though, that Judy's off-hand remark was revealing. By then she saw me as her warden, at least some of the time. I knew otherwise, and I understood her frustration. It was a role I had little appetite for. Husband, lover, chief of staff, concierge, personal assistant…no problem serving her in any of those capacities. Jailer, not so much.

Pat enjoyed the challenge of teaching Judy one of a stack of board games she regularly brought along. The steadily increasing aphasia hobbled Judy when trying to find a "right" word or to get that word out in games that once spotlighted her previously quick mind and linguistic prowess—Scrabble most notably. For Judy, the fun in it now was embedded in her back-and-forth with Pat and in the increasingly loosey-goosey rule bending and procedural improvisations they would devise.

Occasionally, *A Trusted Friend* sent one of a handful of substitutes when someone from her regular team couldn't make it or was ill or otherwise unavailable. I met most of them, usually crossing paths as they arrived and I left home for campus. Judy wasn't enthusiastic about new faces and could even be hostile, especially when they came on short notice or I wasn't on hand to introduce them.

This note appeared one September day in the caregiver's logbook: *"Please, if you don't already, talk with Judy about the caregiver, by name, who will be here in the afternoon. She was totally unaware that I was coming and was quite cool to me for a couple of hours."* In fact, it's likely I had told Judy, probably even written it down on her daily "what's happening" sheet. Inputs like this often failed to stick, and the written lists lost usefulness as time and her disease advanced. We could try to cover all bases, but her day-to-day state of mind became so variable that I couldn't always predict how things would sort themselves out.

The caregivers' logbook offered me some real insight about how Judy managed when I wasn't around, and that usually relieved me of some of the stress I felt whenever I had to leave the house. Their entries were usually brief, written on the fly at the end of their shifts.

> *Super day, walked and laughed lots, started organizing Judy's studio as planned—labeled thread & button drawers. Listened to the CD of Celtic music that your friend recorded, Judy seemed especially happy/silly.*
> —Deborah

> *Good day for walk this afternoon, Judy thought it wasn't as "drafty" as this morning when it was really blowing. She responded to the birds, geese, and saw a heron on the neighbor's dock. The music that was playing when I arrived seemed to help her mood—good thing to set up for the start of each shift. She was moving in time to*

the beat, so I knew she was really listening. We folded origami until she lost interest. I think the music is great.

—Evelyn

Such a great day w/Judy—we put new pictures in photo book and took some more. She was really interested in fall leaves, also in the tomatoes in your garden, especially the ones the squirrels got. We laughed lots and went over pictures of your weekend activities. Talked about her birthday coming up next month. She couldn't remember her age. She laughed and said it was a 'pigment' of her imagination. We laughed again and I asked her what color that 'pigment' would be. She said, "It must be gold." We finished the afternoon cutting different gold squares from some fashion magazines and made a collage (left it on kitchen table). She seemed good as I got ready to leave.

—Deborah

They also commented on less-than-great days.

Judy was very upset when she answered the door. She was angry at Michael. She said she wanted to kill herself, then began throwing things on the floor from the table. I calmed her down by talking quietly & letting her have some time to chill. I sat with her at the kitchen table. She said she was hungry. I found some quinoa in the fridge & warmed it up for her. She ate 100% of it. Judy then went to her studio, so I phoned the office & talked to Carmen. She gave me a couple of suggestions. Judy walked from her studio to bedroom and then back to kitchen. I got her to look at a magazine with me and by 3:00 she was feeling much better. We went outside and picked some shriveled day lilies, put in compost. A neighbor saw us & came over to say hi, Judy couldn't bring up her name.

Older lady. We went back inside at 3:30 p.m. Rest of the afternoon was very good.

—Pat

She was very hostile and argumentative for most of my visit. Judy told me I could sit on the couch but not in the kitchen with her. She shouted about how she didn't want anyone here and told me to leave repeatedly. The next hour she spent going from bedroom to sitting room and back. I checked on her and she was quietly sorting through her stuff, so I let her be. She seemed to calm down the last hour but wasn't friendly. Something upset her and she just wasn't herself. Hope next time is better.

—Maureen (an occasional substitute provider)

Became agitated with me as soon as Michael left. Didn't understand why I was here. Didn't want me here but didn't want me to go. I gave her some space and went to kitchen area. She raised her voice from the other room, very angry. Then she came into kitchen and stood next to me yelling, wanted me to leave. I spoke calmly and she agreed to let me call Michael.

I called and left a message. Then I phoned the Trusted Friend office and spoke with Joellen. She said Judy had been like this a few times recently, to just let her be, suggest she go to her studio or bedroom. She went to her studio and stayed there the rest of my shift but seemed to calm down. She said bye when I told her I was leaving but didn't leave the room.

—Shirley (occasional substitute)

I'd known for a while that Judy was incubating a measure of resentment toward me, most of it coming from her loss of independence. Even though I tried to get her buy-in for any major changes ahead of their happening, I'd had to make the hard decisions along the way, and she blamed me each time. Naturally, since I was the one standing there alongside her. I think, though, that her occasional outbursts, while aimed at me or at one of the care providers, were really aimed at the disease. Acknowledging this helped me to see her anger as what it was: enormous frustration and grief over all that she'd lost. That she could contain it so well, despite the outbursts, amazes me still. I really doubt I'd have the wherewithal, were it me.

Part of that resentment lay, too, in the fact that I was able to leave home each day, to head to campus, leaving her and all my cares and worries behind (or so she imagined). I think that's where the idea that I had a love interest was rooted, some other woman out there that I was with when I wasn't with her. Lisa wrote me this email one evening:

> *Hi Michael. Not such a great day today...When I arrived, Judy's eyes were red, she'd been crying. She told me you were gone and weren't coming back. She said, "I'm just in a bad mood today." Later I thought she was pulling out of her melancholy state while we were looking at the photo album in your library that has your house renovation pictures but seeing people at the end of that book triggered something. She stood up and said, "I don't want to do this anymore." She told me I could go, and that she was going to bed. I let her be in the bedroom for about 15 minutes, then I went in and convinced her to come help me scoop snow. I thought exercise and fresh air would help. She came reluctantly, and when we were working, she'd stop and say, "I don't know why I'm doing this for Michael because he's with another woman." I can't persuade her at all to think otherwise—she says, "You're wrong." After we came in, I tried to get her interested in my lap harp, but she said no and went into the bedroom again. I just left her alone, then 10 minutes later, she came out with a cup of cold coffee in her hands, and it was as if nothing had gone wrong! We visited, looked at that picture book on your ottoman, made tea,*

I was grateful that Lisa and the other care providers shared details like this with me. It prompted me to reassure Judy that I'd never leave her, that there was no other woman, nor would there be, that I'd always come home, as I always did. I don't think she really believed that I had someone on the side. She knew how much time I needed to spend on campus; she'd been part of that work environment for nearly ten years and still came with me to campus often enough that it remained one of her comfort zones. Her insecurities sometimes got the better of her, and her vulnerabilities, thanks to the disease, were constantly staring her in the face. It's not surprising that she'd sometimes lose herself in a muddle of sadness, abandonment, hopelessness. That she always managed to pull herself out of it is the amazing thing. She had an essential inner strength that may have wavered but never abandoned her. That strength of hers helped me a lot too, and I was grateful for it.

Whenever I'd discussed with Judy my feeling that having in-home companion care was going to be necessary, her usual response had been "I don't want anyone here with me" or "I don't need someone to be here all the time." She had another response, less frequent but no less insistent. "We can't afford it." That probably went back to those many years when we were both self-employed, when, in fact, there were times when we couldn't afford extras. The reality was we needed to be able to afford this. If we were to have a reasonably well-financed retirement, I needed to keep working at least another six or seven years, so retiring early to care for Judy wasn't on the table. We'd made good headway with our financial advisor Roxanne's help. She'd moved confidently to help us position ourselves more favorably with our retirement savings and investments. Between those and the university's retirement plan, we were cautiously optimistic. This optimism was contingent on my continuing to work, at least until I turned seventy.

We hadn't factored into our retirement plan a terminal illness for which there was no cure and no effective treatment, that would eventually render Judy unable to manage self-care and the myriad daily activities to which—when life was "normal"—we hardly gave a thought. Lacking long-term care insurance, her dependency would come at a heavy cost—physically, emotionally, and financially. Figuring out how we'd deal with the Alzheimer's price tag became my wee hours bête noire, intruding on my sleep when competition for that annoyance was already shared by a host of concerns.

When we signed on with *A Trusted Friend* homecare in 2013, the estimated median household income in largely urban Lancaster County, Nebraska, where we lived, was $58,009,[12] with 18.9 percent of the population earning within a range of $50,000 and $74,999. Nationally, the median household income that year was a bit lower than in our home county and was estimated at $52,250. I'll use $55,000 as a rough average; that translates to a monthly income of roughly $4,600, likely not enough for many households to manage more than their essentials.

How fortunate we were—and how ironic it feels saying that now—that when Judy was first diagnosed, I had an annual income three times the national average. We were fully able to meet all our financial obligations and maintain what anyone would have called a comfortable lifestyle. We still had a mortgage, but its payoff was in sight. Our credit was excellent, and the loans we secured to complete repairs and renovations to our home were quickly discharged. We weren't running any credit card debt, and we were long past financing our son's education and career launch. So at least in the short term, paying for in-home care would be doable.

At the outset *A Trusted Friend* billed us at $21.00 an hour plus incidentals that included mileage and occasional admission fees or outing expenses. A couple of four-hour afternoons a week quickly doubled to sixteen weekly hours, and after about a year's time we'd increased the team's hours to roughly twenty-five per week, charges equivalent to about $1,100 biweekly and over $2,000 monthly. When we reached the point at which Judy needed help bathing, dressing, and feeding herself, we needed thirty-five hours of in-home care each week. That coincided with an increase in the agency's hourly rate to $22.00. Even with a monthly take-home salary of roughly $8,000.00, assigning $3,400.00 of that to her team's services was both financially and emotionally stressful.

If we'd been facing this level of caregiving expense with only that median monthly income of $4,600, with mortgage, real estate taxes and insurance, auto loan payments and car insurance, utilities, groceries, medical care, and all the rest that had to come out of that $4,600, paid in-home care would have been far beyond our reach, impossible to even consider. So it was for a large percentage of the caregivers of the more than five million Alzheimer's sufferers in the US when Judy was first diagnosed, a number that has grown to more than six million today. The costs are staggering.[13] And the numbers will only increase absent effective treatments or a definitive cure.

Every case of Alzheimer's and similar dementias is unique. As a husband caregiver friend of mine likes to say, "You know one case of Alzheimer's, you know one case of Alzheimer's."[14] It's much the same when it comes to how primary caregivers finance the costs associated with the disease. A lucky few have the foresight and the means to purchase long-term care insurance that, depending on the specifics, can greatly reduce their personal outlay. In our case, by the time we could afford long-term care insurance it was too late for Judy. Her symptoms were already measurable, so we couldn't insure her at any price.

One of the first things I did after her diagnosis was to apply on her behalf for Social Security Disability Benefits. Our application was approved in less than two months, and that additional $900 monthly would be an important part of underwriting the expenses of her care as they increased by the month and by the year. Roughly 22 percent of my net salary went toward care expenses in the years that she remained at home. I anticipated that we'd need to tap into retirement savings, and we eventually did, but while Judy was at home, we were able to cover the costs out-of-pocket. A friend's unanticipated generosity also factored into the financing strategy.

We first met Kitty in the 1980s. She'd grown up in Michigan, and like us had gone to art school, eventually finding herself co-owner of a small craft gallery in Alexandria, Virginia. Shared interests in art generally and art textiles specifically had nurtured our friendship, and her second marriage to a real estate entrepreneur and investor based in Washington brought symmetry to our deepening bond. Martin too had midwestern agricultural roots, a background that had led him in a roundabout way to collecting folk art. He also admired textiles and applied them creatively in all the commercial projects his firm developed. Through the nineties we met up with them for a few days or a week nearly every August, at their Chesapeake Bay cabin. While their DC townhome was well appointed, it wasn't showy, in keeping with their modest, midwestern sensibilities. Their cabin cum beach house was downright rustic and lent itself perfectly to the type of comfortable informality that seems to fertilize healthy and long-lived friendships. Kitty and Martin's hospitality was always bighearted and sincere, and Judy loved spending time with them as much as I did.

Martin's death in a boating accident in 2006 convulsed Kitty, convulsed all his family and his many friends, us included, and convulsed his business. Kitty's grief was profound, but slowly she recovered to a new version of the life they had built together, accepting that while it wasn't what either of them had anticipated, it was her task as his survivor to move forward, and she did.

After Judy's diagnosis, Kitty visited us a couple of times,

wanting to spend quality time with her while Judy still knew her and understood the friendship that we shared and how much it meant to each of us. She was faithful in keeping in touch with us by phone and rarely did a month or so pass without a check-in. It was during one of these calls, after Judy handed the phone off to me, that Kitty asked me what Judy's care was costing. I explained that we were averaging $2,200 monthly at that point and that I expected it would be increasing steadily as the next year played out.

"Let me help you with this, Michael," Kitty offered. "I'd really like to do something concrete, and given the half-continent stretching out between us, this is a great option."

"That's generous of you, Kitty, but I think we can manage this, I really do. The big anxiety for me is simply that we don't know how long this will go on."

"So let me help, if only to reduce your anxiety a bit. Listen, Martin left me in great shape, better than I ever thought I'd be. The truth is, I'll never live long enough to exhaust the financial resources I have. You know me, I have this frugal streak and I make no apologies for it. Most of our estate will one day go to various organizations that we've supported over the years, and I won't be around to see the benefits. So let me do this; it will comfort me to know that I can play a small part in Judy's care and well-being."

I told Kitty I'd think further on her proposal and talk with Judy about it. Her response when I did was accepting and appreciative. "It's really wonderful that she's offering this," she said. "It makes me feel really good. She's been such a great friend for all these years."

So, we accepted Kitty's gift, a thousand dollars each month transferred automatically to our checking account for what would turn out to be an eighteen-month term, to support our expenses for Judy's expanding care needs. It was an instance of very good fortune following on bad, and we understood that. Our friendship with Kitty was already strong and didn't need any additional outward affirmation, but this special generosity enriched it even further. I know that Judy was as moved by it as I was.

The yoga practice Judy had been faithful to since the mid-nineties continued until Annaliese let me know that Judy seemed increasingly disoriented in that class at the fitness center. Apparently, she'd mistakenly claimed two other folks' mats during a regular routine, and she refused to give up the second one when its actual user challenged her. A few times she'd drunk from water bottles that weren't her own, and no one found that amusing. Annaliese assured me that people weren't unkind, that they understood Judy's situation, but some were becoming impatient. "Maybe it would be better to get her into a one-on-one class," she suggested.

We were friends with a popular yoga teacher with whom Judy had taken classes many times in the past at a different location, but whose class schedules hadn't worked with ours for some time. "What would you think about having Maura come to the house once or twice a week for an hour of yoga?" I proposed. She loved the idea, so I emailed Maura. Would she be able to squeeze in a private class, in our home, once or twice a week? She was willing to give it a try.

Judy really loved those sessions with Maura. Once their yoga routine was completed, Maura would make tea, and the two of them would chat for another half-hour or more, a gift of companionship that the small per session fee she charged us didn't come close to justifying. It was pure, unqualified kindness on her part, and it was genuine. I could see that Maura liked spending time with Judy and that Judy gave something to her as well. Maybe it was her receptivity, her genuine appreciation of time spent with someone that she liked and trusted.

Loneliness is one of the most damaging consequences of Alzheimer's. When family and friends pull away, as they sometimes do, that loneliness expands and amplifies the negative impacts of the neurological changes the sufferer is experiencing. I could see early on how loneliness demoralized Judy and threatened her quality of life, almost more than the disease itself. So, while there were moments when she felt I was controlling her life too much, the deep connections she made with people like Maura and with her *Trusted Friend* team members were worth the efforts it took to lay the groundwork. I'll never regret reaching out on her behalf when she could not.

12

*Either know, or listen to someone who does.
To live, you need understanding: either your
own, or borrowed. But many people are
unaware that they do not know, and others
think they know when they do not…Asking
advice won't diminish your greatness or cast
doubt on your talent. To the contrary; it will
strengthen your reputation. To combat mis-
fortune, take counsel with reason.*

— Balthasar Gracián, from *The Art of Worldly Wisdom*

Dear Judy,

*Saying that we finally consummated our relationship on an
unseasonably mild late December evening in 1971, during a
holiday get-together near our former undergraduate campus, in
an unoccupied bedroom in a rented house where college friends
tentatively launching the rest of their lives were still room-mat-
ing or cohabiting, makes it sound a bit too formal, maybe too
"genteel." I'd come back from my first semester of graduate school
having missed you wildly and wanting you badly, and if I'd been
too timid to make a move four months earlier when we'd said
goodbye, that reticence had evaporated in the interim.*

*I knew we were of one mind about sealing the deal as soon as
I picked you up that night at your parents' home. After catching
up with them as minimally as politeness allowed, we signed off
and headed to the interstate that would deliver us to what we
and all our friends called "The Yellow House." A beer or two and*

forty minutes or so into the party, we disappeared, though in that tight and intimate milieu I doubt anyone had second thoughts as to what we were up to. Losing my virginity with you was a huge relief, an urgent need ticked off a checklist of life experiences I was ambitious to realize. I didn't see in the heat of it how you guided me, how you steered the course for both of us.

What I hadn't anticipated was the degree to which sex with you transformed not just how I loved you, and you me, but how both the physicality of it and the enormous emotional release seemed to alter something at my core, something essential that I hadn't recognized until that moment. It committed me to you, a pledge of body and soul about which I'd have no second thoughts. It seems unlikely from this distant vantage point. We were in our very early twenties, two slight young adults with uncertain handles on our futures, yet so ready to commit to one another, little experience necessary.

Did we maybe surprise ourselves, that the sex felt so right from that first time? It's been too long now to remember. Across the forty-three years that we were married, though, sex was always important, often urgent, a priority that we always maintained, regardless the complications that life set before us and the natural ebb and flow of sex itself in any lifelong relationship. It was a key part of how we communicated and of how we conceived of our partnership—until Alzheimer's callous intrusion.

In the first couple of years of your illness, fooling around, as in "You wanna fool around?" continued to provide reaffirming and restorative carnal interludes once or twice a week, as they always had. We continued to enjoy one another, the physical closeness a balm offering mutual solace and reassurance.

Having been relieved of the pressures and distractions of wage earning and career, you seemed to bring more focus to it and take more pleasure from it. The world fell away, and cocooned together, skin to skin and heartbeat to heartbeat, we could feel safe and, for a little while, in control. There were times, too, when sadness slid under the covers with us, and you'd weep silently, unwilling or unable to explain despite my whispered

After the clinical trial was behind us and Judy entered the middle
stages of the disease, a fast-increasing number of activities of
daily living were being affected. She who'd always prided herself on putting together outfits in which each item—whether
tee, pullover, slacks, jacket, scarf—complemented every other,
began to falter as soon as she'd slide the wardrobe doors open.
The options seemed to stymie her, even though she'd made so
many of those garments herself and had worn them in various
combinations over many seasons. That's when she started wearing the same items over and over, three or four consecutive days
without variation, despite my reminding her or suggesting other
options. I took photos of her wearing different outfits and taped
them to the wall inside her closet where she'd see them as soon
as she opened the doors. It didn't really help, her capacity to understand their purpose having been completely muddled by that
point. I finally realized that it wasn't really something to spend
time addressing, deciding instead that if she was dressed in a way
that was comfortable for her, maintaining her past standards was
wasted energy. It did feel like capitulation, though—another win
for the disease.

Her lifelong interest in clothing and fashion and my interest
in social history had steered us to the British television series
Downton Abbey from its debut season's first episode, broadcast
on our public television network in early 2011. By the time the
fourth season was appearing in 2013, we remained faithful view-
ers even though Judy had long since given up trying to keep the
storyline and the characters straight. She loved the costumes,
their fabrics and construction details, as much characters for her
as the actors who wore them. Even if she could no longer sew,

her past technical prowess came through her still critical eye and her visceral understanding of fit and of what constituted good fit on a particular body.

Her high regard for *Downton's* costumers, then, wasn't surprising. "Look at how straight that hemline is," she'd remark admiringly about a silk chiffon shift Lady Mary might be wearing. She'd note the drape of a particular fabric and how the actor's movements animated it. She'd exclaim about a layer of sheer lace and how it fell over an underskirt, and seeing a use of pin tucks, she'd recall "I used to do pin tucking a lot when I was sewing," a decorative and textural strategy she'd also taught over many years. That she could express that degree of technical appreciation with such clear-mindedness and authority, yet stand frustrated at the closet door, unsure about what top might go with which pants or indifferent to the fact that the short-sleeved linen shirt she was trying and failing to button was inside out, was both dissonant and alarming.

Because all the hands-on skills and the tacit knowledge acquired over a lifetime of sewing her own clothes had become too compromised for her to successfully complete a project, we were purchasing more of her clothes. She liked to shop, and a weekend excursion to a local clothing boutique or department store was an easy destination when getting out of the house seemed like it might have a beneficial effect on her mood, or simply break up the monotony of an otherwise uneventful day for both of us. We'd navigate to the sales racks, and if something appealed to her, I'd put it over my arm. When we'd selected five or six items for her to try on, we'd head over to the dressing rooms. That something so seemingly simple and straightforward could devolve into an entirely confused and stress-inducing fiasco reflects Alzheimer's insidious talent for subverting the best intentions.

"Sir, sir, ladies only in the dressing rooms!"

I'm stopped in my tracks by an earnest part-timer just doing her job.

"But—" I start, and Judy interrupts.

"It's okay, I'm fine, just give me the clothes."

"Start with the jeans and the sweater," I advise, placing the gray tweed cardigan and the black stretch jeans on top. "I'll wait right here."

Judy disappears around the corner, reappearing a few minutes later wearing the store's gray cardigan with the black pants she'd left home in.

"The sweater fits you well, so if you like how it feels we should get it. But you didn't put on the stretchy black jeans."

"What black jeans?"

"The ones you took into the dressing room. They must still be there. Go back and put those on, and try the long-sleeve printed tee shirt instead of the cardigan."

Again, she disappears around the corner. This time the wait extends until I finally call out, "Judy, how's it going in there?" No response. Another couple of minutes and she returns. Gray tweed cardigan replaced by printed tee shirt, over her original well-worn black pants.

"What happened to the stretch jeans?"

"What stretch jeans?"

"The ones you took into the dressing room, that you haven't tried on yet."

"There aren't any stretch jeans in there!" Her voice rises along with her frustration.

"Look, I'm coming in there with you, it'll be a lot easier."

I turn to the young saleswoman at the nearby register. "If you're hoping that we'll be purchasing anything this afternoon, then you're going to have to wrap your head around my being in there with my wife. She needs my help." Her eyebrows lift and her mouth begins to open, but she reconsiders. She returns to her task without saying anything, and I find Judy three louvered doors down, in tears, seated on a small bench, the stretchy black jeans on, naked from her waist up.

"Why are you crying?"

"I don't know. I'm stupid! I can't remember anything!"

"What happened to your bra?"

"I don't know. Maybe I didn't have a bra?" She sounded

painfully insecure just then.

"I know you wore a bra, so it has to be here somewhere." I moved a small pile of other customers' rejected items alongside which she was sitting and saw the strap of her bra sticking out from under her.

"You're sitting on it," I said. "Put it back on and we'll try the Eileen Fisher tank top with those jeans. It should look good on you."

It did. Even at sixty-five, Judy wasn't more than two or three pounds over her weight in college, and her slim silhouette flattered the clothes she wore as much as they flattered it. I loved her for far more than her looks, but they were certainly an important part of what had attracted me to her in the first place. That attraction held across decades and renewed itself each time I saw her comfortable in her own skin and proud of whatever it was she chose to clothe that skin in.

We bought her the jeans, the tank top, and the cardigan. The other items she'd brought into the dressing room hung where she'd first placed them, but by that point I realized they'd fallen off her radar. I didn't mention them. Still embarrassed, she didn't notice. *My bad*, I thought to myself. "I'm sorry," I said, "I shouldn't have loaded you up with so many clothes and with too many instructions." I was finally learning that with Alzheimer's, the sooner I let go of whatever the complication was, resolved or not, the easier things would be for Judy. Better yet, I told myself, don't set things up for complication in the first place.

Around the time that she started favoring the same clothes day after day, Judy began to develop an aversion to bathing and showering. When time allowed, long, hot baths had always offered her respite, especially at the end of busy and sometimes trying workdays. Now, somewhere in the disease's middle stages, slipping into a tub full of warm water unlocked in her some kind of phobia. Rather than seeming relaxed, she'd become uneasy as soon as her legs entered the water. Reclining backward as the water rose around her torso would bring a look of alarm instead of relaxation to her face, her hands reaching out to hold the sides of the basin as if she might tip out of it. I wasn't sure what was going on. "Just relax," I'd say. "I'll stay with you; I'll wash and rinse your hair. It's fine; nothing's going to happen."

Did the evident fear rise from some weakening of her ability to parse out the space around her? Did she feel as if she'd slide below the water's surface, as if the water would somehow consume her? When she started having difficulty getting out of the tub, unable to conceptualize a sequence of movements that would lift her back up onto her feet and then out over the side of the tub, that basic pleasure joined other forgotten parts of her former routines, historic artifacts of a past life collected under the heading "that was then." I struggled to help her hold on to as much of the day-to-day as possible, but the disease inevitably outwitted me. "Ha! Figure this one out, buddy," it seemed to snidely taunt me with each new debility.

To get her to agree to shower, I had to start taking showers with her. Once upon a time the erotic possibilities attached to getting in the shower together would have spontaneously altered a morning's agenda, a reset worth whatever tardiness resulted. Her anxiety under the shower head's spray now began to explode in cries of "You're killing me! You're killing me!" as I massaged shampoo over her scalp. There was anger there too, sometimes physical as she tried to push me away. "I don't need to shower! I hate this! Let me out of here!" I tried to be as calm and gentle as possible, tried to reduce her distress with encouraging words and a step-by-step narrative in as soothing a tone as I could settle on. "I'm going to rub some conditioner in now" after I'd rinsed the suds from her hair, and "Turn a little, I'll scrub your back, just relax" and "Lift your right foot now, I'll wash between your toes."

Once the disorientation took over, though, each session in the shower stall became something to get through as quickly as possible. Only when I wrapped a warm towel around her and sat her down to comb and dry her hair did she manage to find her center again. She continued to put her hair in curlers until the mechanics of that process stopped making sense. Then I took over that task too. I'd seen her do it often enough over many years, and I knew how much that daily styling had meant to her.

Same with her makeup, though she'd always kept that to a minimum. When lipstick appeared as eye shadow, I took over that
operation too, my long-ago painter's practice a helpful training
in wielding her small collection of makeup brushes and sponges
to cosmetic advantage. When she looked in the mirror, I wanted
her to see the person she was most familiar and comfortable
with. I hoped she'd always know she was still herself, and if hair
and makeup could help her hold on to that recognition, then
we'd carry that on too, as before.

*I remember a Sunday evening, the end of a busy weekend and
the prelude to what promised to be another challenging week
spread thin by work demands, caregiving, the household, lack of
sufficient sleep—the list went on. You and I were side-by-side on
the sofa, our legs stretched onto the coffee table, alongside wine
glasses, their last sips abandoned. The PBS Masterpiece Classic
musical theme was playing as the episode's credits rolled. We'd
both taken turns nodding off during that last half-hour, so I knew
we'd welcome being fully prone.*

*"Ready for bed?" I asked. Your yes was unhesitant, tinged
with relief. I clicked the remote off, and we started down the
hallway to our bedroom.*

*"Deb's coming at 9:00 in the morning, so let's get your clothes
ready." We'd taken to laying out whatever you'd be wearing the
next day—one less thing to distract me when I'd be hustling to get
out the door to head to campus.*

*I pulled two shirts on hangers from the closet's interior and
the idea to affect a refined British accent struck a split-second
before the question came out "Would you prefer to wear this
milady, or this?" as I held up the two options. You grinned
broadly, getting the joke, and it made me feel good that you did.
"This one," you said. "Thank you," you added.*

"Thanks for what?" I asked.
"Just thank you," you replied.
That warmed my heart.
Before I turned off the light, it occurred to me to write down
my "milady" question. It went in my notebook, tucked back into
the bedside table drawer. Sometime later it got its second wind in
this poem.

OUR OWN PRIVATE DOWNTON

We pretend that I'm your valet
although, a lady, you'd have
a lady's maid,
a Baxter.

Would you prefer to wear this
milady, or this? I ask.
You're usually quick
to choose. You still know
what you like more,
and less, and how
you like to look,
more or less.

We shower together.
No valet or lady's maid
would do this, except
in the most dissolute
household.

Your reprimands are high-pitched
and ricochet off the shower's
walls when I rinse away
shampoo and then
conditioner. You're killing me!

You're killing me!
(A soft towel comforts
and dries.) You survive
to have your hair parted
and combed, dried and
rolled over pink tubes
of foam. I am your coiffeur
as well, having developed
skills, like Baxter's, I did not know
I possessed.

At mealtimes I channel Molesley,
placing silver and linen
at your lady's place.
Then in Mrs. Patmore's role
I prepare your favorite dishes
though you seem to like them
less and less.

After dinner
we have no Violet Crawley
to make acid asides and
keep us amused, so we sit
by the flat screen until you
signal your exhaustion
and I pull again from
Baxter's bag of tricks
to change you into
night clothes and
triple absorbents.
You resist slipping
off your top and
insist that sleeping
in your bra is
perfectly comfortable.
Your dreams must take you

My sleep had been compromised for so long that when I finally walked into our primary care physician's office hoping to get a prescription that would gain me an hour or two more a night, uninterrupted, I knew my health wouldn't tolerate a continuing deficit. As active as I was—gym workouts two or three times a week, rounds of golf usually on foot, movement around campus chasing the next meeting, chauffeuring Judy on errands or outings—I didn't remember the last time I'd slept solidly for seven-and-a-half, eight hours. Typically, I'd sleep for three or four hours, then wake in the middle of the night, my mind in overdrive, a turmoil of worries and fears. I'd get up without waking her, make an herbal tea, read until I started to feel drowsy again, and then maybe fall asleep for another hour or half-hour before the alarm tweeted me back to consciousness. I envied Judy then.

Unlike many Alzheimer's sufferers, she certainly wasn't insomniac, and she rarely woke prematurely, typically enjoying eight to nine hours of sleep a night. That symptom of the disease was present, though it wasn't Judy who was manifesting it.

Dr. Breyer, true to form, listened quietly and then responded thoughtfully.

"In terms of diet and exercise, you're doing everything right. Cutting back on alcohol consumption in the evening will probably help. That extra glass of wine may help you get to sleep, but it's probably contributing to not staying asleep. I do think that your worrisome frame of mind and the anxiety you're feeling, while not unexpected given your home and work situations, are also impacting your sleep cycles. Rather than have you take a sleep medication, I'd like you to try an anti-anxiety medication called Clonazepam. You'll take a one-milligram tablet each day just before bedtime, and you'll need to give it a bit of time, maybe up to two weeks, to start to see an improvement in your sleep patterns. Give it a try and I'll see you back here in four weeks."

A week later I was sleeping through the night. It felt almost miraculous. Lights out at 10:00, and I wouldn't stir until the alarm intruded again at 5:00. I stopped nodding off in campus meetings and at my desktop's keyboard. I had more energy, and my mind didn't seem as wound up as it had been most of the preceding few years. The annoying impatience with Judy that I'd been struggling to control subsided; it seemed easier to pay attention to the moment and ignore what had just been or what was coming next. I felt centered in a way that I hadn't in a long time. There seemed to be just one thing missing now: my libido. When I checked in with Dr. Breyer for the follow-up a month later, that libido was 100 percent checked out.

"A change in a patient's sex drive is one of the possible side effects of the drug," Dr. Breyer confirmed. "It's hard to say for sure, and in your situation, there might be other factors at play. I'd recommend you give it another month, see how things go. If you opt to stop taking Clonazepam, you might find it helpful to meet with a psychologist or a therapist, someone who understands what you and your wife are going through and might be able to help you address the anxiety without medication."

"What if I were to reduce the dosage?"

"You could try taking three-quarters of a one-milligram tablet for three or four days, then drop to half a tablet for another three or four days, and see if the sleeplessness or the libido, or both, return. It may take a while to determine if we can make this work, but I'd like you to try before prescribing an alternative. And if you're willing to consider talking with a neuropsychologist, our office can set you up to see Dr. Paul Snyder. He has a lot of experience working with Alzheimer's families, and it may be helpful to you to have someone that you can discuss all of this with. You're carrying a heavy load."

Later that day I shared with Judy the general details of my visit with Dr. Breyer and the referral to Dr. Snyder that I left the office with.

"You're going to have an appointment with a psychologist?" she asked by way of confirming what she'd just heard.

"You heard right," I said. "Maybe it'll help me to deal with my worse-case-scenario anxieties without having to be medicated."

"Hmmm. Well, you are pretty intense. Maybe you should have seen a psychologist a long time ago." She chuckled at that remark, proud of herself for her witty retrospection. She was evidently having a rare good day, her sensibilities level, at least briefly. Something else I could bring up with Dr. Snyder: how unnerved I could feel when clear-headedness made an unexpected appearance and the former Judy surfaced. Each time was like a flashback, and my optimism would surge, though not for long. We'd accepted that this disease would go in only one direction, good days notwithstanding.

"Don't be a wise ass, or I'll bring you with me," I chuckled back. The fact was in the Medical Center's memory clinic and their Center for Successful Aging, she had all the psychological and medical support she needed.

"Well, I don't think seeing your doctor...uh...Doctor...whatever his name is, will help me. I'm already losing my mind. If he can keep you from losing yours, though, you should go." Smart lady she was. Smart-ass sometimes.

Dr. Breyer's office had made the referral knowing that Dr. Snyder's neuropsychology practice had earned him a solid reputation and successful track record diagnosing and counseling Alzheimer's patients and their caregivers. I'd never been in therapy, nor had Judy, but we both had family members, friends, and colleagues for whom psychotherapy had been life altering, even lifesaving, at different times in their lives. If nothing else, it would give me the opportunity to talk with someone who was very familiar with the type of situation we were in and maybe offer some useful guidance or strategies to help navigate the road ahead.

He and I clicked from the outset, another instance of good fortune. Dr. Snyder was all business, though backgrounded by his warmth and empathy, he never seemed standoffish. He quickly put me at ease, and over the course of the four years that I met with him, the comfort that I felt in our first sessions never lessened. I enjoyed enormous relief in being able to talk openly about how I was feeling relative to the neurological changes that Judy was undergoing, the changes in our relationship that resulted, the fears of what was ahead of us.

Snyder was adept at attaching descriptive labels to certain types of behavior—Judy's or mine—and to different manifestations of the disease that helped me better understand first, that these were entirely predictable and experienced widely by dementia sufferers and their caregivers, and second, that I could adapt to them positively so that I could offer her better support and at the same time release a lot of the stress and anxiety I was internalizing. I'd never heard the term *Othello syndrome*[15] until he explained that the fear Judy harbored that I wanted someone else was a typical expression of delusional jealousy in an Alzheimer's patient. I should do nothing more or less than reassure her that I had no relationship with anyone else, that she was the only partner I needed or wanted.

If I hadn't had the word *aphasia* as part of my own everyday vocabulary, I'd nonetheless understood what it was before Dr.

Snyder used the word to describe the breakdown of her vocabulary and her struggles to find the right word for a thing or action. I'd been aware of that symptom almost from the start. She could get frustrated in situations where the right word just wouldn't come, and it was important that I not add to her frustration by betraying any impatience. Be calm, be steady, he advised me, and when I wasn't sure what to do or say, best to do or say nothing. Take in the situation as an observer would, and if reaching out for Judy's hand or putting an arm around her was all I could think to do, that was enough. She would know that I cared, and if I didn't have a solution or a remedy, she wasn't expecting one. She simply needed to know, and deserved to know, that she was loved and supported.

Dr. Snyder had apologized the first time he and I met, regretting that 7:00 a.m. was the only time slot he'd had available, though that contributed to the value of the experience for me. My head was always clearest first thing in the morning, and at that hour the world had barely begun to intrude. I'd get to the gym by 5:30, work out for about an hour, shower and dress there, then head the half-mile or so to his office. When I got home to Judy at around 8:00, she'd often still be sleeping, so I'd rouse her, get us both breakfast, then head off to campus. The sessions fit smoothly into our routine from the outset, and that helped me to stick with them.

Early on Dr. Snyder assigned me the task of spelling out the goals I had for treatment: goals for myself, goals for caregiving, and general goals. This provided a host of insights that guided our conversations and established a kind of scaffold for the long term. How to accept or overcome the ongoing sense of loss and mourning, what he identified as *ambiguous loss*, a term that until then I hadn't registered but that both Judy and I had been feeling profoundly since her diagnosis. How to change the negative script in my head, and how to manage the feelings of guilt about not doing enough that I was experiencing, along with the resentments I held that she wasn't sufficiently appreciating everything I was doing for her. How to accept that we no longer had a partnership of equals, that increasingly our relationship was moving toward something that resembled more closely that of a parent and child.

"Try to think of this entire experience as an opening into aspects of yourself and your relationship with Judith that haven't come into the light before," he recommended. "Everything is changing, so you naturally feel unstable. Concentrate on the moment, whenever and wherever, and when you feel your anxieties pulling you into that 'what if' zone, step back into the moment. Stay with the present."

Our weekly appointments became biweekly after a couple of months, then eventually we settled on a monthly session that offered reinforcement of the coping skills and strategies that we'd been developing. As my confidence as a caregiver increased, the sense of being adrift and vulnerable lessened. By helping me to identify challenges within two main categories—practical on one hand, emotional on the other—Dr. Snyder helped me see that I could keep the two separate and better respond to challenges reasonably and constructively. Almost as soon as I learned how to do that, Judy's own anxiety levels seemed to drop. It made sense. Dependent children pick up on their parents' anxieties and express their own reflexively. As her dependence on me increased, exacerbating my already fraught anxiety levels, so did her own anxieties. What a pair we'd become!

The disease would progress; we could do nothing to stop it. We could, however, plan rationally and coolly, anticipating our eventual needs and seeking solutions that, when we needed them, would be ready and waiting. That I had her unquestioning trust made this a lot easier for me. That she had my undiminished love made it all, I hope, more bearable for her.

13

...we can hope that science will come to our rescue sooner rather than later – but hope is not a plan of action.

– Susan Jacoby, from *Never Say Die*

In the immediate aftermath of Judy's initial diagnosis in 2009, we speculated about a single 1960s snapshot of her grandmother sitting in the foreground, with Judy's mom and dad behind her. She was an aging widow at that point, near the end of her life, a faint smile on her face and a hauntingly vacant look in her eyes—the kind of look that many Alzheimer's sufferers eventually manifest. I first saw that look in Judy's eyes at what I'm estimating was somewhere in the late middle stage of her disease, toward the end of 2013, four-and-a-half years or so into her diagnosis. It was an ambiguous kind of ocular vacancy and distancing that seemed to complement the other disconnections—her increasing aphasia and apraxia and the anosognosia that started to be noticeable at about the same time.[16] She stopped registering that she had Alzheimer's, and if I reminded her of that reality, she'd react with surprise, as if it were news to her. That she experienced this phenomenon didn't worry me, but it could be unnerving. She'd already lost so much to the disease, and yet there were times when she had no clue at all.

In the first year or so after the diagnosis, her impulse to hide it away, to deny it, was insistent. It became difficult for me to respect her wish that we not share it within our social circle, and there were instances when I felt sharing the information was the best thing all around. When I overheard her one evening telling a dinner guest openly and unashamedly, "I've been diagnosed with early onset Alzheimer's disease," I knew that she'd accepted it. As unfortunate as her situation was, I felt a degree of relief that she finally seemed willing to acknowledge it honestly and move forward as best she could. That outward acceptance held for a couple of years, until one day it was subverted, like nearly everything else, by the disease itself.

I was trying to sort out a story she was struggling to tell me. She was confabulating its details and timeline in a way that I think made no more sense to her than it did to me, although she was qualifying her narrative with a surprising assuredness. I wanted to get the story straight but knew that if I interrupted her or asked too many questions, she'd just get confused and frustrated. I preferred a more self-confident Judy than a defeated one. As her story came to its indeterminate end, I summed it up for her as best I could. Trying to sound matter of fact and nonjudgmental, I added, "It's interesting to me to see how Alzheimer's puts obstacles in your way when you're trying to tell me something."

"What do you mean?"

"Well, you've got some parts of your story right, but other parts are missing, and so I have to guess what those missing pieces are. I think Alzheimer's hides them from you so that they're not within your grasp when you want them."

"What do you mean?"

"I mean that because you have Alzheimer's it's sometimes difficult for you to communicate as easily as you once did."

"I have Alzheimer's?"

"Yes, sweetie, you do have Alzheimer's. It's been more than four years since your diagnosis."

"Wow, I didn't know that."

Better that she doesn't, I thought to myself. She was moving almost imperceptibly into a state of unknowing, and that might bring her greater peace of mind. I told myself to let her be, to let her tell her stories however she could, to let her believe that she was in fact fine, as she so often insisted. I needed to follow her example: accept whatever comes along, then forget whatever comes along. Acceptance I could will in myself. Obliviousness, on the other hand, was not among the options I could choose from. At least in the abstract I knew that this would all go in just one direction, that if it ran its course the disease had just one thing to stop its progress. Too much water under the bridge, too much experience gained, to let even the most under-the-radar form of denial hold any sway.

Friends and colleagues often asked me how Judy was doing, and these expressions of interest and concern were appreciated if not particularly helpful. Inviting her out for coffee or lunch, or offering to walk with her around the lake, or dropping off a casserole as meal relief—things like that would have been helpful but were rare. Occasionally, someone serendipitously delivered new information just when it could be useful, and if it smoothed the path, I was grateful. Such was the case the day that one of my colleagues, Dr. Cruz-Vincent, stopped by my office unexpectedly.

"I think you know one of my neighbors, Kay Larsen," she said. I had interacted several times with Kay, an arts professional working for a local nonprofit, relative to a fundraising project but didn't know her well.

"Well, Kay's husband Richmond Baker also has Alzheimer's. I wondered if you knew."

I'd never met Kay's husband, though I knew he'd been a successful architect whose firm was closely involved in several urban redevelopment projects here in town. Judy had crossed paths with him too, as one of his membership terms on the campus's independent cinema "Friends" board had overlapped with the terms she served before she was diagnosed.

"I'm sorry to hear that," I said. "Do you think she'd be amenable to my reaching out to her?"

"I know she's open to that since I mentioned to her that I would let you know about Rich. You might find you're going through some of the same stuff, and maybe there'd be ways you could help one another."

I had Kay's email address and sent off a message to her that afternoon. A week later she and I met for lunch at a small coffee shop near campus.

"Rich was diagnosed a couple of years before Judy," she told me after I'd given her a barebones outline of how we came by Judy's diagnosis, our experience with the clinical trial, and her general middle stage status.

"He had no family history of dementia that we were aware of," she explained, "though he did play football through college and had a couple of concussions during those years. We wondered if those may have caused it, but like you and Judy, it's all speculation. We'll never know. For the last year-and-a-half, he's been going to adult daycare since I'm still working full time. He was always a very outgoing and social person, so he was willing to go from the start, and he likes the folks there as much as they like him. That was a huge relief, and it's worked well for us until recently. He's fallen a few times this past year, and he wanders the house most nights, so it's reached the point where I can't manage him at home anymore. He'll be starting full-time memory care as soon as an opening comes up. He's been on the waiting lists of a few places for a couple of months now, and two of them are telling me it shouldn't be much longer."

While I'd been mentally mapping the various memory care facilities around town for a few years at that point, I wasn't aware that there might be nonresidential adult daycare options for someone in Judy's situation. If that were something that worked for her, it would certainly reduce, at least to a degree, the costs of in-home companion care. We were managing those, but I feared that their financial toll would eventually over-strain our budget.

I shared with Judy the details of my lunch conversation with Kay Larsen. She vaguely remembered having served on the film center's support board, I think because we continued to see films there a couple of times a month. She couldn't remember Rich.

"He's been going to a day program at the rehab hospital where you did your driving test," I told her. "Kay says he really likes the people there, and they have different kinds of activities through the week. Does that sound like something you might want to try?"

Her reaction was instantaneous and unequivocal.

"I won't go to any kind of daycare! I'm not going to do that! No! No! I won't do that!"

Tears spilled out as she pulled away and buried her face in the sofa's cushioning. "I don't want daycare! I don't want anyone! I just want you to leave me alone!"

"Do your homework," Dr. Snyder counseled me when I met with him a few mornings later. "Visit some of the facilities that provide day services for people with dementia to get a feel for how they're set up and what they offer. You know your wife well enough to have a sense of what might work for her, but you won't be able to gauge that until you've checked them out. Talk with the staff at each place you visit and talk with some of the clients too. Once you've done that, you'll understand the lay of the land better, and you can broach the subject with your wife again. If you reassure her that she'll have final say, she may be more agreeable to giving it a try."

Kay Larsen had told me who to contact at Gateway Rehabilitation Hospital's Adult Day Services division, and I made an appointment to meet with Andrea Svoboda, its director of Senior Outreach. I resisted the impulse to feel guilty that I was doing this behind Judy's back and against her loudly proclaimed opposition. "Keep your emotions in one place," Dr. Snyder had advised, "and don't let them complicate carrying out as logically as possible the practical tasks ahead of you. It's reasonable to feel grief about what you and your wife have lost, to feel sad about her condition and anxious about her future and yours. But you want to provide her with the best quality of life and care available, and that will take clear-headedness and resolve. You can be strategic and pragmatic in ways that express your love and compassion.

That'll be easier for you to do if you keep her best interests on the front burner."

His recommendations made sense, but the physical reality of Gateway Rehab's Adult Day Services center was sobering and destabilizing. Following Andrea from her office down a long, sterile corridor of institutional green tile walls on the day I visited, I felt overwhelmingly alien. When we reached a wide steel door, she tapped a keypad above its handle, and a loud beep cleared us to pass through. The door locked behind us. *Of course,* I thought, *folks with neurological impairments or with mobility issues need to be secured and protected.* Nonetheless, it was unnervingly like imprisonment. None of the day services clients here could exit the place without a staff member making that possible. How would Judy react to that, I wondered. Would she grasp what was going on?

We'd entered a large space furnished with numerous upholstered chairs and sofas, all showing signs of wear from long and hard use, especially at pressure points where aging hands and arms had sought leverage in lifting their bodies to full and more-or-less upright positions. "This is our largest room," Andrea explained, "where our clients can relax on their own or hang out together, and where we often have guest presenters. Right now, everyone's in the activities room, so let's head in there."

We crossed the space and passed under an archway that opened into another room, smaller and congested by comparison with the first space, but equally well used and abused. Around four or five plastic-covered banquet-style tables sat a diverse assembly of male and female seniors, about twenty altogether, including two wheelchair-bound individuals, one asleep and the other holding court at the lead end of one of the long tables. Two staff attendants were busy helping their charges apply glitter to colored paper collages-in-progress. Most turned in our direction as we entered, greeting us with facial expressions ranging from welcoming smiles to head tilts of curiosity to blank stares of indifferent passivity. I tried to imagine Judy in their midst, sitting at one of the tables, cutting and pasting odd rectangles, squares, and triangles. My spirits sank.

As we moved closer to admire their artwork, a smiling woman possibly in her mid-eighties reached out and took my hand. "I remember you," she said. "I remember you."

I smiled down at her, then dropped to one knee so that we met at eye level. "Yes, it's been a long time," I replied, though I had no idea who this gentle soul was. "How are you these days?"

"I'm well, thank you. It's nice to see you again." She patted my hand without releasing it.

"It's nice to see you again too," I said. She smiled, and I smiled back. After a minute or so I caught Andrea's eye, signaling that we were about to move on. "Andrea's going to show me the rest of your Center now, so I'll say goodbye."

The kind lady cupped my hand in both of hers, repeated, "I remember you," then let it go. "You come again now," she said. "It's been too long."

On my drive home that day I again tried to picture Judy in that little community of failing bodies and minds. Most of them had looked to be in their seventies and eighties. She not only looked twenty years younger, she was in fact twenty years younger than some of them. How would she feel about that? Would she take to it, and to the group, the way that Kay's husband had? Maybe with the staff's help we could set the stage in such a way that she'd feel she was there to lend a hand, that she'd have a role to play, something like a staff assistant maybe. Would that be disingenuous? Would she see through that? Was I overthinking all of it? Andrea's parting words made more sense than any of my subsequent muddled thoughts. "Just drop her off for a few hours some afternoon, and we'll see how she does. It's worth a try, and there's no commitment. Let me know when you want to do it; I'll be here."

I postponed bringing up the subject with Judy for another couple of months, unsure that Gateway's Adult Day Care would be the right fit for her and fearful that broaching the subject would prompt another meltdown. Finally, I did make the proposal.

"Let's just stop by and meet the staff there, look around, just to get a feel for the place. I'd like to know what you'll think. We're not making any kind of commitment; we're just doing a little exploring."

Nothing had changed in her feelings about the idea of joining any kind of adult daycare program. When I did insist that we get in the car and take an hour to visit the place, her resistance held. After I'd parked in their lot, she refused to get out of the car, though I finally coaxed her into the building. She returned Andrea's welcome with a stone-faced silence. After some small talk and Andrea's overly enthused summary of their programs and modest amenities, she led us toward the Center's entry. As she reached to punch in her keypad code, Judy bolted, running toward the building's main door but collapsing onto a settee just as I caught up with her. She sobbed uncontrollably.

"I don't want to be here, no, never, never! I don't want this. I want to be home. Leave me alone! Just take me home!"

It was heartbreaking, and I was responsible. Andrea sat down alongside Judy, but her effort to comfort her by recounting her kindergartner daughter's tantrum at the outset of her first day of school a few weeks before was entirely irrelevant and inept. Her patronizing tone struck me as so unprofessional, and I wondered how she could hold a "senior outreach" leadership position in this kind of service organization. *Maybe this works with the very aged or the very demented*, I thought to myself, but I knew Judy wasn't so far gone that she'd submit to that kind of infantilizing condescension.

"I want to go home," Judy repeated. "Just take me home."

Kay Larsen and her husband Rich's positive experience with Gateway had me feeling both envious and puzzled. Nonetheless, I was glad that it had worked for them for as long as it had. The cost savings over in-home companion care were significant, and with subsidies available to help qualified clientele and their families negotiate those expenses, it was affordable to a broader socioeconomic segment of the community. At that point, though, it just wasn't going to work for us.

I shelved the idea and returned my focus to *A Trusted Friend* and to helping manage Judy's care team as their members came on the scene, got to know her, and settled into regular weekday schedules. As their hours in our home increased, though, I worried again that the expense would eventually strain our budget beyond what we could tolerate. Without mentioning anything to Judy, nine months or so after the misfire with Gateway Adult Day Services, I located a couple of independent full-time memory care residences that offered day client services and made appointments to visit them. I reasoned that finding a non-resident day program within a 24/7 memory facility would offer services tailored to the specific needs and capabilities of folks with marked cognitive impairment. In addition, it could provide an experience of residential care to which Judy might gradually adjust, lessening the strain or trauma of that transition once we reached the point when there would be no alternative.

Attached by an enclosed breezeway to a large assisted-living retirement home incongruously named Garden Vista, Bel Gardens Mansion was a memory unit that limited itself to twenty full-time residents and four day clients, promised a high staff-to-client ratio, and boasted access to the Vista's indoor pool. But the cramped, dark, and low-ceilinged Alzheimer's building and the lack of nearby gardens raised the question "How did they come by the name Bel Gardens Mansion?" The memory care section had a distinct "out of sight, out of mind" feeling, tucked away as it was behind the larger main building and accessible only through it. The absence of an activities room and the ubiquity of wall-mounted televisions suggested that staring blankly at quiz shows, old movies, sports events, and Lawrence Welk reruns was the typical agenda. "Whenever they have guest presenters and music groups over at Garden Vista, we take our memory folks there," the unit's manager cheerfully informed me. I wasn't sold. I couldn't picture Judy there, and I felt that if the tables were turned and it was me being shuttled to adult daycare at Bel Gardens Mansion, I'd either stage a revolt, fall into a deep depression, or both. I passed on that one, reporting nothing to Judy.

When I visited The Lodge at Heritage Ridge not far from our home, I came away with fewer reservations. The Lodge's main communal areas were spacious and laid out so that someone guiding a walker or moving around in a wheelchair could easily and safely navigate them. Abundant natural light streamed in from high clerestory windows. A sprinkling of residents relaxed quietly or napped in several large parlors furnished traditionally yet comfortably. Some of the residents were isolated in their private rooms along two corridors extending from the main parlor area, and some were gathered in a roomy activities space that abutted an open plan kitchen where staff members were facilitating a chocolate chip cookie bake.

Its proximity to our home would be convenient for Judy's *Trusted Friend* team. If it worked out, I planned to have them drop her off a couple days a week after lunch, and I'd pick her up myself at the end of those afternoons. I intuited that she'd be less likely to resist passing time there if I weren't the one delivering her. Both Lisa and Evelyn agreed to keep her company there for an hour or so the first few times, hoping that would reassure her and help her adjust.

Kelli, The Lodge's director, seemed a bit harried and distracted as she showed me around, though she was clearly proud of the amenities and interacted warmly with the clients we encountered. The three young female attendants on hand, all in their mid-twenties, greeted me with wan smiles that betrayed a profound, though probably understandable, boredom. Paid hourly at or close to minimum wage, with charges who were at best mildly interested in the goings-on, at worst entirely non-communicative, they would be challenged to ignite and sustain any kind of collective energy. That they didn't seem to perk up when their supervisor and I crossed their paths left me wondering about Kelli's expectations of them, but I didn't pursue that. I wondered how Judy might take to them and they to her. When she was teaching, she loved working with young women and men their approximate ages. With the tables turned, with Judy as their responsibility, how would she react? Could she get used to being confined with a group of folks mostly her own mother's age or close to it, all—like herself—suffering from some degree of mental impairment? I wouldn't know until we tried.

Things at home had been working out so well with the team from *A Trusted Friend* that had it not been for the increasing costs of that in-home care, I'd have left things alone. Most of the time Judy enjoyed their companionship, and they seemed genuinely keen to help brighten her days. The problem was that as her care needs increased over the course of what could be years—we had no way to anticipate the duration of her disease's eventual course—we risked being derailed by the financial pressures. A full day at The Lodge, 8:00 a.m. to 5:00 p.m., lunch included, would cost $75.00, $40.00 for a half-day without lunch. That was less than half the cost of her *Trusted Friend* team's services. We had to explore it.

Lisa had been the first to chauffeur Judy from home to The Lodge, and shortly after she left her there, she texted me a message that all had gone well and that Judy seemed comfortable. When I arrived at the end of that first afternoon tryout and entered their glass-enclosed vestibule, I saw Judy through the locked main door, already in her coat and hat, gloves on, purse over her shoulder, motionless. I wasn't sure who'd taken pains to make sure she was ready and waiting, but it reminded me of picking up Trevor after an afternoon of preschool some forty or so years earlier, he and other kids eager for their parents' arrival. It also struck me as I looked in at her that Alzheimer's was putting up more barriers between us, invisible and impregnable. I was on the outside looking in, an observer anything but impartial, one who could do nothing to rescue her from the strange new world that was offering her an unwanted citizenship.

Judy didn't notice me, nor did she hear the buzzer I activated when I reached that door. Her expression was impassive, and she appeared distant, lost in thought or in non-thought, I couldn't tell. She'd been at The Lodge for about four hours, and I'd not had any calls from their staff, so I tentatively concluded that the tryout had been successful. A video camera above my head clicked audibly, and "Come in Mr. James" sounded just as an unseen party released the magnetic lock. As I opened the door,

Judy turned and saw me entering.

"How'd it go?" I asked.

Her eyes blinked and she stood. Whatever thoughts she'd been lost in were gone. "Fine. "It was fine. Can we go now?"

She wasn't too forthcoming as we drove home, and I wasn't sure whether her afternoon at The Lodge had left her entirely unimpressed, she'd already forgotten much of what had taken place while she was there, or she simply didn't want to think or talk about it. Later I tried to coax some impressions from her, but she wasn't cooperating. "I'm tired" is all she offered.

Two days later she returned for a second afternoon, Evelyn reporting to me later that Judy had interacted well with the attendants on duty that day and that she seemed friendly with the other day clients and residents. I arrived to pick her up a little after 5:00, and again she had her outerwear on and was ready to go. This time she saw me before I'd reached the vestibule, and when I stepped to the door she was standing just at its interior side, her face almost against the glass that separated us. As soon as they buzzed the door open and before I could stop her, she shot past me and out of the vestibule into the carport area, then into the parking lot and toward the rush-hour traffic just beyond. When I caught up with her, she turned angrily and shouted, "I'm never going back there! I won't go back there! Take me home, I'll never come back here!"

This time there were no tears, her anger so fiery and consuming that it allowed no space for their release. I was hugely disappointed and confused, second-guessing both the wisdom of pursuing this option and my hopefulness that we could make it work.

"Look, if you really don't want to go back there, I won't force you. I hoped you might like it, but if you don't, then I'm not going to make you go. We'll stick with your *Trusted Friend* team; you won't have to come back."

In the few minutes since she'd bolted her anger had subsided, replaced by tears and a crushing sadness that seemed to fill all the space in our car.

"Just take me home," she said. "Just take me home."

I phoned Kelli the next day to follow up, concerned that something may have taken place that upset Judy or that triggered her anger. She assured me that Judy had seemed relaxed and interested in the various activities the staff had scheduled. Apparently, she spoke with two of the other day services clients on and off through the afternoon, and she said Judy had thanked her when she helped her with her coat not long before I arrived to pick her up. She was as surprised to hear of Judy's "escape" as I'd been when it happened. "I think she'll get used to it, but it does take some clients longer than others. If you keep reassuring her, she should settle into things here, and we'll do all we can to make her feel welcome and comfortable."

That night I thought long and hard about it, concluding that forcing Judy to return would be counterproductive. She clearly understood what was involved, and if she couldn't fully articulate her feelings, she had no trouble demonstrating them. I suspected she felt that she didn't belong there and wanted no part of it. I felt I had no choice but to respect that. I decided again to abandon the experiment at least for the time being. I figured that down the line I could revive it and hope for a different outcome.

There's no denying that my art practice took a hit in the years following your diagnosis. While there were exigencies requiring that I work in my studio at least a few hours a week—as a faculty member at a Research 1 university, I was required to be actively involved in research or creative activity, and I had a studio assistant employed by my college whose on-the-clock hours I was responsible for filling with meaningful work—between my teaching and administrative obligations and caring for you, for myself and for our home, it was often difficult to squeeze out the time and to induce the mindset I needed to trigger ideas worth

exploring and developing.

The self-reflection that filled a good part of my therapy sessions with Dr. Snyder helped me realize that you and I had arrived at a kind of qualified, if not full, acceptance of our respective circumstances. For you, that acceptance was a kind of resignation, not in the sense that you'd go through the rest of your life defeated and diminished, but rather, you'd let your losses recede and give your thoughts and attention to whatever moment you found yourself in and whatever small pleasures and satisfactions those moments offered. For me, there was resignation as well. I knew I couldn't change your condition and that it would only get worse. I no longer felt any resistance to our fate. Rather, I committed myself to giving you all the support you needed, to protecting your quality of life in every way that I could, and to learning as much as possible from every part of the experience.

Understanding what my recast role in our marriage was helped me to reframe my relationship to the studio. While I'd always found solace and comfort within that space and in conversation with the processes of conceptualization and execution that I engaged with there, my impulses and explorations had long been driven by a career-building ambition and a general competitiveness that no longer felt relevant or useful. If I were to resurrect any degree of genuine enthusiasm for the studio environment and my work in it, the work would have to rise from the grief and pain that we were both experiencing, as well as from the revelations and insights—about myself, about you, and about the disease—that I was gathering as your primary caregiver.

Employing A Trusted Friend *caregivers both filled up some of your time and freed up some of mine. As often as I could, I'd block off mornings or afternoons when you'd have one of the team with you so that I could retreat to my basement studio with far fewer distractions than I'd have had on campus. I began to visualize ways to transform our respective feelings, our shared experience, into visual patterns, textures, and movements that privileged a more poetic kind of expression. My studio work had always been about visual sensation and how colors, marks, and ambiguous spaces could be integrated in ways that evoked the emotional and psychological undercurrents coursing through our inner lives. If I could apply the visual vocabularies and technical processes I was working with to an intentionally metaphorical purpose, if I could take the measure of our Alzheimer's experience from the perspective my studio offered, I might manage to pull from the work some degree of transcendence, if not for you, then for myself. I set about trying.*

14

But one day, I know, it will be otherwise.

— Jane Kenyon, from *Otherwise*

In late 2013 we drove east to spend Christmas with Trevor, Veronica, and the twin granddaughters, six years old by then. Along the way we stopped for overnights with longtime friends, catching up on their lives, revisiting our shared pasts, unaware that several of these visits would turn out to be valedictory.

In Hershey, Pennsylvania, where Veronica's family lived, we all holed up for three days in a hotel, connected rooms letting the girls move freely between ours and theirs. We'd always loved having time with Clare and Francesca, and both of us regretted that living half a continent away meant that those times were too few and far between. Since we'd last seen them, they'd been learning to read. By that point, though, Judy had been struggling with text for quite some time, and though she'd been a lifelong reader, those days were behind her. It saddened me to hear her hesitate over the pronunciation of a syllable or a word, but I don't think the girls noticed. They pointed at features in the illustrations and at odd words they'd try to parse out, Judy trying alongside them, less guide than peer.

The girls' unselfconsciousness and genuineness refreshed any space they occupied, and Judy had always loved moving into that space with them, easily and willingly viewing the world through their eyes and at their level. That hadn't changed. The teacher in her reveled in showing them how to do things, and I always enjoyed seeing the three of them bring shared focus to whatever the activity was, to the exclusion of everything and everyone around them. That came naturally to Judy. My efforts were sincere, if inadequate. She'd sometimes chide me for lacking the patience for or interest in their fun and games. On this occasion, she demonstrated a genuine enthusiasm for Legos equivalent to theirs, though while their manual dexterity was ripening by the hour and the day, hers was diminishing. I don't think they noticed that either. I sensed her sadness at the struggle, and maybe at the irony too. As they were learning, she was unlearning.

When I started planning that trip, spending a few days in New York City was part of the program. It had been a few years since we'd been to Manhattan, and we missed it. Through the years when Judy and her partner Kathy owned their fabric business, they made frequent buying excursions to the Garment District, and Judy and I drove down for cultural immersion weekends two or three times a year. When I suggested we plan to take the train from Harrisburg into New York for a few days, she liked the idea. I booked Amtrak seats, the hotel, and tickets to a performance of *Tosca* at the Met. Just like old times.

Judy really surprised me that weekend. I went into it with my anxiety level ramped way up. What if we got separated somewhere? What if I had a heart attack or a stroke or something and had to be hospitalized? How would she manage that? What if she got overwhelmed or exhausted, the traffic and the people and the sounds all too much to process? Instead, it all turned out to be much more like a homecoming for both of us. Judy hadn't seemed that relaxed and present for many months. Her longstanding familiarity with the city and its rhythms and cadences resurfaced. Despite her impairments, it was clear that she felt comfortable and not the least intimidated.

Exiting the cab in front of the Grand Hyatt alongside Grand Central Terminal, I got held up by the cab's slow credit card processor, and in the minutes it took to complete the transaction and collect our bags, Judy stepped out of view. I panicked for a few seconds until I saw her on the other side of the hotel entrance's glass doors, signaling me with a wave. The doorman had ushered her in, and in fact, it was she who'd kept her attention on my whereabouts. *This is going to be fine*, I thought hopefully.

With this weekend in mind, a few months before our trip I'd signed us up with MedicAlert, a nonprofit that, among other services, offers wearable identification that links individuals with specific medical conditions to their primary caregiver or other responsible individual. At first Judy objected to wearing the functional bracelet that matched one I'd also have around my wrist, and it irritated her that she couldn't remove it with one hand. Eventually though, like a lot of other things, it fell off her radar. The bracelets provided me with a bit of reassurance that in some emergency, first responders would be able to access information critical to her safety and mine. New York City would be our first testing ground. Fortunately, nothing came up that put it to the test.

Knowing we'd be there between Christmas and New Year's, our Providence friends Corie and Bill came down for one overnight, long enough to share dinner together and brunch the following morning. They were like family, and Judy relaxed into the warmth of their love. Another longtime friend, Jillian Raymond, happened to be visiting her daughter Hannah in the city that weekend, and we met up with them at the Metropolitan Museum to catch up over lunch and to view a couple of exhibitions. Judy had always been especially fond of the Raymonds and loved any occasion to spend time with them. The galleries were crowded with tourists, the museum's buzz was high energy, yet it all felt normal, ordinary. Her ease and peace of mind were noticeable. We could almost forget that Alzheimer's was along for the ride.

The matinee performance of Puccini's *Tosca* at the Metropolitan Opera that Saturday had me reminiscing about the many operas we'd seen together over the years. We both came to opera in young adulthood, largely thanks to the Met's Saturday afternoon live radio broadcasts that introduced us to the history and repertoire of this singular genre. The first performances of the Met's annual tour that we saw in the entirely unsuitable Hynes Auditorium in Boston in the early 1980s confirmed our love of the form and led us to Lincoln Center. Over the years we saw dozens of operas performed there, sometimes driving down from Massachusetts to binge on three-performance weekends—aural, visual, and narrative excess that both satisfied and inspired us.

We were seated in the Met's Grand Tier Restaurant well in advance of the performance and enjoyed a satisfying brunch before we headed into the theater. I went over the main points of the opera's plotline, and though I realized Judy wasn't really following me, I expected that once the curtain rose it wouldn't matter. The music, the singing, and the drama would make sense generally, and in the darkened theater, she would connect with it on some level. That's just how the afternoon played out. At intermission it was clear to me that she was enjoying it, and I again felt grateful. Waiting in line to use the ladies' room, she got into a conversation with the woman just ahead of her, older by at least twenty years, stooped, friendly and kind. I wasn't close enough to hear what passed between them, but I admired Judy's capacity to make small talk with a stranger when, increasingly, the effort involved in even that type of lightweight chitchat could exhaust her.

We returned by train to Harrisburg, where we picked up our car, then detoured to Maryland to see our granddaughters one more time before the long drive home. The girls were giddy and silly, typical six-year-olds. They teased Judy, and she teased them back. Her pleasure in being with them again was evident. It was as gratifying to witness as it was bittersweet. It would be their last time together.

The following autumn, ten months after the Christmas trip East and five years into her diagnosis, we visited her family in the Houston area, another of the road trips that seemed to provide a temporary reprieve from the disease. While we didn't know it at the time, Judy's mother and brother would never again see her moving confidently on her own two feet, and they'd never again have real conversations with her. Those they had during that visit would be their last. None of us had any idea how quickly things would progress from that point.

On that trip, unlike the previous ones, Alzheimer's did manage to catch up with us. Midway to Oklahoma City during our return drive, we stopped at an oversized rest area—Texan in scale—with generous parking areas and identical east and west entrance-exit facades. The absence of any private family restrooms and the potential that she'd exit via one door and I'd go out the opposite stimulated my anxiety, and, our MedicAlert bracelets notwithstanding, I cautioned her before she walked into the ladies' room. "Just wait for me right here when you come out, don't go outside. You got that?" "Wait for you here," she repeated. *Okay*, I thought, *fingers crossed.*

Hurrying to leave the men's room, I didn't notice my wedding band slide off the finger on which I'd been wearing it for some months, fault of an arthritic joint in my ring finger which made for some discomfort any time I needed to remove the ring. It had fallen off my left pinkie a couple of times before, each time while drying wet hands, but then I'd heard the clink of metal on tile flooring. This time the delicate sound didn't register in the hubbub of the busy men's room. I hurried to get out to the lobby, relieved to find that she'd waited as I'd instructed. I didn't realize until hours later that the ring was gone.

Hoping that it had fallen into the trunk when I'd opened it at the rest stop to retrieve some bottled water, we continued to that night's destination. A thorough search of the trunk and the car's interior turned up no ring. I felt a huge disappointment and sadness, that piece of forged metal custom made for us by an artist friend and metalsmith more than forty years before, a wedding set that symbolized so much. I blamed myself for my carelessness, yet it felt as if the disease had stolen one more thing. If I hadn't been in a hurry. If the rest stop had only one entrance. If I'd trusted Judy to wait for me. If...

Tired from the day's long drive and with another eight hours or so ahead of us, we went to sleep early that night in an undistinguished but serviceable interstate-adjacent motel in an Oklahoma City suburb. Sometime in the wee hours, my sleeping self sensed movement in the room, and I forced myself awake. Before I could begin to make out her standing form near the foot of the bed, I knew she wasn't next to me. I rose, and she said, dejectedly and on the verge of tears, "I don't know where the bathroom is." By then it was too late, she'd wet herself, her bottoms, the carpet.

"It's alright, let's clean you up. It's no big deal. Don't think about it."

She wept.

"Let's get back to sleep. We'll be up in a few hours."

I lay there wondering what this meant. She'd had a couple of similar accidents in recent months, but those I blamed on lack of proximity to toilets and my inattention. Here we were in a cookie-cutter style motel, hundreds of thousands of rooms just like it abutting interstates across the country, and she'd failed to locate the bathroom door just where they all were, six feet or so from the hallway door, next to the closet, steps from the foot of the bed. Mental note to self: bring along a couple of night lights next time we travel.

In the next week she wet our own bed one night, necessitating our decamping to the guest room and the subsequent purchase of a waterproof mattress protector to simplify the cleanup of any recurrences. I tried to keep it lowkey, no big deal. *This happens, she sleeps soundly, don't worry about it.* I'd learned by then that holding her to account for things like this was a fool's errand.

A few days later she disappeared down the hallway and into our bedroom, and when I hadn't heard any sound for the next five minutes or so I thought to check on what she was up to. The bathroom door was closed. I tapped on it and then turned the handle. She was standing in front of the toilet, her slacks down around her feet, a mildly bewildered expression on her face.

"What are you up to?" I asked.

"I had to poop."

I glanced into the empty bowl. I hadn't heard the toilet flush. "Did you do anything? I didn't hear it flush." That's when I noticed three neat little turds sitting innocently in the commode's shadow. "Oh Judy, how'd you do that?" I asked.

"Do what?" she replied. She wasn't even aware. Obviously, she hadn't managed to seat herself. She'd likely waited just a few seconds too long before heading down the hallway.

I cleaned her up, disposed of the evidence, helped her pull her slacks back up. She looked at me vacantly.

"It's okay, don't think about it. Not your fault. Next time try to get to the bathroom as soon as you're aware you need to go. You don't want to wait."

It struck me that this was potty training redux but with little likelihood that any gain would be achieved. I wasted no time locating a home health supplies vendor convenient to campus and making their acquaintance. Over time they would prove to be unfailingly helpful and kind to both of us. Judy came with me a couple of times when size or fit questions were considerations and seemed to enjoy strolling around their showroom and taking in their eclectic inventory of useful devices and equipment intended to make homecare more sustainable.

Hell, I thought to myself, *where is this taking us?* I didn't like what I sensed was in the offing. Was there a deal breaker around the corner? Was this it? Were we really turning this page?

The good thing, I guess, is that most days it didn't seem to matter much to Judy. She no longer saw herself as ill, she was just going along for the ride in neutral, neither resistant nor unresistant. She needed help now with most of the activities of daily living, and most of the time she was willing to accept that help. I was still struggling with the notion of becoming her parent, a condition to which I was feeling a lot of resistance. For over forty years I'd been her partner, her lover, her spouse. I had no practice parenting her and didn't welcome any.

When we came of age, at least in the working-class milieu in which we grew up and passed our adolescences, the "first time" was pretty much a big deal. The younger one was, the more likely the event was revealed in one way or another to one's closest friends. The older one was, the greater the likelihood that a perpetually pending deflowering remained a secret tightly held. Today, in a hyper-sexualized and hyper-eroticized media culture that offers sex up as a smorgasbord of seemingly endless variety, in forms and on platforms we'd never have imagined in our youth, the significance of the "first time" may have lost its luster. Not such a big deal to many young people today. Something that happens. Now what?

For me, with you, it was a big deal. I knew I wasn't your first, and that was fine. I knew I loved you; I believed you loved me, and having sex for the first time with someone that I loved was an unparalleled kind of shared fulfillment, singular in its force and transformative in its results. You were more measured about it, maybe more realistic, pleased but unsurprised—a counterbalance to my exaggeratedly romantic self.

In pregnancy and new motherhood, though, you found your version of fulfillment and located your truest emotional core. Once that inner warmth was kindled, you brought it to bed with us every time we made love over the next four decades and some. It was there for Trevor whenever you and he were together, watching television and chatting late after I'd called it a day. It radiated from within you whenever you two squared off across a Scrabble board, a bowl of popcorn between you, and your inevitable victory claimed matter-of-factly, but lovingly. Breastfeeding Trevor the first years of his life had given you another outlet for that inner warmth, and you always held those memories tenderly. Your body and heart gave and received, and I know for you those were points of pride. Intimacy and reverence remained deeply entwined.

And then, the final time…

I knew it would come eventually, wasn't sure how I'd know, but figured that Alzheimer's had a date in mind. Turns out it did, not long after those first incidents of incontinence.

"Wanna fool around?" I asked. Tried and true, that invitation had rarely failed to get things going.

"Fool around?"

"Yeah, as in make love. Hot sex. Fun and games. You know," I teased.

"Sure," you said, as indifferent a "sure" as you'd ever uttered.

We undressed, we laid together, but the warmth you'd always brought to it wasn't there. Then I realized you weren't there. Well, your body was there, but the lover in you had checked out. The warm core was extinguished. You returned a distant look. That door had closed.

"Let me just hold you," I said.

"Hold me," you replied.

The onset of incontinence meant that the caregiving workload would increase substantially. Judy now needed someone with her twenty-four hours a day, and the multiplying costs associated with that round-the-clock care—costs in dollars for *A Trusted Friend* providers and the physical and emotional toll it took on me as her primary caregiver and our full-time wage earner— meant that the writing was on the wall, unmistakably legible. I wasn't ready to retire, nor could we have afforded that option at that point, given both the healthcare and retirement benefits programs that came with my position.

Although my earlier search for adult memory care day services hadn't produced the results for Judy that I'd hoped would relieve some of the stresses, it had given me the opportunity to begin to form an idea of what was available in our community, of what my optimal wish list for her full-time care included, and of what I wouldn't consider under any circumstances. From the start of the search I ruled out any dimly lit, low-ceilinged facilities lacking secure outdoor spaces for its residents' and their families' use; residences that offered only shared bedrooms and baths for their clientele, a recipe for endless confusion and tension; facilities that relied principally on ever-present television screens to distract or anesthetize their occupants and that offered only minimal daily activities beyond the essentials; and facilities that eventually forwarded their advanced dementia clients to skilled nursing facilities when the demands on their staff members approached some ill-defined threshold.

What I hoped to find for Judy was a memory care residence with well-trained, experienced, and skilled personnel who demonstrated a sincere commitment to their clients, who learned about their lives and personal histories, treated them like family, and whose empathy and compassion were genuine, revealed in the relaxed naturalness they brought to engaging their charges. I realized even then that this was asking for a lot. No facility would be perfect or ideal. Care providers in these settings aren't all cast from the same mold; they're as individual as the residents for whom they're responsible. I'd learned by then that by observing care providers on the job and listening to their interactions with their residents, I could make some general assumptions and could form impressions reliable enough to trust. My first question to myself was always "Can I see Judy in this place, and do I think she could be content here?" My second question was "Can I see myself here? Do I think I would feel comfortable and be treated lovingly if I were a resident here?"

I wondered then what her own criteria would be, were the tables turned and she found herself in my position. I knew that after more than four decades together, we each understood the other's likes and dislikes. I felt that I could trust myself to locate a workable situation in which Judy could feel at least somewhat at home, with people that she could trust and even feel genuine affection for. In any case, this is what I told myself. I said nothing to her at the time, doubtful that she'd understand why placing her in full-time memory care was looming as our only realistic strategy.

In the end I made deposits that secured our place on waitlists at two memory care facilities, both of which met many of my preferences. Fairview Senior Community did indeed fulfill the promise in its name. Located on a tree-shaded property that had once been a dairy farm, overlooking a small pond that was part of a creek network on the eastern edge of the city not far from our home, Fairview was a large and sprawling senior living complex that included independent, assisted living, skilled nursing, and memory care options. Its many amenities included both indoor and outdoor pools, a small gym, a yoga and meditation space, two main building dining rooms—one operating cafeteria style and the other with a full wait staff—a large library, a small theater, and an activities program that was weighted heavily toward musical events presented by outside performers.

Its memory residence hall sat apart from the primary complex, so although any of those amenities could be accessed by memory care residents, they needed to be accompanied and supervised either by staff members or by a family member. Given the ratio of staff to memory clients, I figured that it would usually be a challenge to schedule a time for a swim, for example, that wouldn't conflict with staff members' responsibilities to other residents. Nonetheless, since I expected that I'd spend some time with Judy most days, I anticipated that we'd be able to take advantage of some of those offerings together, at least for a while. At approximately $280 a day or $8,500 a month, Fairview would be the more expensive of the two options I was considering.

The one complicating factor was their expectation that memory residents be able to feed themselves. Once clients reached the point at which they couldn't manage that task— common enough among Alzheimer's sufferers—they'd be required to move to skilled nursing. While those services were located on the property, moving to unfamiliar living quarters would sever any relationships Judy might have made and would surely impose some degree of stress on both of us. My hope was to get her settled and secure from the outset and to keep any disruptions to a minimum.

Northside Manor Memory Care, like Fairview, sat independent of its parent retirement complex in a quiet residential neighborhood less than ten minutes from my university office. Northside Manor included independent and assisted-living options but lacked a skilled nursing facility. General nursing care was available in the memory unit, however, with two registered nurses on staff. When I first visited, I expected that we were still a long way from needing nursing care. Their reassurances that once admitted as a resident, Judy would be able to stay until her natural death, that being able to feed herself wasn't a requirement of residency, lessened some of the qualms I'd felt when I learned of Fairview's policy in that regard.

The architects who'd designed Northside Manor's memory facility had thoughtfully laid out a spacious floor plan that included two large dining rooms adjacent to equally generous parlors that formed the central and more public core of the building. After passing through reception, residents, their loved ones, and other visitors were buzzed through locked doors that opened into a wide and brightly lit corridor linking the wings containing the residents' private suites with the dining and parlor areas. A combination ice cream, popcorn, and coffee shop, nostalgically decorated to evoke something out of a small-town heartland childhood, opened from the main corridor and offered refreshment and a meeting place to residents and visitors. I imagined that young grandchildren dragged along to visit resident grandparents or great-grandparents would find that attraction particularly appealing.

When I first saw the Manor's large floor-to-ceiling aviary and its colorful winged boarders, I thought it was something Judy would really enjoy. She'd always loved watching the annual cycling of bird life from our home's back porch and from her studio. Sightings of hummingbirds, woodpeckers, egrets, Great Blue heron, and Eastern screech owls occasionally enlivened the more predictable activity at our bird feeders and around the lake, and we both appreciated it. The aviary's occupants were on the diminutive side, finches primarily, but very fascinating to watch at close range. Built-in banquettes facing the structure offered seating and opportunities to socialize with other residents and staff. It seemed like a nice touch in a facility whose residents lived in permanent lockdown.

As I was being led on my first tour of Northside Manor's memory residence, I was surprised to see Kay Larsen's husband Richmond Baker's name on one the private bedroom suite doors. *So, this is where Kay ended up placing him*, I thought to myself. As for each of the full-time residents, a shallow wood and glass cabinet at the doors to their rooms displayed some biographical information, a portrait and some family photographs, and other ephemera intended to help staff and residents alike become familiar with their in-house neighbors. It was a way to acknowledge everyone's personhood and past life and have that life seen as important. I began to imagine what we'd collect to represent Judy's life if and when…

Northside's memory building and its two long wings enclosed a well-tended and nicely landscaped garden and lawn. Seating built into and along retaining walls was integrated with pergolas that provided shade in the growing season, and two large, covered patios guaranteed protection from the elements. The Manor's memory compound backed up to one boundary of the neighborhood's city park, and that proximity meant that residents who were still ambulatory, accompanied by their loved ones, could easily and safely access an expansive green space quite literally in its backyard. Judy and I were still walking together almost daily, so I appreciated that Northside's location would encourage us to venture beyond its enclosures.

While Fairview programmed frequent performing arts events and screened vintage films in a small theater a few times a week, it didn't offer a structured daytime activities program. Northside had a dedicated activities room that was staffed twelve hours daily including weekends, and which offered art and craft projects, bingo and other games, gentle yoga and other exercise sessions, film screenings, birthday or holiday celebrations, and more. As a strategy to help eventual residents transition to its facility, Northside also had a day program in place. We'd tried and failed twice before to get Judy on board with adult day services, but months had passed since our last attempt, and I felt it would be worth trying again.

When I visited Fairview and Northside in early fall 2014, I felt good about each facility and hopeful that Judy wouldn't reject them out of hand. At home we revisited the subject of her eventual need to move into full-time memory care. She listened quietly as I described what I'd seen at the respective institutions and how eager their staff members were to meet her. "I've scheduled a couple of visits," I told her. "So, you can meet the people there, get a feel for each place, see what appeals to you and if you prefer one place over the other."

"Okay, that's fine," she said. "But I don't know what's wrong with just staying here."

"Look, this is important. We have to plan ahead, and I'll feel a lot better if I know what you like or don't like about these places and the people we'll meet there."

"Well, whatever," she replied unenthusiastically. "I just think I'm fine here at home. Except for you, always trying to control my life."

She was right about that, but she didn't always understand that controlling her life was the last thing I wanted to do. Alzheimer's didn't give me a choice. If I were being forced by circumstance to have to be her guardian, it would be with the goal of providing her the best quality of life possible for as much remaining time as we would have together.

Sometimes, though, I think she did understand.

By Christmas 2014 I'd taken her to visit the memory care residences at Fairview Senior Community and at Northside Manor, and those visits had gone relatively well, all things considered. Certainly, she still resisted the idea, but that resistance was weakening, maybe because she'd lost the emotional and cognitive strength that had fed her earlier opposition. She broke down during the interview at Northside, her sadness triggered by what she must have felt was the pending rupture in her everyday life. I know that my reassurances and those of the staff that discussed it all with us were small consolation. We had finally approached the limits of what homecare we could manage, both practically and financially, on our own. I sensed she felt defeated, broken. I ached for her.

During the holiday week, with the university shut down and family distant, we decided to make a quick road trip to visit the Crystal Bridges Museum in Bentonville, Arkansas, an undemanding day's drive through Kansas City, where we stopped for lunch and to see an exhibition at the Nelson Atkins Museum. Looking at art of one kind or another had always been a major preoccupation in our lives, and the enjoyment she continued to draw from that activity was one thing that Alzheimer's never managed to cheat her of. Even when her language skills, spoken and written, were permanently damaged and she struggled to tell a story or relay a thought, her eyes continued to work at admiring and interpreting almost any art that she saw before her.

I'll always warm to the memories of those few days in northwest Arkansas, our first time traveling to that state. She was so relaxed and content that it made me feel likewise. I'd reserved a room for us at the 21c Museum Hotel near the town square, ideally located within walking distance of Bentonville's entire center as well as Crystal Bridges and its grounds. We'd barely settled into our room when the front desk rang to tell us that they were upgrading us to a suite on another floor due to loud renovation work they anticipated would start early the next morning. We relocated with little fuss, feeling that good luck had decided to come along for the ride. After the misfortunes of our

Texas–Oklahoma road trip a few months earlier, this was much more to our liking.

The three days in Bentonville played out as satisfyingly as we could have hoped for any spur-of-the-moment getaway. Alzheimer's kept a very low profile, and our time there as tourists seemed normal in every way. We slept well, we dined well, and we were amazed and inspired by so much of the art we saw, both at the Moshe Safdie and Partners-designed museum, and at the 21c. The hotel chain's brand mascot, four-foot-high fiberglass penguins—fluorescent green at the Bentonville location—appear randomly and unexpectedly all around the hotel, and they really tickled Judy's funny bone. It was deeply heartening to see her that happy after all that the previous years had laid on her.

We arrived back home on New Year's Eve. It was the last road trip we'd make together. After dinner I lit a fire, and we sat side by side on the sofa, positioned so that we could see it and the live Christmas tree in our library. We reminisced about the many ornaments on it that we'd made ourselves or purchased together, some from the first year of our marriage, more than forty years back. Silence came. We watched the fire gradually slow its progress.

"I think you should give them to the girls," Judy said out of the blue.

"Give what to the girls?"

"The ornaments we made. I think they should have them."

That took me by surprise. What prompted that? What did she sense in that moment?

"For sure we'll give them some of the ornaments," I said. "Especially those that Trevor grew up with. That's a good idea."

The flames subsided, passing their earlier energy to the embers that now glowed in the darkening recess of the fireplace.

"Happy New Year," I said.

"Happy New Year," she returned.

15

You put together two people who have not been put together before. Sometimes it is like that first attempt to harness a hydrogen balloon to a fire balloon: do you prefer crash and burn, or burn and crash? But sometimes it works, and something new is made, and the world is changed. Then, at some point, sooner or later, for this reason or that, one of them is taken away. And what is taken away is greater than the sum of what was there. This may not be mathematically possible; but it is emotionally possible.

– Julian Barnes, from *Levels of Life*

Dear Judy,

Two weeks into 2015 I signed the papers enrolling you in Adult Day Services at Northside Manor Memory Care. I'd brought up the subject one way or another nearly every day since we'd returned from our holiday week escape to Bentonville, hoping you'd warm to the idea. To my cautious relief, you didn't protest. I think you weren't really processing it. From your inside looking out, the notion of going to a place where strangers would oversee you just wasn't a situation you had any way to wrap your head around.

"We're just going to try this out, see how it goes. I'll drop you off on my way to campus in the morning, and you can have lunch there each day. I'll come by at the end of the afternoon to pick you up. They'll have plenty of things for you to get involved with, and they're looking forward to your being able to help them with some of the residents." I wasn't sure just how much help, if any,

you might be able to offer, though I hoped that they'd find little things for you to do with or for the older residents, most of whom appeared to be about your mother's age. That was an age bracket that you'd always indulged and enjoyed sharing time with.

At sixty-six, you'd be the youngest client in Northside and close in age to some of the longer-term staff who'd be caring for you. Since you looked a lot younger than your age, I wondered that you might even be mistaken for a staff person at some point. I mainly hoped that this time you'd somehow manage to get comfortable enough that flight wouldn't be your impulse when I returned to pick you up.

"Where are we going?" you asked the first morning I drove you there.

"I'm going to drop you off at Northside Manor; you're going to spend the day there."

"I am?" you asked. "What am I going to do there?"

"They have lots of things to do, puzzles and games, exercise, you can have lunch there, they show movies, and they have people come in to play different kinds of music sometimes. I think you'll enjoy it."

"Do I know anyone there?" you asked. I reminded you that you'd met several of the care providers on staff and that you'd sat in on a Trivial Pursuit-*type game in the activities room when we'd visited.*

"You've met Shawna there—she's the activities program director—and she's looking forward to your joining them. That day you seemed to like her and being with the group. I think it'll be fun for you." I tried my best to sound upbeat and enthusiastic, though now I wasn't sensing the resistance you'd expressed the previous times we'd attempted a day services situation. While I wouldn't say you were eager to try it out, I did sense a small measure of curiosity on your part.

That first full day went well, and the next, and the one after that. Each morning you'd ask where we were going, I'd repeat that I was dropping you off again at Northside Manor, you'd roll your eyes and say, with a sigh, "Oh, that place!" but you didn't object.

Like The Lodge at Heritage Ridge's non-resident day services program, Northside Manor Memory Care charged $75.00 a day for nonresident services, including meals. While I wasn't planning for Judy to have breakfast there while she was a day client, she would have lunch each day and occasionally dinner when I had campus business that extended into the evening. So, I expected she'd be there most weekdays from 8:30 or so to about 5:00 or 5:30, eight or eight-and-a-half hours typically. That daily rate was a hundred dollars less than eight hours of *A Trusted Friend* care, by then $22.00 an hour. I'd been completely satisfied with her Trusted Friend care team, and she'd come to really like them and look forward to being with each of them. We were moving toward full-time placement at this point, though, and while the financial savings were undeniably attractive, there was enormous benefit in her acclimating herself to Northside's environment, staff, and residents.

Because Judy's *Trusted Friend* providers had, in fact, become so trusted, I asked to continue with Lisa, Evelyn, and Deborah three mornings a week each for three hours so that Judy could maintain those relationships even after her Northside Manor days became the new routine. Their arriving at home at 7:30 those mornings to help her have breakfast, get washed and dressed, go for a walk or run an errand, and then to drop her off at Northside at about 10:30 kept her connections active and allowed me to get earlier starts on campus. Even with those continuing *Trusted Friend* hours, the total weekly cost for approximately fifty hours of care in the first months of 2015 was less than what we'd been paying for thirty hours weekly in-home over the preceding year.

Unquestionably, $2,300 out-of-pocket a month was, comparatively, far more than the average single wage earner family in this country could afford for daycare of any kind, whether for pre-school children or for ill or aging adults. We were very fortunate that we were able to manage it despite not qualifying for federal Medicaid coverage or having had long-term care insurance to pick up some or all of the tab. Because the care that we were able to get for Judy was such high quality, I felt doubly thankful. I may have had some concerns about how long we could sustain it, but at the time my overriding feeling was relief. If, eventually, I'd need to turn to retirement savings, at least we had retirement savings to fall back on. At the end of the day, we were in far better financial shape than many people facing the costs of a disease like Alzheimer's.

The day-by-day process of becoming a part of Northside's community made an initiate not just of Judy, but of me as well. We went into it as partners, she and I, and I was determined that we keep it that way. We were also clients, and while her presence there would be far greater than mine, I understood that the more present I could be, the more I could serve her interests as her advocate, the better her overall experience would be. It helped that Northside's management and staff endorsed that approach. When a family member might show up unannounced at any time of day or night, there was an added incentive for staff to make sure that their clients' needs were being met promptly and thoroughly. That always seemed to be the case, and nothing that Judy ever reported to me about her days there gave me reason to think otherwise.

About two weeks into her day services experience, Fairview Senior Community's director phoned me unexpectedly. An opening for permanent residency in their memory unit was available, and they wondered if we were ready to take advantage of the opportunity. Judy's name had been on their waiting list for just shy of six weeks but had moved to the top relatively quickly. "Let me think about this," I responded. Things were already going quite well for her at Northside Manor, and I liked their promise that she'd be able to stay there through her life's course, even after she could no longer feed herself.

When I phoned Fairview back to explain that Judy's day services situation was working out far better than I'd hoped, they were generous and understanding. They agreed to hold our deposit, keep us at the top of their wait list, and as openings materialized, they'd continue to offer us placement. It was reassuring to know that we'd have two options should the need become urgent. That left me feeling both relieved and optimistic. I like to think that some of that optimism rubbed off on Judy.

Some of the full-time female residents at Northside took to her quickly, and she to them. They were all much older than Judy, and she might have reminded them of daughters of their own, or other younger family members, or maybe themselves, a decade or two earlier. Judy was unfailingly kind and gentle in their regard, and vice versa. We slowly picked up details of their lives, from stories they shared whose factual basis I couldn't always determine, or from members of Northside's staff, or from relatives who visited regularly or infrequently. I made it a point to have lunch with Judy there at least once or twice a week, and that helped me to get to know who was who among the residents, as well as among the staff. If eventually she'd be living there permanently, I wanted both of us to feel comfortable and accepted.

I arrived earlier than usual to pick her up one January afternoon during that first month of day services. She was in the activities room, and one of the staff had a pop music trivia quiz in progress. While these types of games were beyond some of the residents' capabilities, for some they unlocked caches of arcane knowledge that could be surprising and sometimes downright hilarious. Judy seemed keen to stay in the game, so I retreated to the outer perimeter of the group where a friendly and petite octogenarian named Vera was watching the goings-on, her bemused and skeptical expressions alternating as a function of the answers being voiced by the game's participants.

"How are you doing today, Vera?" I asked.

"I'm well, thank you," she replied without looking up.

"You're not interested in playing the trivia game?"

"I'm not one for popular music," she answered flatly. "My father was an opera singer. That's the kind of music I grew up on."

"Wow, that's great! My wife Judy and I love opera too. Can you tell me a little bit more about your father's career?"

Vera proceeded to sketch out a rough chronicle of her Italian baritone father's early years singing minor roles in European opera houses before coming to the States just before the Second World War, a wife and three teenagers in tow, Vera being the oldest. According to her, they eventually settled in Kansas City, where he patched together a living as a soloist with church and community choruses and as a private voice teacher. She'd met her husband in Missouri, and they'd eventually landed in Nebraska. She never left.

"Sounds as if you've had a very interesting life," I said.

"I've had a good life," she agreed, "and now they're all gone. It's just me. We never had kids of our own."

I started to empathize, but before I could finish, she interrupted. "Who's your favorite baritone?" she asked.

"Well, I've heard quite a few," I answered. "We heard Sherrill Milnes at the Met a couple of times; he had a terrific voice. And we heard John Shirley-Quirk once with the Tanglewood Festival Chorus and the Boston Symphony. That was memorable. But I think my favorite baritone was…" and I drew a blank. "He was in the very first Met production we ever saw, Rigoletto. And I heard him in other roles on Met live radio broadcasts. Oh…his name just won't come to me." I rubbed my temples, hoping to coax the singer's name out of hiding. "Darn, I just can't think of the baritone's name."

Through her reminiscences of her father and her own life, Vera had kept her eyes on the trivia game group. Now she turned to look at me, paused, and after a few long seconds during which I continued trying to come up with Cornel Macneil's name, she said cleverly, "Well, you've come to the right place."

Midway through a second month of day services, I arrived to pick Judy up as darkness settled in and the evening meal was about to be served in the dining room. As I approached the carport at Northside Manor's main entrance, I noticed a sheriff's vehicle parked just out of the fire lane. *Curious*, I thought, and I wondered what might have prompted a sheriff's visit. As we walked out through the front door to head home five minutes later, it was still where I'd first seen it, still unoccupied. I asked Judy if she'd seen an officer inside the building just before I arrived, and she hadn't. *Curious*, I thought again. I looked back to the carport as I opened my driver's side door. A yellow light faded toward darkness; a damp chill lay over everything.

Later that evening my curiosity was satisfied. Among a dozen or so personal emails that had accumulated through the day was one from Kay Larsen. She had sent it to numerous email addresses, most of which I didn't recognize, though some members of the local arts community and my colleague Dr. Cruz-Vincent, her neighbor, were known to us. The subject line read, simply, Rich Baker. Kay was sharing the news that her husband of forty years had died that afternoon, of complications of Alzheimer's, in Northside Manor's memory unit, where he'd resided for a year-and-a-half. Like Judy's, his disease had been younger onset, had interrupted a still active professional career, and had dropped the final curtain on his life. The sheriff's office had sent an officer to confirm the death, and we'd nearly crossed paths.

By the time Judy started day services at Northside, Rich's condition had deteriorated to the point where his interaction with other residents was minimal, so she hadn't had the chance to get to know him. I saw him only a couple of times, once in the activities room where he leaned forward in a wheelchair, present but absent. Never having met him, I had no way to gauge the degree to which his physical self had changed, but I knew the disease, and so I knew that the man I saw poised between worlds was not the man that Kay had known and loved for more than forty years. I did know the grief that they had lived, though, and my heart went out to both of them.

I was in my office on campus the following morning when my cell phone rang.

"Michael, this is Karen at Northside Manor," the memory unit's director said. "Do you have a minute to talk?"

My first thought was that something had happened to Judy. She'd started the day more discombobulated than usual, and had it not been for a meeting I felt I needed to attend, I'd probably have opted to keep her at home.

"A room has come available here, and we're calling to ask if you and Judy would like to have it."

So, Rich Baker's exit would launch Judy's full-time occupancy. The opportunity felt simultaneously welcome and unwelcome. His death had cleared a pathway for her, but now I knew there was no way to deny or underestimate that pathway's ultimate destination. I wanted to say, "Let me think about it," as I had to Fairview Community's offer a month before. I wanted this call to come six months, a year, three years or more from now. I wanted Judy at home with me each night; I wanted to be able to look forward to that each day, at least. Yet, I knew. She'd adjusted so well to Northside, she liked everyone there and they reciprocated that affection, and her outlook on the life she was living seemed relatively good. The moment felt unfortunate yet serendipitous, and I knew it was time.

"We'll take the room, Karen," I replied.

When I arrived to pick Judy up a few afternoons later, she was sitting by the aviary with a couple of the full-time residents, her attention held by the busily hopping and darting finches. After greeting everyone, I sat next to her and decided it might be a good moment to broach the subject that I'd been thinking on most of the day.

"Judy," I said, "did you know that many of the people you're with all day, like Ruth here, and Carol, have their own rooms down the hall?

"They do?" she replied.

"Yep, they live here at Northside full time, so they sleep here, and they have a lot of their things here. What would you think of the idea of having a room of your own here?" I had no idea how she'd take that question, but in thinking about ways to put the prospect of full-time residency on the table, it was the one approach that seemed relatively low impact and noncommittal. And maybe a little devious.

She thought for a moment before replying "Where would the room be?"

"Let's take a walk," I said. We left the bird watchers and turned to walk down a long hall, toward the room that Karen had told me would be vacated that afternoon.

"If you like the room, we can bring some furniture from home and hang some of your artwork and make it comfortable for you." She listened but didn't respond. What was she thinking at that moment, I wonder.

Rich's emptied room was brightened by a large window that faced a small, landscaped alcove separated from the parking lot by a wide sidewalk. About the size of a standard hotel room, it was carpeted and featured a couple of closets and a large bathroom with a walk-in shower. At about waist height, moulding split the walls into upper and lower sections painted in contrasting colors.

Judy took in the space silently. "If you'd like, we can paint the walls to brighten it up a bit more," I said. "I was thinking that we could maybe do something like the pale robin's egg blue of our bedroom at home, if you'd like that."

"That sounds good," she finally said.

To say that I was relieved by her tacit agreement would be an understatement. Not many months before, she'd unequivocally and angrily rejected joining an adult day services program, the second one that she'd nixed. Fast forward to the start of a new year and, in a relatively short time, she'd fully accepted Northside Manor's small community, and each new day she was willing to return. Now she was accepting the notion that this was a place in which she could, and would, live. I'll never be sure that she was thinking of it this way, but not once did she voice the slightest objection. Somehow, she'd come to terms with it.

I think that yet again, the disease was responsible. It stole whatever resistance to an institutional setting that she'd felt previously. Her world had continued to shrink, and now it was very much centered on her daytimes at Northside. Her waking hours at home were fewer, and her social life now played itself out in Northside's activities room, in its lounges and corridors, in its dining rooms, and in its walled garden. She'd made new friends and acquaintances and clearly felt comfortable among them. All that remained was to outfit a room of her own and settle her into it.

"So, you're okay with bringing some furniture from home and some of your clothes and stuff, and making this your own private room?" I asked as we exited East number one.

"I like it here," she said. "I can have some peace and quiet with my own room. It's a good idea."

Her recurring capacity to think lucidly and levelheadedly when it most mattered never failed to surprise and humble me. So much of the time she thought and maneuvered through a dense haze or fog, a kind of cerebral cushioning that distanced her from the real world whose clarity was taken for granted by those of us looking from the outside in. There were moments, though, when from her side she did see clearly, and I think this was one of those. I was grateful for it.

It weighed on me, during those weeks when the room that would become your new home was being repainted, and I was piece-by-piece moving in furnishings and some of your clothes, that our long life together was about to undergo another major and irreversible change. This felt different from how I felt—we felt—six years earlier when your diagnosis cast us adrift. Then, we were the two of us, and while we might have felt very alone, we had one another. We slid under covers on opposite sides of our bed, but we shared that bed. Whatever happened, that physical and psychic closeness would bolster us.

Now it was as if a fissure had appeared in the ground beneath our feet, and we were standing on opposite sides of that fissure. We could still reach across it, we could still hold on to one another, but the crevice would soon widen, and at some point, it would widen beyond our reach for one another. I knew this in the abstract. I didn't want to afford it reality.

When we were at the point of moving Judy full time into Northside, many memory units typically recommended that the family deliver their loved one on whatever day designated as the start of permanent residence, get them quickly settled, and then leave and not return for a week to ten days. The rationale was that this would allow the client to adjust more smoothly, minimizing any disruptive impulse to leave the facility with returning family members. Karen had mentioned to me previously that at Northside, they found this approach often worked best.

It felt wrong to me. I had misgivings that sudden abandonment by close loved ones would increase the confusion and disorientation that the patient was already experiencing. That belief was part of the reason why I felt that being in Northside's day services program would smooth Judy's way to that ultimate transition. It had also motivated me to involve her in the preparation of her Northside room so that if there were any initial strangeness or discomfort, she'd have time and exposure to help her get past it. That calculus turned out to be the right one for us.

Late winter and early spring 2015 brought an unusually high number of days with above-average temperatures, and the Sunday we'd settled on to start her full-time occupancy of E-1 was one of those. It dawned sunny and by noon would reach 81 degrees. The evening before, we packed the last of the clothes that we'd be bringing to her Northside room. She asked a few times where we were going, and I reminded her after each query that the next day we'd be settling her into her new digs. It wasn't registering, but by Sunday morning it had. When she came from our bedroom to join me for breakfast in the kitchen, she sat down, looked up at me, and burst into tears. Her tears brought mine, and I sat alongside her, heads together and hands clasped, neither of us able to speak. "I love you," I finally said, "I won't abandon you."

"I know," she replied, "I love you too."

16

In the vast sky the sun is setting;
the path home is far
and the bag is already heavy.

> – Ryōkan, in *One Robe, One Bowl*

Dear Judy,

Despite the day's unusually high outdoor temperatures, our home felt cold and unwelcoming when I returned after settling you into your Northside room, joining you for supper there as the sun went down on the outside world, and helping you change into night clothes. "The staff will be in later to see if you need anything, and I'll be back tomorrow night after dinner," I said to you by way of parting. You never objected, only asking, "Will you come back?"

It felt bizarre that every noise I made in our empty house that evening seemed somehow amplified, larger than life, as if to remind me that there was no one else to hear and absorb those sounds. "So is this what it'll be like when she's finally gone forever?" I asked myself. In the complete privacy of our kitchen and living room, in my studio and in our bedroom, I felt that all the world's eyes were staring at and judging me, exaggerating how exposed and somehow guilty I felt that in contriving to protect you and give you the best care that I could, I'd somehow failed both of us.

While your adjustment to Northside's nonresidential day program had been mercifully uneventful, I nonetheless half-expected a phone call from the staff that night, imagining you having a meltdown, or lashing out and hurting another resident or an attendant, or somehow disrupting things to the extent that they'd recommend I return to take you home. That you'd done none of these things to that point, that you'd accepted this new station in life without protest, made no difference in my irrational imaginings. I felt I'd abandoned you, and I just wanted you home.

The phone never rang.

With Judy no longer at home, "home" became more of a pitstop, the place to which I headed late in the day after I'd kissed her goodnight or sometimes tucked her in, and the place I left from each new morning, heading to the gym, to campus and work, and once or twice a day, to her. Sometimes I'd join her for lunch, always I'd come to her as soon as I'd had my evening meal, to keep her company for a couple of hours, to take her out for walks in the neighborhood, to sit in the garden and enjoy the evening's raking sunlight, before getting her ready for bed and bidding her sweet dreams. Not once did she ever ask to come home, not once did she ever complain. The Northside staff had been so welcoming and loving from the start that she'd warmed to their embrace, never, that I was aware of, looking back. I felt happy for her and for us, and sad too.

While I wrapped up furnishing her Northside room, I moved most of the contents of my studio to campus. The college had generously agreed to my relocating my creative operations to an underused basement-level room two floors down from the department, and with that consolidation I could optimize holes in my administrative and teaching schedule by secreting myself down there to pick up with whatever work-in-progress was underway. Having worked from a home studio over the course of my entire career, I'd had misgivings about how separating from that comfort zone would impact my working habits, but it proved to be more conducive to concentrated production. Since she was no longer at home, that was no longer the center of our lives.

Her new center was Northside, and mine split with Northside Manor and the university campus. Again, I felt enormous relief and gratitude that finally, the pieces of our lives were falling more harmoniously into place.

Loyal friends and family members showered Judy with cards and notes and flowers during her first weeks at Northside, giving us those expressions of love and concern to read and reread when we were together in the evenings. Sometimes she could bring a sense of recognition to a name or pair of names and seemed genuinely pleased and flattered that so-and-so had thought of her and made the effort to reach out. Alone together in her room, it may have been just the two of us again, but we both knew that we were surrounded by many caring souls who, whether at a near or far remove, were now sharing this journey with us.

Ten days after she took up residency, I flew to Washington, DC, to participate in a weekend-long conference that would give me the opportunity to carve out some time to visit with Trevor and his family and to have dinner with our friend Kitty, whom we hadn't seen in nearly two years. Kitty's monthly contribution to the costs of Judy's care continued, and its impact meant even more now that those costs had increased to about $7,200 a month, including six hours a week that I continued to pay *A Trusted Friend* so that we could maintain Judy's contact with Lisa and Evelyn. Our financial advisor, Roxanne, had set up automatic withdrawals from one of my retirement accounts to cover the lion's share of that monthly total, and I continued to feel very grateful that we had the means, at least in the near term, to secure for her the quality care that Northside provided. To care for their loved ones, many dementia caregivers face an unanticipated early retirement or impoverishment, or both, to provide for their charges' everyday needs and safety, at the risk of their own health and peace of mind. Judy and I were far more fortunate than many, and I continue to appreciate that.

That Saturday afternoon in DC I skipped the conference's final program to tend to personal relationships. Being with Trevor and his family for the first time without Judy was strangely disquieting, though our granddaughters' energy and unfailing curiosity—they'd turned eight a month earlier—and their tentativeness with me, the grandfather they spent time with only infrequently, made them even more endearing. We explored an exhibition together at George Washington University's Textile Museum, walked around GW's Foggy Bottom campus enjoying the mild weather, then passed an hour or so catching up at a busy coffee shop where, for me, Judy's absence seemed even more pronounced.

In the middle of dinner with Kitty later that day, my cell phone rang and Northside's ID scrolled. I took the call, and it was Janie, the nurse on duty that evening. Nothing to be alarmed about, she assured me. They had to let me know that they'd found Judy on the floor of her bathroom, conscious and apparently unhurt, though they weren't sure whether she'd slipped and fallen or had sat herself down where they found her about a half-hour after a staff member had changed her into night clothes. If I thought that she should be seen by a doctor, they'd arrange an emergency room visit, but they felt confident that she wasn't injured, and they just needed me to be aware. By then my trust in Northside's care team was solid enough that I accepted their assurances and promised to check in with them first thing the next morning.

"Thanks again, Kitty, for the financial support you're providing; it means an awful lot, and I know that if she could, Judy would thank you from the bottom of her heart."

"Don't mention it. I want to do it and it's a gift to me too. It means a lot that Judy has such good care, and I'm so glad that she's comfortable where she is."

As usual when longtime friends meet only once in a blue moon, we caught up with one another's lives, me sketching out for her how we'd come to find Northside and how Judy's initiation had unfolded, and she painting the broad picture of her day-to-day, the recent sale of the Chesapeake Bay beach house that, over the years since Martin's death, she'd found herself going to less and less, and her general contentment with the life she'd fashioned for herself.

"But I think my life's about to change again," Kitty added as we started in on the desserts we'd ordered. "I've met a man; his name is Leslie—Les—and we've been dating now for about half a year. We've kind of fallen in love. It feels pretty nifty, maybe a little strange, at my age."

My surprised expression quickly changed to one of irrepressible happiness for Kitty. "This is great news," I said.

"Well, it wasn't something I was out looking for, and nothing I expected." Kitty then shared the details of how they'd met: through a friend named Ellie, one of Kitty's bridge partners, who happened to be Leslie's sister. "The weekend we met he was staying here in DC with Ellie and her husband, she was hosting bridge that Saturday, he and I started chatting over a glass of wine after the game was over, a couple of hours passed, and he asked me for my phone number. He lives in Richmond, Virginia, so we spent a lot of time on the phone those first weeks, and now we're doing this back-and-forth thing, alternate weekends there or here, but since he'll be retiring this summer, we're starting to talk about a future together."

As I sipped on the last bit of wine in my glass, I thought about Martin, about how devastating his death had been for all of us who knew him, and about our admiration for Kitty and how she'd handled it. Now, in the ensuing years, she'd intentionally and gracefully put her life back together.

"I'm so happy for you," I said.

"Well, you know, I'll always love Martin, I'll always miss him. But I came to realize something these last few years. I still have a lot of love in me yet to give. It doesn't seem right not to give it."

After I returned from Washington, I shared pictures of the girls and their parents with Judy, told her about our visit together to the museum and our downtime in the Foggy Bottom coffee shop, but I wasn't sure what she was registering. There was that distant, sort of clouded look in her eyes, and she didn't even seem to be aware that I'd just returned to her after five days away.

I showed her the selfie I'd taken with Kitty outside the restaurant where we'd met for dinner, then proceeded to summarize her news about meeting Les and finding herself in love again. Judy's alertness returned as she looked from the selfie to me and back, and I detailed the specifics of their still-developing romance. "Kitty feels she has a lot more love in her to give," I explained, "and she seems really happy."

Judy's eyes focused again on the photo on my smartphone's screen, and she smiled as her brow relaxed.

"Martin would want her to love again," she said, uncoached and unprompted, as lucid as she'd ever sounded. "He would be really happy too."

I certainly agreed. Someone who loved Kitty as much as Martin did would certainly want her to love again and to be loved. At that moment, applying such a scenario to myself was about as far from my consciousness as anything I might imagine. Did the thought cross Judy's mind though? Was she subtly telling me something?

Other than that distant, hazy look in her eyes that had become more pronounced as her disease advanced, Alzheimer's hadn't affected her physical appearance very noticeably. She'd gained about twenty pounds as she became more sedentary, but she'd never been a large person, and in fact she'd always tilted too thin rather than too heavy. She'd never been a snack person, and even after the move into Northside Manor, she'd continued to eat lightly, and rarely between meals.

By early May, though, her gait was changing, and changing relatively fast. She'd always carried herself straight-backed and erect, but now I and the staff noticed a slight lean of her head and shoulders to the side and a shortening of the length of her steps. While she could still navigate the hallways on her own two feet, she began hugging the walls and gripping the railings that lined them. Only when I or a staff member held her arm or elbow or waist to provide a little support did she move with something like her former sureness. I'd read and been told that her mobility would eventually be compromised, and now I was seeing it happen.

As the spring semester on campus wound down, I decided to accept my golf buddy Paul's invitation to join him and two other devotees of the sport for a weekend golf excursion to a remote and moderately exclusive links-style course at the northern limits of the Nebraska Sandhills. Time and its passage no longer seemed to intrude on Judy's consciousness, and I accepted that it was unlikely she'd miss my daily visits. She was living now by the memory care unit's rhythms and routines, and she seemed perfectly adjusted to those. I made sure the staff knew where I'd be, and I arranged weekend visits for her with a couple of friends so that she'd have some distraction and contact with people who loved her dearly.

While the weekend at that isolated course was energizing, inspiring, and restorative, I couldn't help but regret that you and I hadn't been able to discover its pristine beauty together. You'd have loved the abundance of western meadowlarks and their clarion whistle, sounded from fenceposts and the tops of gently swaying sand bluestem, penstemon, and milkweed. The still coolness of the pine forest abutting the edge of the Snake River canyon offers the kind of serenity and space for reflection that you'd have appreciated. You and I had driven across the Sandhills together several times, but on that club's course, travel by golfcart would have set you squarely inside that topography, with miles of grass-covered dunes and their sandy blowouts extending outward from beneath your feet to the horizon. I think you'd have liked, just as I did, the feeling of being fully exposed to the forces of nature but at the same time being entirely in harmony with them.

When I was first learning the game, I enjoyed having Judy ride our local course with me as I played with and against myself, no partners' balls to account for, just my own, no partners' judgments of the through-ness of my swing or the height of my ball's trajectory to contend with, just my own. In that sense I'm a solo player at heart, comfortable within myself as she always seemed to be within herself. I guess that's why having her riding sidekick with me once in a while completed the picture in my head of what an ideal round of golf should be.

I don't want to diminish that weekend's golf excursion and the pleasures it afforded. The camaraderie of our little group of players and the soul-satisfying beauty of those pristine surroundings were the stuff of enduring memories. By then I was getting used to having my own life in an outside world that Judy no longer inhabited, and I was allowing myself to take genuine pleasure in it. In any case, I knew she no longer missed any of that, nor could she even imagine it. Yet, I sometimes pined to have her by me, and I regretted no longer being able to share the kinds of new experiences that, over the course of our long marriage, had always kept it exciting and fulfilling.

I had planned to bring her a card and some flowers on our anniversary, Wednesday, May 20, that year, but otherwise intended to keep the event lowkey. I wasn't feeling particularly celebratory, and I knew that marking our forty-three years of marriage would likely have little significance for her, given her condition. It would be enough to see her for a while, to hope that maybe a moment of clarity would let her in on the meaning of the day for us.

That all sort of fell away when I got a call mid-morning from Karen, Northside's director.

"Michael," she started. "This is Karen. I've just come from a weekly staff meeting that included our director of nursing and the two nurses that Judy's most often interacted with since she moved in. Everyone's noticed a steep decline in Judy's mobility these last couple of weeks, and now she's having a much harder time holding herself upright. I'm sure you've noticed how much she's leaning to the right, and it's becoming harder for her to make eye contact with anyone or anything above waist level."

It had, in fact, startled me a week earlier when I returned from the Sandhills and noticed how off-balance she seemed. I found myself cradling her shoulders sitting next to her, trying to keep her from leaning away.

"Yes, I'm aware of that," I replied. "She seems very unsure of herself when she's standing and walking, and she's slowed down a lot. It occurred to me that maybe she's going to need a walker soon?" phrasing it as a question since I felt I needed some guidance.

"We don't think Judy's going to be able to learn to use a walker; she's past that point. She's close to needing a wheelchair."

This was sobering, and I paused. A month before she'd had no problems walking around on her own, her posture seemed as good as it had always been, and at that point I wasn't thinking we were anywhere near needing a wheelchair. Her disease had always seemed to progress in fairly lengthy stages, changes occurring at intervals, but those intervals separated by long plateaus. Now the changes were accelerating and the plateaus shrinking.

"The team agrees with me that our best advice to you right now is to speak with a hospice agency and get that level of care set up for Judy as soon as you can. They will be able to provide you with different kinds of equipment, like wheelchairs, as Judy's needs develop, and they are very skilled with providing for her comfort and monitoring her condition from day to day."

Wow, I thought to myself, *we've come to this already?* I'd read some about hospice care and associated it with end-of-life preparations. While she'd lost some ground, she was still eating normally and still able to feed herself. Her aphasia had increased such that now she could rarely form a complete sentence, and the ability she'd held of describing something or substituting a different word for it when she couldn't think of the correct one was now gone. I had to intuit some of her wants or needs by way of her gestures or a clue in a syllable or a part of a phrase, but I'd become good at interpreting things like that by context, and in any case, I knew her so well that I rarely misunderstood. She still listened to me when I spoke with her, and often she seemed to understand what I'd be talking about as we looked through a picture book or a magazine together, or a photo album. This didn't feel like end of life, so why would we need hospice care?

Karen was reassuring. "Hospice can provide several personalized services that our team just doesn't have the time or wherewithal for. They'll monitor her vitals closely and adjust or change her medications as the situation warrants. They can provide her a wheelchair, and if Judy needs a hospital bed at some point, they'll arrange that. They can even do things like arrange for regular massages when that would soothe her, especially her limbs. After six months, they'll reevaluate, and if they determine she still qualifies, they'll extend her care for another six months, and so on."

I asked for a recommendation and Karen apologized that they couldn't recommend any one agency. "I'll email you a list of hospice organizations in the area, and you'll need to contact them yourself. Our residents have used all of those on the list at one time or another, and I can't think of any instances where the patients or their families failed to have their needs met. You'll just have to reach out to them. One thing to know," Karen concluded, "this won't cost you anything in addition to what you're already paying for Judy's room and board. Medicare will cover all the costs."

The list appeared in my inbox a few minutes later, and I went straight to the various agencies' websites. Their general mission statements and specific services matched closely, but I didn't want to use a coin toss to land on one. I decided to give Kay Larsen a call, guessing correctly that she'd used hospice during her husband Rich's final months and could offer guidance.

"We used Salt Creek Hospice Care, and they were great. We never had any problems, and I'd use them again in a flash," Kay said. "They're professional and very caring, and they were always on top of things. You won't be disappointed."

That was all I needed to know. Kay's past experiences had proven helpful to me, and I trusted her without reservation. By 4:00 that afternoon I was sitting in the director's office at Salt Creek Hospice's headquarters. By 9:30 the next morning Judy had had her first full assessment, Northside had received our primary care physician's endorsement, and she was officially in hospice care.

This wasn't how I'd expected to mark our forty-third wedding anniversary, but for her I knew that it was the best route forward. She was struggling physically, and anything that would help to alleviate some of the debilities she was experiencing had to be positive. At least that's what I told myself, though it felt premature. She was past objecting, and at that point I think she was past understanding the implications of transitioning into hospice care. To others' kindnesses and expressions of concern and caring, she typically responded with what I took to be appreciation, so I anticipated that she'd be receptive to any increase in that kind of solicitous attention. If Alzheimer's was going to continue to strip her of everything that made her who she was, then we'd exploit every form of care that we could get for all it was worth.

The first year after your diagnosis was hands down the loneliest and most isolated part of this journey. Back then you'd forbidden me to tell anyone of your diagnosis, and so only a handful of close family members and friends knew. Few among those lived near us, which meant that the up-close support we got early on, while important, was minimal. We struggled to map out and begin to navigate an entirely new emotional, psychological, and lifestyle territory into which we were unexpectedly thrust and where we felt abandoned.

*Fast forward five years and that sense of near total isolation
was a distant memory for me and long erased from your consciousness. We had a solid support system around us, one that
developed through the spontaneous desire to help extended to
us by many friends and acquaintances, in countless direct and
indirect ways. That was bolstered and greatly enhanced by the
professional care providers and programs that I'd engaged to
help me help you. I know you felt as grateful as I did, even if you
couldn't always express it.*

*As word that you were now receiving hospice care spread
through our social network, support swelled in many ways and
from many corners. No question this was good, but I began to
realize that it could be problematic. Physically, you were increasingly fragile. Emotionally and psychologically, you seemed—at
least to me—more vulnerable. Should I try to protect you from
the merely curious, to keep you from becoming an object of
others' pity? You'd always been a very private person. Would you
want to be on display for anyone who might want to spring an
impromptu visit on you? Would you recognize visitors you hadn't
seen in some time and wonder who these people were? Was I
over-thinking all of this? Should I simply trust you to accept
whatever offerings of friendship and concern might come your
way, and step back from trying to manage them? You'd always
held me to account for obsessing over stuff like this. "Lighten up,"
you'd say in the face of my anxieties and insecurities. "It'll all
take care of itself."*

Trevor flew from Maryland a week after Judy's hospice care
started to spend time with her at Northside. Over the course of
those four or five days he had lunch with her and spent the better
part of those afternoons by her side. She enjoyed it, and the special bond that they had was front and center, even if she could

no longer articulate her thoughts and feelings in that regard. She laughed quite a bit while he was with her, his wit still able to amuse her, and the silliness lifted her spirits.

While he was on hand, her first wheelchair arrived, as generic and, I'd learn soon enough, ineffectual as the medications for Alzheimer's relief she'd taken all those years and would soon forego. Trevor helped her to adapt to it and to having someone else control her mobility. She didn't resist, but gave herself to it willingly—or maybe resignedly? I didn't yet understand how uncomfortable she often was, especially when on her feet, but also sitting and even lying down. It wouldn't be long before she'd make that discomfort plain and unmistakable.

There were two episodes that I can recall when her frustration resurfaced and exploded. One lunchtime she flung a meal that had just been placed in front of her halfway across the dining room for no reason that the staff could determine. At that point when words almost entirely failed her, captive to a wheelchair, I think she'd simply had it, and she needed to express that somehow. A few weeks later, possibly prompted by some unseen pain or discomfort, she grabbed an attendant's inner thigh as she was being transferred from her wheelchair to her bed and squeezed with every ounce of strength she could muster. It took another attendant to release her fingers' grip, leaving a badly bruised patch of flesh in her wake. That was totally out of character and shocked us all. It wasn't Judy; it was the disease.

Whenever I visited Judy—once, often twice, even three times some days—I'd update her on where I'd been, who I'd seen, what I'd done. We'd sometimes sit on the edge of her bed, or on a commons room sofa, and I'd scroll friends' Facebook postings, my own too, sharing this one's latest selfie and that one's chemotherapy update and another's note of encouragement. Usually none of this elicited from her more than a weak smile or a murmur of accord, though there were one or two brief moments when clarity shone through the fog to stunning effect.

Barely two weeks into hospice care, she brought me up short and sharp with an understanding so acute and unexpected that I felt like a clap of thunder had exploded beneath the ceiling fixture in her room.

The evening before, I'd joined a hundred or so guests, mostly friends and colleagues, at a campus museum for a preview reception of an exhibition of the new work I'd completed over the course of the previous two years. Working with the invaluable help of my studio assistant Sam Vaughn and employing the team from *A Trusted Friend* had allowed me to bring renewed focus to my studio practice. I'd felt real inspiration to translate into visual form the Alzheimer's experience that we were living, and through trial and error, I'd figured out how I'd do that. Now the fourteen pieces that resulted from that fertile period were beautifully installed against the gallery's gray walls.

I spoke in the gallery for fifteen minutes or so, explaining the roots of the work in our shared Alzheimer's journey. I expressed regret that Judy was unable to be there but shared the memory of how, before she'd moved into full-time memory care, she sometimes sat halfway down my studio stairway and watched the progress of a good number of the exhibited works. When I ended my reflections, the visitors applauded generously. I stopped them just as they began to disperse. "Wait!" I said. "Let me take a photo of all of you." Holding my smartphone above my head I did just that. And the reception played itself out.

Later that evening, after going back to Northside and helping Judy with what were by now well-established nightly routines, and seeing her comfortably put to bed, I headed home. Before putting myself to bed, I reported the evening's exhibition reception on Facebook and uploaded the photo I'd taken of my audience. It was an acknowledgment to them of my appreciation and encouragement to others to think about seeing the show.

Early the next morning I headed back to Northside, intent

on talking with one of the hospice nurses when she checked in. While we waited, I scrolled the latest batch of Facebook postings. Sitting alongside me as usual, Judy watched images and text comments come and go. Suddenly the photo of the gallery visitors from the previous evening slid by. I returned to it, spreading my fingers across the smartphone's screen to enlarge the photo. "Here's everyone who came to my exhibit opening last evening," I said. It was the first time I'd mentioned the event to her.

She'd known most of the folks who'd been at the opening, and she'd seen much of the work as it came into being in my studio. She'd made art herself and exhibited it, both in this country and abroad. We'd gone to countless artists' exhibition openings over the course of our life together, always connected in one way or another to arts communities. No question, she knew that milieu.

She looked at the photo, then looked at me. There was a sudden brightness in her eye, a sharpness as if some thin scrim had been pulled aside and light allowed to cleanse the air, to bring everything into focus. She looked back at the photo.

"Why wasn't I there?" she asked, with as much presence of mind as I'd ever known her to display.

The piercing appropriateness and logic of the question, how it revealed her full if momentary comprehension, left me guiltily speechless. In fact, I'd considered bringing her along to the reception, but I'd decided that was wishful and wistful thinking. Her aphasia was advanced, apraxia and ataxia had combined to badly compromise her mobility, and I feared she'd be regarded more with pity than with empathy. Her disease and its devilish machinations, its relentless and rude transformation of the life we'd built together was, after all, the subject of the work, and therefore, so was Judy. To expose her vulnerability in that context would have been grossly unfair, maybe even abusive. I intended for her to see the show, but I intended to choose a day and time when we'd most likely be alone in the gallery, when we'd be able to view it with some assurance of relative privacy.

In that shockingly insightful moment, it felt as though she'd caught me in a lie. Unprepared, I came back with "I'm taking you tomorrow. We'll see it together tomorrow," trying to sound as reassuring as possible. All she said was "Okay." I scrolled upward and the previous evening disappeared.

Dementia caregivers often suffer feelings of inadequacy and guilt, and even the most devoted can be derailed or blindsided when some vestige of the person they knew reappears, even fleetingly, and asserts their identity, their autonomy. I knew that the clouds that had just parted for Judy would quickly recast their dense shadows and that minutes later she'd retain nothing of our exchange. It was crushing nonetheless, being given this glimpse of her former lucid and assertive self. Doubly crushing because there was no hope that it could be more than momentary.

The following morning, an overcast and typically quiet Saturday in the museum's environs, we arrived just as the building opened. Kitty had flown from DC to see the show and to spend time with us over the weekend, as had our dear friend Robin, with whom Judy had bonded while they were doing graduate work together at the university not long after we'd first arrived in Nebraska. She'd flown up from Texas where she'd settled herself as a public school art teacher after completing her degree. They helped to transfer her into and out of the wheelchair, into and out of the car. She seemed to recognize each of them, even if she could no longer address them by name. They understood.

Once in the gallery, she slowly took in what hung on the walls. I told her the titles of the pieces and pointed out some features I thought she might have signaled herself if she could: the subtle nuances of some of the gradations of color that served as backgrounds for more graphic marks and strokes on the printed fabrics, the abrupt fractures of linear patterns whose disconnections evoked for me the cerebral disconnections she continued to suffer, and darkened passages of sky and cloud that lent a moody, lonely, or introspective tone to some of the works. Leaning rightward in her chair, her viewpoint wasn't optimal, but she did seem interested. Finally, I asked her what she thought.

"Nice, yes nice," she whispered. The effort she made to turn her head upward toward the large rectangles and squares hanging before us must have been tiring. When we finally managed to get her back in the car, she slumped into her seat with a groan.

I don't really know whether the visit to the exhibition made sense to her then, though I like to think it did. I hope it did. I drove her from the museum to our home to share lunch with our two friends, to sit out on our lakeside deck and listen to birds and other late spring sounds, to just be, quietly, peacefully. If I'd learned anything in the six years since her diagnosis, it was how to just be in the moment.

That weekend museum visit and the lunch in our home that followed turned out to be her final outing beyond Northside's locked doors. She cried out in pain as Kitty and I worked to move her from her chair into the passenger seat on leaving the museum, and the same maneuvering brought her to tears in our garage, near the end of the afternoon. It was too challenging now to move her safely and comfortably, too anxiety producing for both of us. Her world and her life were now concentrated at Northside Manor. I understood that we'd never reprise any part of the life we'd once shared. That's when the finality of it all really sunk in.

Word had spread through the Northside staff that Judy's mother, Florence, and brother Russ were flying up from Houston to visit her. Flo was ninety-one at that point, and we hadn't seen her since our drive down to Texas the previous autumn. I'd been texting and emailing them periodic updates on her condition, though I anticipated that they'd be a bit shocked to see how much ground she'd lost in the interim.

Russ phoned me from the airport as he was about to leave the rental car lot. "We'll be near the front door when you arrive," I told him.

"Your Mom and Russ have just landed," I said as I disconnected.

"They'll be here in fifteen minutes." She didn't respond.

From her room, I saw them pull into a parking space, so I took the handles of her chair, and we started down the corridor. At that time in the afternoon, Northside's "main drag" was busy with staff and residents moving about—purposefully for most of the former, aimlessly for some of the latter. We carefully wove our way through the corridor's traffic. As we approached the main entry area, the door opened and her mother and brother passed through, turning in our direction as the crowd seemed to tune into what was going on and came to a halt.

I rolled Judy closer and bent down to ask, "Do you know who this is?" as her mother approached and reached out to touch her face.

"It's my mother," she answered through tears, unsuccessfully choking them back as a smile fought to dislodge the sadness that quivered on her lips when she recognized her. "My mother."

Judy's weren't the only tears through which their reunion was witnessed. I wondered about the emotional toll scenes like this took on Northside's staff, women and men who invested so much in building relationships with those they cared for, sometimes over the course of many years, always to lose those people whose lives their own had become a critical part of.

Over the next few days, Judy was with her birth family again, and she seemed to draw comfort from them. Her mother had always been outgoing, and despite her age she was sharp and still curious. She enjoyed the goings-on in the activities room, and several times that's where I found the three of them when I returned to Northside. They spent time together looking through albums of family photographs, and they joined her for lunch in Northside's dining room each day of their visit. If they harbored doubts they'd ever see her alive again, neither of them said so. I thought it unlikely, but I didn't want to voice that. *Just stay in the moment,* I told myself.

17

Lest in our grief we lose our way,
The dead lead back to light of day.
Not their absence from us we mourn,
But ours from them, and this we learn.

— Wendell Berry, from *This Day: Collected & New Sabbath Poems*

Three weeks largely wheelchair bound took a toll on Judy's strength and ability to help move herself from her chair to her bed or onto her bathroom's commode. She'd soon become a two-person assist, though I and most of the staff were still able to handle getting her in and out of her chair singlehandedly. My greater concern was her sideways lean that had grown more exaggerated. Despite attempts to keep her propped up with folded pillows or rolled blankets or both, there were moments when I feared gravity would propel her out of the chair.

Janie, one of the dayshift nurses who regularly worked the east wing where her room was located, took me aside one afternoon after she'd helped me reposition her and the pillow wedged against the chair's right arm.

"No one's likely to tell you this, but she needs a tilt-in-space wheelchair."

I'd never heard that term, though I realized later that I'd seen that style of wheelchair often.

"The problem," Janie continued, "is that they're considered a type of restraint, and we aren't allowed to restrain our residents." She went on to explain that occupants of such wheelchairs, when they're in a reclined position, are usually unable to lift themselves out of the chair. Ergo, that type of chair is prohibited.

"Well," I replied, "Judy's already unable to get herself out of the chair she has unaided. She's at risk of falling out of it," I continued, "and I think this is really a safety matter. If she lands on the floor, there's a good chance she'd be injured. I'd rather she be restrained." I've always chafed anytime I get a whiff of illogic or bureaucratic red tape, and this was one of those instances.

"I think you should talk with the nursing director, Jess, tomorrow," Janie said as she retreated. "I think you have a good case."

When I finally caught up with Jessica late the next afternoon, she'd already heard that I was on a new mission.

"I've discussed this with Karen, our director. We agree at this point that Judy is pretty much restrained by the wheelchair she already has and can no longer get herself in and out of it without help. Her leaning is so pronounced and her balance so uncertain that falling out of it is a real risk, which apparently you mentioned to Janie. So, we're on board with your asking hospice to get her a tilt-in-space chair."

Janie had evidently advocated for us, and I was relieved that reason had won out over the powers-that-be. From the start of our relationship with them, Northside Manor and its staff had consistently lived up to their pledge to recognize the humanity and worth of each of their residents and to protect their safety and well-being. Judy had been embraced warmly and sincerely from the start, and I appreciated that they still saw me as her primary caregiver and their partner. While Northside wasn't our real home, it had certainly become our refuge.

It's an early July evening, about half an hour or so until sunset. In the short video I made of you and me sitting under a pergola in Northside's garden, you're in your new chair, and with its help you're holding yourself up fairly well. You're wearing an

aqua cardigan that didn't belong to you over a pale pink cotton nightgown with lace edging around the collar opening and some smocking on either side of a buttoned front, also not your own. You'd never have worn either color in your previous life, nor did you ever wear nightgowns, but at this point, the Manor's hand-me-downs worked for the staff and kept you comfortable. Although it's mild and I'm short-sleeved, you've got a fleece blanket spreading downward from your waist to your ankles.

In your hands is a piece of ruffled polyester organza, its shade of deep magenta one that might have shown up in someone's prom dress but again, a color you'd never have gone near in your own work, nor when you were buying for your fabric shop so many years earlier. You seem intrigued by it though, and your fingers move to fold it, one fold lapping over another, until the folds reopen, and you start again.

"It came out," you say.

"What came out?"

"These."

"These? What, the stitches?"

"These are...these are that way...But um...I didn't come into that...But I'd like to...stay that way." You look toward me. "But I don't know...what we're going to go over..."

"You don't know what you're going to do with it?" I ask, trying to guess at your meaning. The sounds of birds chirping background my question. The setting is peaceful, we're alone, I'm trying to make sense of your spoken thoughts.

"Would you make something out of it?"

"Yes."

"What would you make with it?"

"I don't know..." you begin to sing. "I don't know, da da da da... da da da da..." Maybe you're picking up on the birdsong overhead.

"You seem to like edges," I say. "Like the edge of this blanket... see, it's done with a blanket stitch."

"I like that," you say definitively.

"You like the way it looks, the way it feels?"

"Mmm...mmm..." you nod.

"Let me take your glasses off," I say, reaching for your sunglasses, "so I can see where your eyes are looking."

"This is wet," you say, lifting and flipping the magenta fabric swatch.

"How'd that happen?" I ask.

"I don't know."

"I think I know. You used it as a handkerchief a little while ago."

"Oh, it was up then," you reply, "probably from the pop...I don't know, it worked up something..."

"You wanna wash it after? We can put it in your laundry basket."

"Yeah, that's true...that true..."

Thinking we may have exhausted the possibilities of the magenta fabric, I place in your lap a small bundle of fabric swatches that one of the staff had put together for you with a metal ring and reach for the organza, accidentally pinching you in the process.

"Ouch!" you say.

"Oops! Did I pinch you?"

"Yeah..."

"Can't take me anywhere," I say with a laugh. "Oh, man, can't take me anywhere. I'm sorry, didn't mean to pinch you."

You're grinning too now, and you turn to me, and there's recognition in your eyes. You reach out to pat my arm.

"No, you're good, you're good," you say, still smiling, "you're good good good good good good good..." You start a kind of whistling; you seem to be trying to push air through your almost closed lips. The birds continue their evening song. You turn away from me, returning to your interiority.

That "good, good, good" was the nicest thing you could have said to me in that moment. It felt to me like a kind of thank you, a type of acknowledgment that you'd withheld for so many months, so many years of what you'd seen as my controlling you, controlling your life. The last thing, of course, that I'd ever wanted to do. I was just trying to care for you.

And I think you knew.

The summer days passed, one by one. Local friends brought thoughtfully curated and delicious picnics to share in the garden or in the private dining room when Nebraska's heat precluded being outdoors. Some were paying their last respects, and it was often painful for them. They cared so much for Judy; they hated seeing what Alzheimer's had wrought. Any self-consciousness on her part had long ago evaporated. She enjoyed their visits, she laughed and enjoyed their hugs, they held hands, she accepted the love their visits represented. I appreciated the support, the simple fact that they were there and in being there helped us both feel less alone.

By late July she was sleeping more, and getting solid foods into her was becoming more complicated and time-consuming, in part because she now needed some help to feed herself, and more generally because she was losing interest in whatever appeared on her plate. I made her some dishes that she'd always enjoyed, and those met with partial success. One day she devoured a full slice of a frittata I brought in; the next day she wouldn't look at another one. I couldn't help but think of how it had felt to train a one-year-old to eat; likes and dislikes change from day to day, and unpredictability often reigns.

I started bringing her smoothies, several a day, mini meals with names like the Slam Dunk, the Triple Crown, the Power Play, each boosted with nutrients that I hoped might give her a little more energy or strength, or at least satisfy any hunger that she felt. She enjoyed them and had no trouble drawing on the straw whenever I offered her the container.

Since the episodes of discomfort and pain she'd experienced being moved into and out of her wheelchairs, she'd been on a low dose of morphine that made a marked improvement in her overall tone. She was going to bed earlier in the evening, waking later in the morning, and napping on and off through the day. Yet, she seemed aware of what was happening around her most of the time, and her alertness and attention span when it came to such things as videos that I'd play for her on a smart TV I'd installed in her room remained good. I landed on some video discs of nature scenes filmed in various parts of the world, each with a meditative musical score, that she watched intently when I played them for her. Even I found these therapeutic, the pristine settings—waves lapping at a low-tide shoreline, gently flowing streams rippling over gravelly creek beds, slowly changing cloud forms moving over vast expanses of field and plain—inviting quiet contemplation and offering momentary escape. They required no intellectual commitment; it was pure visual and auditory sensation. She opened herself to them, and time moved along quietly and peacefully.

It was both interesting and heartening whenever she entered a period of wakefulness, that she appeared to have things to say and do that seemed clear to her, though not to me. I'd get her attention, she'd look right at me, and then suddenly she'd be distracted by something unseen. Her eyes would dart toward the left a bit, or the right, in either case away from me, and then she'd stare intently into space, maybe at someone or something that only she saw. Sometimes she'd reach out at the same time, squeezing something unseen between her thumb and forefinger, or touching a fingertip to…what? The air? To something hanging in space that only she saw?

Once she mimed threading a needle, moistening the thread end between her lips before carefully guiding it into an invisible needle held between the fingers of her dominant left hand. That one was rather astonishing and very, very familiar.

I think that as she moved closer to death, she was also traveling to earlier places in her life, maybe reviewing her life, maybe reconnecting with people in her past with whom she'd once been. I favor thinking that she was mostly pleased and satisfied; at least in those moments, she seemed so.

On the last day of July, she was awake when our friend Linda Esterling arrived to spend a little time with her. I was by her bedside when Linda walked in. As she approached, Judy recognized her, and a big smile rose from her lips into her cheeks. "How are you?" she asked her, as clearly and sincerely as any greeting she'd made since she'd first arrived at Northside. It was touching to hear that and to see the pleasure Linda's visit gave her. Linda, too, was pleased to be on the receiving end of Judy's warm welcome. I left them gratified at that genuine expression of friendship.

That evening I was sitting alongside you, writing a journal entry. I turned toward you and your open eyes surprised me. You'd been sleeping so much, I wasn't expecting your gaze. I smiled and moved my face to yours, almost touching, as close and intimate as I could make it. Your eyes were clear, as if the fog had lifted, and my instincts told me that I'd better take advantage of that momentary clarity.

"We've had a great life together," I said, almost whispering. "We've been awfully lucky. We traveled together all this time, and we'll travel together until the moment when you're ready to let go." You looked intensely at me, and I returned that stare.

"No need to be afraid, you won't be alone. There's nothing to worry about, I'll be fine. I'll take good care of myself. I'll always love you. Our spirits will find each other again, and in the meantime, yours will live in the hearts and minds of everyone who knows and loves you."

Your eyes stayed locked on mine for a good ten minutes longer. You said nothing, and I didn't really know what else to say. The room was quiet and calm, and I think you knew how

The New York Times ran an article in the following Sunday's print edition that drew my interest. Written by Jennifer Hollis, it was titled "Providing the Soundtrack for Life's Last Moments."[17] Hollis is a thanatologist, someone who offers musical care to people on their deathbeds, vigils with harp and often voice accompaniment. In her article she explained the effects her vigils often had on the patients and their loved ones and on herself. It made so much sense. I thought that it was something that Judy might like.

"Do you happen to know if there's anyone here in Lincoln who's a trained thanatologist or who does this sort of thing?" I asked Lisa from *A Trusted Friend* when she arrived the following afternoon to spend a few hours with Judy. Lisa had studied music at the university years before, and I knew she paid attention to the local and regional music scene.

"Let me ask around," she replied. "I think we should be able to find someone."

That evening I asked one of the hospice nurses the same question. By Tuesday she'd located a young harpist named Tyler and had arranged for him to be at Northside to play for us two evenings later.

In the modest dimensions of Judy's room, Tyler's instrument seemed to grow larger than it was as he slid it from its carrying case. There at the foot of her bed, it didn't need to make a sound to impress. It seemed massive. For a few seconds I worried that its sound might be too much for her, that it might overwhelm the room, but my fears were unfounded. Tyler played with a deftness and delicacy that were unexpected in a university engineering student who could have passed for the football team's quarterback.

He played for about a half-hour, and Judy slept through it all, though she didn't seem to be in a deep sleep. I hope she was listening, that she heard the Bach "Prelude in C Major" that he played as precisely and seamlessly as its composer might have. Tyler played seven or eight pieces in all, their melodies drifting out of her room, down the corridor and into the other residents' rooms. The on-duty staff told me later that they loved hearing the music. It was a special gift to Judy, to both of us, that this young stranger would volunteer his talent and demonstrate his empathy in this way. It felt to me as if we were inside the music, inside its resonance. It was a fitting coda to a life enriched by music of many kinds, and I hope she felt it.

The following day, August 7, Judy was awake and sitting in her wheelchair when I arrived with her morning smoothie. One of the staff members was remaking the hospital bed that had been delivered to her room at hospice's request six weeks earlier. What the bed lacked in visual appeal it made up for in adaptability and ease of use. She was spending so much time in bed by then that sores had become a definite risk. The hospital bed made it easier to reposition her and to configure bolsters so that pressure points could be varied throughout each day. While her speech was no longer comprehensible, she was able to express any discomfort she might be feeling, either with sounds or with facial expressions or both, and we were all learning to interpret those.

I returned at lunchtime with a second smoothie and again found her in her chair. Staff told me she'd been alert the last couple of hours, and although she was in a semi-reclining position, she didn't seem sleepy. I slid the chair into its upright setting and brought the paper cup's straw to her lips. She turned her head away.

"You're not hungry?" I asked. "Maybe you can have a little now, and more later?"

She turned toward me, and I offered the straw a second time. Again, she turned away.

"Okay, then, we'll let it go for now. Maybe you don't have much of an appetite today."

She never sipped through that or any straw again. I tried one more time later that afternoon, and she was resolute, refusing the offer.

Had she made up her mind to take in no more nourishment? I wasn't sure at the time just what she was trying to tell me, if anything. She'd clearly decided she was done with smoothies. In hindsight, I think she'd decided for herself that she'd take no more nourishment.

Over the next four days she mostly slept, rarely stirring. We swabbed her mouth with water, hoping to relieve the dryness that she had to have been feeling, especially when her mouth eased open on its own.

Northside Manor's staff and the Hospice team were fully with us. They'd seen the last days of the Alzheimer's journey many times before and understood what was happening. The edema that swelled Judy's feet and lower legs for many weeks had lessened, and now she was showing signs of mottling, splotchy discoloration of her feet and shins. Normal, they confirmed, the body gradually "shutting down," the functioning of the heart in slow retreat.

I phoned Trevor on that Tuesday morning. "I think you should probably come now. They're telling me another few days maybe, no more than a week."

I'd accepted the idea of this ending some weeks before, finally realizing that no exceptions would be made for Judy or me. Now I was beginning to accept it concretely, the physical evidence before me undeniable and irreversible. She'd clearly given herself to it; now I had to.

"Trevor's flying out today; he'll be here this evening," I whispered to the sleeping Judy when I returned to Northside. No reaction, and she slept for the balance of the morning.

Evelyn from *A Trusted Friend* arrived after lunch and set herself alongside her, a poetry collection open on her lap. She read, and I let myself get distracted with emails in the background. After a half-hour or so, Judy began to stir, and her discomfort was unmistakable. "I think maybe I should stop reading?" Evelyn hesitated.

"Yeah, I think that may be a good idea. She doesn't seem like she's enjoying it," I said. Though her eyes remained closed, her expression revealed distress, audibly at times. She alternated between sleep and restlessness for the next couple of hours. Just after Evelyn left, I fetched Charlotte, the nurse who'd just come on duty, and after repositioning her, she decided to call hospice. Toni arrived about 7:00.

"Her breathing is a bit labored right now; she seems to be struggling with that. It's normal at this stage. We can try giving her some oxygen; it might help her to relax, calm her down. At some point, though, it likely won't make much difference. Her body is slowly letting go." I agreed we'd give it a try.

By the time Toni left, Judy was connected to oxygen, and her morphine dosage had been adjusted. I hoped that would help, but her discomfort continued. Her eyes opened, and until Trevor arrived at about 10:00, they stared blankly into the space above her. When he walked in, he brought his face close to hers, and she focused on him.

"Hi, Mom, I'm here," he said gently. "How are you doing?" Judy looked back at him intently, he held his face near hers for what seemed like many minutes, and then she closed her eyes. His was the last face she would register in her sweet lifetime.

The next three days of your ebbing life were unremarkable, and then suddenly, mystically, almost unbelievably, it was over.

The nurses came and went, the sheriff's deputy likewise, and I was left alone with you. It felt strangely comfortable and right, somehow, being in that room with your lifeless body, still beautiful to me. I didn't feel overwhelming grief; in fact, my sense of relief surprised me. I did feel sadness for all that we'd lost, but I was relieved for you. This terrible journey we'd been on for six years had finally ended. If you'd been able to, you might even have encouraged a celebration of some sort.

Bach's cello suites played for the next couple of hours. I fine-tuned the obituary I'd been working on that last week, waiting for the crematory driver to arrive. First, he'd take you to the Pathology Department at the Nebraska Medical Center in Omaha where, later that Friday morning, a diagnostic brain autopsy would be performed. I'd discussed this possibility with Dr. Langfeldt, believing that in the interests of science, and those of our immediate family, it would be helpful to have a final con-firmation that it was, in fact, Alzheimer's that had taken your life. He'd confirmed that they would find the information helpful as well. A month later I would have their report, confirming the original diagnosis. Any doubts we may have had along the way were finally put to rest.

The driver arrived before sunrise. A congenial fellow with a gentle Hispanic accent, Carlos introduced himself before outlin-ing the last procedure you'd be part of at Northside. Once Kristie and Audra had returned, he directed us to positions at each corner of your bed.

"We'll each take a corner of the sheet that Judith's lying on, and Michael, you and Audra will bring your corners up and over, toward us." We followed his instruction and then folded excess fabric over your head and feet. "Now Kristie and I will fold our ends over to your side, and we'll just lift Judith part way

so we can tuck it under." With a minimum of movements, your shroud was secure.

It struck me how fitting this was. Fabric, the physical substance of pretty much everything you'd done career-wise through your entire adulthood, now snugly cocooned your pale, still body. It was just a sheet stripped from your bed, but there was something ageless in its transformation into shrouding for your corpse. It seemed almost magical to me and so appropriate. That it was just an ordinary, generic bedsheet seemed doubly fitting. You'd always been a modest person, unassuming, unpretentious. This was about as unpretentious as it gets.

Next, Audra and I rolled you on your side facing us, and Carlos slid a rigid full-length board onto the mattress. We settled your shrouded body against it, and then he unzipped a large black sleeve of a bag that filled most of the wheeled gurney that had accompanied him into your room. With a minimum of movements and the experience of having done this dozens if not hundreds of times, he and Kristy slid you into the bag, zipped it up, and lifted you onto the gurney.

"I think you should stay here," Carlos said to me at that point. I wonder if he thought I might crack if I walked with you to the service bay, to see your packaged form glide into the back of his van. I'd been in that garage door entrance area before, when we'd moved some of your furniture into Northside. Very functional, very loading dock. No red carpet. As ordinary as ordinary could be.

Kristie opened your bedroom door, Audra stepped out of the way, and you were rolled out of E-1, out of my sight, out of Northside Manor, and into the first light of that new day.

18

*Death is final, but grief is ongoing. The extent to
which we experience it may or may not depend
on the depth of love or even the depth of regret
we feel. In fact, perhaps grieving, at some level,
is the ongoing effort to continue to live with those
we've lost.*

— Diane Rehm, from *On My Own*

Dear Judy,

*When I walked out of Northside, got into my car, and drove
to our home, nothing about the world you left me in seemed
normal. Everything was familiar, but everything had changed. I
was still me, but I didn't feel like yesterday's me. You left a huge
hole inside me, and I wondered if that hole would ever fill.*

*Trevor came up from the guest room once he heard me in
the kitchen, and I told him you'd died, where you were just then,
what we'd do later in the day, then I went to bed to try for a few
hours' sleep. No tears; I was too exhausted for that.*

*Early in the afternoon we returned to Northside to start emp-
tying your room. To help with larger stuff, I lined up our friends
Paul and Ben to meet us there the next day, Saturday, and rented
a small moving van to make that job easier. Until your room
was entirely vacated, we'd be paying the daily rate, so delaying
would be wasteful. In any case, I knew from our own experience
that someone else was on their waitlist, soon to occupy E-1, likely
very eager to learn of an opening. That person's caregiver would*

appreciate the respite that placement would offer.

Jonathan and Margo Parker came later in the afternoon of that sunny and sad Friday to sit out on the deck with Trevor and me, over a glass of wine, to talk about you and about the memorial service I'd started planning. We'd known them almost since first arriving in Nebraska, having met them through the arts community in which they are both invested, Jonathan as a supporter and Margo as a maker and supporter. She had faithfully visited you at Northside weekly through the five months of your residence there, and despite your condition, it always seemed that you recognized her and understood the bond of friendship you and she shared.

Since neither you nor I were believers, I'd initially scouted out a few secular meeting spaces, but for one reason or another those proved impractical. Our years as members of the Unitarian Church drew me to the local one, but after attending services there for a couple of years we'd eventually distanced ourselves. I had doubts that their sanctuary would seat the number of folks I thought might join us. When I began having trouble getting their building manager to return my calls, I took that as a signal I shouldn't ignore.

At Margo's suggestion I spoke with a minister at a prominent Congregational church here in town, to inquire about the possibility of our holding the memorial service in their sanctuary. That I was an unapologetic nontheist didn't qualify the minister's sincere invitation to hold it there. It was a familiar space since over the years we'd attended numerous musical events the church had hosted, and I knew you'd admired the church's architecture, and especially the Art Deco detailing of its interior spaces. We'd also attended their annual Christmas Eve festival of lessons and carols several years running, a nod to tradition and an embrace of community that satisfied some seasonal need for fellowship.

From the start of planning your service, I imagined hearing your voice in the background, "This is silly, it's a waste of time and money. I don't need any kind of memorial service. Just scatter my ashes somewhere and leave it at that." You never wanted to be the center of attention and were never comfortable in that spotlight. As an introvert, you liked keeping to yourself, you cherished your privacy, and you didn't like any kind of fuss.

"The people I cared about will remember me," I kept hearing you say in the back of my mind, "and that's good enough. They don't need to be dragged to a public service. They've got better things to do."

Knowing you as well as I did, those thoughts reflected what I believe you'd have said had we ever discussed it—and we never did. Nonetheless, I decided that I needed some way to honor your memory and that it would be good for our family and friends to be able to join me in that undertaking. I hope you'd have been pleased, in the end.

I was cycling on the bike trail two days later when my phone rang. I came to a stop out of the way of other cyclists and walkers and answered a split-second before it went to voicemail.

"Hi, Michael. This is Andy at Cottonwood Crematory. How are you today?"

Odd, I thought, *that he's asking me this. I just lost my wife. I'm grieving. I'm bewildered. I'm trying to take one day at a time.*

"I'm fine," I replied.

"I just wanted to let you know that you can pick up Judith anytime."

Wow. I paused. Pick Judy up anytime. As if she'd just had her hair or her nails done or had just finished getting a massage. I could pick her up anytime. All ready to go, she was.

I thanked Andy and hung up. That was weird. I thought, *Pick up Judith...*

Which I did, a day later. Inside a small, rectangular plastic box was a clear, four mil plastic sack, her snow-white ashes pushing against its stretched membrane. Five pounds' worth, if that. Her physical being incinerated into powder, grains of dust swept into maybe a hundred cubic inches of container. *So, this is all there is*, I thought to myself. Sixty-six years of breathing, thinking, growing, eating, learning, loving, mothering, teaching, creating, being. In a little navy-blue plastic box. Ready for pickup.

A week passed before I finally slept through the night. Though she hadn't been in our home or our bed for more than five months, they hadn't felt as empty as they did those first days after she died. Every time I walked from our bedroom down the hall to our living area and kitchen, I'd look in the room that had been her studio, hoping somehow that she'd be sitting there in the sturdy wooden Eastlake rocker, looking at me, waiting for me, happy to see me. It's bizarre, really, that I so much wanted her to appear, to return, given that I long ago stopped believing in any kind of afterlife, have disdained superstition with equivalent certitude, knew beyond a shadow of a doubt that her death was final, permanent, irreversible. I even imagined the practical and pragmatic Judy, watching the scene with a wry smile on her face, thinking to herself, "Michael, you hopeless romantic…this isn't *Truly, Madly, Deeply* or *Ghost*. I'm not coming back."

For some reason, the notion that I was now a widower didn't occur to me until the day I returned to my campus office, and I saw that new condition reflected at me in the solicitous facial expressions of staff and colleagues and in the condolences they offered. They seemed to view me a little differently, maybe as they might view an amputee, the thing missing in this case not a limb, but the love of the guy's life. I appreciated their concern, and I knew that I would carry on.

We held Judy's memorial service a couple of months later, a day shy of what would have been her sixty-seventh birthday. A hundred twenty or so people joined us, friends and family from far and near, enough that her unassuming self would have been embarrassed at the attention directed at her and her memory, and gratified, too, that they cared enough for her, for us, to make the time to be there.

Colleagues from the music school played Bach, a sonata for cello and piano and one of his solo cello suites. Maura, Judy's yoga teacher, read a lovely poem by John O'Donohue, "On the Death of the Beloved." Lisa from *A Trusted Friend* enlisted three of her friends to join her in singing an arrangement of Jane Kenyon's poem "Let Evening Come," one of Judy's favorites. Our minister friend Jonathan eulogized her sensitively and knowingly, and our "back east" friend of many years, Jay, shared reminiscences with both humor and insight. Finally, Tyler returned with his harp to play for us once more, accompanied by his own instructor. They played an arrangement for two harps of Jay Ungar's "Ashokan Farewell," a piece that Judy and I both loved. A small exhibition of some of her work hung in a campus gallery through that week-end and the week that followed, an opportunity for those she loved and who loved her to see her art in a different light. She'd have been very pleased.

How I decided what to do with Judy's ashes goes back to our first years together and a shared interest that helped us to reestablish our roots in southeastern New England after the three years we'd spent in western New York State while I was in graduate school.

When we returned to Massachusetts in the mid-seventies,

we found ourselves inspired to learn as much as we could about early colonial history and culture. We'd grown up there surrounded by it, but as adults we could bring purpose to researching the whys and wherefores of that historic environment. This was timely, given the nationwide interest in that history at the advent of the celebration of the American revolution and the republic's founding. We often made weekend excursions to visit museums and historic sites, restored homes that dated from the period, and the cities, towns and villages that were the backdrops for the drama of those years of nation building.

Our shared love of textiles brought us to an appreciation of the rich and varied material culture of the seventeenth and eighteenth centuries. Patterns and motifs that we found in woven coverlets, in quilts and in embroidered samplers riffed on similar decorative ornamentation that appeared in furniture, in architectural detailing, and in other applied arts of the period. That's how we found our way to colonial-era graveyards throughout the southeastern New England region. Whenever agreeable weather coincided with a Sunday morning with no other agenda, we'd pack some snacks, collect some toy diggers and backhoes for Trevor, belt him into his car seat, and head to an old graveyard to take photos, read inscriptions, and sometimes make rubbings. New England is dotted with these cemeteries, often untended and overgrown, rarely visited. We'd find them on those quiet Sunday mornings and spend a couple of hours, usually undisturbed, imagining the lives and experiences of those buried there.

Our favorite graveyard, the one we returned to most often, was the centuries-old Common Burying Ground on Farewell Street in Newport, Rhode Island. Established in 1640, it contains the graves of generations of many prominent Newport families, as well as sections where Newport's Jewish, African, and African American communities interred their dead.[18]

In the mid-1970s, when we were spending some of our Sunday mornings there, the Burying Ground had only recently been placed on the National Register of Historic Places. While work was underway to rehabilitate large areas of the graveyard that had long suffered from poor maintenance, unshorn grass, wayward vines, and other invasive plants still obscured some of the headstones. As Trevor amused himself digging small trenches in the unpaved double-track drives that intersected at the limits of collections of plots, Judy and I would clear tangle from headstones, affix strong rubbing paper, and collect the images and inscriptions carved into the faces of those stones. The death's heads, the cherubs, the stylized portraits of the dearly departed, and the floral garlands and decorative pilasters that often bordered the vertical lengths of those slate slabs spoke to us not only of early American religious belief and social status, but they also constituted outdoor galleries of the stonecutter's art, an art as inventive and expressive as any produced through those years of settlement, industry, trade and expansion, and revolution.[19]

One of the most celebrated of those early New England stone carvers was an English immigrant named John Stevens who, by way of Boston, settled in Newport in 1705 and there opened a shop devoted to stonework. That shop, much restored, expanded and well maintained, remains active in the same location where its founder first opened his doors to neighborhood trade. The shop and the commerce in stonework and stone carving passed through multiple generations of Stevens descendants until it was acquired in the early twentieth century by an artist and calligrapher, John Howard Benson, who rejuvenated the carving enterprise on the very premises where the Stevens family had sustained it for so long.

Judy was as captivated with that history as I was. As undergraduate art students, we'd both studied freehand lettering and calligraphy as part of our design curriculum. She'd studied with Alexander Nesbitt, the author of the book we were assigned in those courses, *The History and Technique of Lettering*. Nesbitt lived at the time in Newport and knew the Benson family. In fact, John Howard Benson's son John Everett Benson had served as a guest presenter in one of Judy's courses with Nesbitt, and she'd had the opportunity to observe as he demonstrated his lettering techniques. Her left-handedness created some challenges for her where calligraphy was concerned, and she found it discouraging. Nonetheless, she admired the grace and authority that people like Nesbitt and Benson achieved in the lettering they executed.

Thinking about those carefree hours we spent among the worn slate markers of Newport's graveyards and of our connections to that part of the country and its rich history helped me to warm to the idea of interring her ashes on home ground. Somerset, Massachusetts, where she'd grown up and we'd lived as a family for twenty-five years, had a few of its own historic graveyards, and in those years of research and study we'd confirmed quite a few Newport-carved headstones among those in Somerset. If I were to inter her remains there, I'd need to mark the location with something fitting and meaningful.

I know you'd have thought it extravagant, and maybe it was. After contacting the Stevens shop in Newport not long after your memorial service, I corresponded with Nick Benson, the shop's current owner and creative director. That correspondence led to my commissioning your stone, its execution by carvers in the shop, and its eventual placement in a historic cemetery in Somerset, within yards of your parents' headstone. Ours is a simple but elegant slate monolith, a lover's knot of interlaced cording carved in relief above your name and dates, my name and birth year below. Some of my ashes will one day join yours in the shadow of that stone. Below all this, four words from a poem by Jane Kenyon, wherein its title: "...so let evening come."

Postscript

*When someone you love dies, you lose them in pieces
over time, but you also get them back in pieces: little
fragments of memory come rushing back through what
they cared about, what brought them joy. If you're
lucky, you get little pieces back for the rest of your life.*

– Anonymous, from *Becoming Duchess Goldblatt*

Dear Judy,

*You knew better than anyone how much I'd struggled through
the course of our life together to focus on the moment. Years of
yoga and meditation practice hadn't completely tempered my
ongoing anxieties about what was expected, what was next,
what would be coming, what needed to be prepared for, what
the future would bring. As you learned to deal with your illness,
you showed me that being in the present was all we really had. I
remember one late summer evening when you were still at home,
sitting together on our deck overlooking our little lake, watching
a thunderstorm move away from us. A rainbow appeared. In
that moment, I thought,* This is what it's all about, this place and
ourselves in it, this moment when our breath is the breath of
the universe. *You occupied the moment, whenever and wherever
you were, and showed me how to do the same.*

*I learned so much from our journey, things I wish I'd learned
earlier in life. Patience, probably more than anything else.
Impatience had always defined me, and you were often victimized by that impatience.*

I once remarked along this line to a colleague, a child development expert, who was quick to reply, "No, in your thirties you probably wouldn't have seen it; you wouldn't have been ready to learn these things that you're learning now." She was right. For years I let ambition lead the way, submitting myself to the tyranny of achievement without thinking much of the shadowed corners of my life where fellow feeling and charity hibernated. Had all this happened a decade or two earlier, I wonder if I'd have taken a route closer to the one Alice Howland's husband John decided to take in Lisa Genova's novel Still Alice. *That's speculative, and I'd like to think not, but then...*

While I never enjoyed the role of warden or ersatz parent, I learned to accept it once I understood that your quality of life depended on it. You might have resented me in those roles, even hated me at points, but I figured out that your resentment was a small price to pay to assure your physical safety and, ultimately, your peace of mind. Alzheimer's excavations were destroying the matter of your mind, and if I could stave off its claiming your sense of security or the tranquility and freedom from worry that I hoped would qualify your days, I felt I had no other option. I suspect that you were as conflicted about this as I was.

At the end I learned that contrary to how I'd always felt, I didn't fear death—neither death in the existential sense nor death in the immediate, right-in-front-of-my-eyes sense. You led me into that awareness since it was evident to all around you that you had no fear in those last weeks, days, and hours. Your acceptance helped my own, and when death came, I was as ready to let go of you as you were to let go of life. There was a lot of gratitude in that moment, and I feel it still.

There's one more thing I want you to tell you. I'm now happily remarried. This is what happened.

You and I both did a lot of grieving through the years of your illness, each in our own way, and sometimes as a twosome. For both of us, there were days that dawned so dark and hopeless that if we'd been able to keep the day's light out and stop time in our black hole, we would have. Fortunately, there were days when we both understood that we could handle it all, and that we would, and that one thing the disease would never take was our love for each other. Therein was the singular victory we could claim.

When your tombstone was planted in hometown turf mid-summer 2016, many East Coast relatives and friends joined me for a small graveside ceremony of remembrance and to bury your ashes. It was a sweltering Wednesday afternoon, the kind of heat you'd always found defeating. In the back of my mind, I could hear you saying to me, exasperated, "What were you thinking?"

A few weeks later, back in Nebraska, I brought another group of friends together to mark the first anniversary of your death. While I wasn't conscious of it, I think I'd begun a long process of wrapping things up, of finding ways to turn my grief and sadness into something different, something more like gratitude, a state of heart and mind in which I could feel pleased as punch that we'd had the time together that we did, in the way that we did. Our marriage, I told myself, was a tough act to follow. Take one day at a time. You've got a life ahead of you, *I kept reminding myself,* find a path. *I knew by then you'd always be with me, and that brought me confidence, much as it had throughout our life together.*

In the shade of a large cottonwood on the edge of Holmes Lake, where you'd once liked to walk and enjoy the comings and goings of passersby, your Trusted Friend *care providers Lisa, Evelyn, Deb, and Pat joined me and Maura, your gentle yoga instructor, as well as Margo Parker and her husband, our minister friend Jonathan, to mark the occasion in a reunion of sorts around an informal outdoor meal that I'd invited them to share. Evelyn and Maura's husbands came too, as did our friend Linda Esterling. Margo and Linda had coordinated weekly visits with you through the five months that you were living at*

Northside Manor, Margo usually taking Tuesday afternoon slots, and Linda, Thursdays. I felt at the time that I had a lot of people to thank for so many kindnesses that were directed at you and me both, and this was part of that effort. It felt very good to see them all again, and you were very much present.

In December I made a three-week trip to India, my first to the subcontinent. It had been in the planning stages since not long after your death, a combination of field work to research a type of traditional painting on textiles produced exclusively in a small corner of the Aravalli hills of Rajasthan and participation in a faculty and student study tour, the first time members of my department would be seeing many aspects of the South Asian textiles and fashion industries up close. While the official objectives of the trip would require all the energy I could muster given the morning-to-night schedule of visits and events that colleagues and I had organized, I went with a secondary and personal agenda. After eighteen months of carrying on, alone in a home where thoughts of you rose no matter where I looked, I needed to put myself somewhere that was entirely unfamiliar. I felt I had to be somewhere that would let me rediscover myself, let me see myself from a completely different angle.

When I stepped from my Delhi hotel on my first full day there, I knew I was in the right place. The assault of wave upon wave of vehicular traffic and the accompanying exhaust, the relentless sound of virtually every wheeled conveyance's horn tapped relentlessly every ten seconds or so, the unruly maneuvering of drivers into, out of, around, through, and over all manner of stationary impediments and obstructions—at times it was breathtaking and nearly heart-stopping. I'd learn that there was, in fact, order in the disorder, but that understanding would come only in time.

With the help of a former graduate student, Raj Kumar, then living back in his home country, I contacted a family of pichwai painters in the town of Nathdwara and over the course of three days got to know them and their family history pretty well. We were welcomed into their home, shown textile paintings that three generations of men in the family continued to produce, and extended a warm hospitality that, I realized, few tourists ever have the privilege to enjoy. The women in the family, grandmother and two daughters-in-law, laid excellent meals before us and added their own unique insights into the family's painting practice. I thought of you and how much you'd have enjoyed meeting these women, proud of their families' accomplishments and, while filling traditional roles in their home life, critical to the success of the business enterprise that made their husbands' and sons' devotional painting viable in an electronic age.

Two weeks into the Indian adventure, I found myself one nightfall on a boat in the Ganges at Varanasi, one of India's sacred pilgrimage cities and one of the oldest in the world. We'd opted that evening to approach one of Varanasi's cremation ghats from the river itself, the better to take in a wide panorama of the smoky scene where multiple cremation ceremonies were underway.

The scene evoked Dante, ten or so small bonfires ablaze as darkness enveloped the clusters of men tending to the remains of their recently deceased family members. We watched as bodies covered in brocades were transported on biers to the water's edge, there to be immersed up to three times, while the sandalwood pyres were prepared. Enclosed by about three hundred kilos or roughly 660 pounds of sandalwood, the bodies would burn for three hours or longer, the resulting ashes commingling on the steps of the ghat, eventually to be swept into the river. From our offshore vantage point, it all appeared otherworldly, ancient, and mystical. I was touched that the family members took everything in hand themselves, that despite it happening in a public space, it seemed nonetheless private and intimate. Not how we do it at home, *I thought to myself, but somehow more satisfying. Only then did I regret not having escorted your body to the crematory. Had I done so, picking up your ashes a few days later might not have seemed so dissonant, so unreal.*

Despite that powerful interface with death and its immediate aftermath, the experience of India seemed mostly about life and the fullness of life. It intoxicated me: the color, all that color; the warm and welcoming people; the harried pulse of large cities and the easygoing pace of small, remote villages; the country's history, woven through vernacular architecture and local cultures, held in ancient walls, in cobbled streets and alleys, in gardens and monuments and in holy enclaves. As a motor coach whisked me along one of New Delhi's major thoroughfares enroute to my flight home, I tried to fix every sight and sound so that I'd never forget all that life I was about to leave behind. On the other side of the world, I'd exit a slim metal tube to the rest of the life I had ahead of me. India helped me realize that living is the point.

That winter merged with spring, and our friend Kitty's words about her finding a new partner resurfaced often, especially on weekend nights when, with a glass of wine in hand, I found Netflix or some other streaming service my only companion. "I'll always love Martin; I'll always miss him. But I came to realize something these last few years. I still have a lot of love in me yet to give. It doesn't seem right not to give it."

As each week and month passed, Kitty's point seemed more and more relevant, more urgent. I knew life was short and precious and found that out the hard way. I believed it had to be lived—no "coulda, shoulda, woulda." I believed you'd have felt much the same, had the tables been turned. "I died," you'd have told me, "and there's nothing you can do about that. You must live your life, so live it." That's what I decided to do.

It was awkward at first, alien and strange, being—at nearly sixty-eight years of age—single again, so unfamiliar with a territory of relationship that hardly resembled anything my youthful self had known. Where does one start? On a short trip to New York, our friend Jay, four times married and unfailingly optimistic in that regard, sat me down in front of his laptop and walked me through the nuances of various dating apps. While they'd served him well, he lived in one of the largest cities on the continent. A far bigger pool, and far less likelihood he'd end up connecting with someone down the block. Not that that would be a bad thing, necessarily. I just wasn't convinced that electronic matchmaking was the route I should take.

So, I started composing a list in my head, single women that I knew, well in some cases, not so well in others, and who struck me as smart, thoughtful, and likely to be worth spending time with. Linda's name kept floating up to the top of the list. I'd add a name, or subtract a name, but hers stayed put right at the top. No other dislodged it. Okay, I said to myself, you're going to have to ask her out.

You and I had known Linda and her ex for several years before their divorce. We'd been casual couples friends, had dined with them a few times, usually with other friends, had crossed paths at the gym, and one Christmas not long after your diagnosis, had spent the day with them and some of their family and friends, a kind gesture on their part knowing that we would be celebrating that holiday alone.

As your disease advanced and our social life shriveled, we lost touch. When we learned a few years later that their marriage had ended, we were too co-opted by Alzheimer's to pay much attention. It wasn't until late in the game that we reconnected with Linda. You'd just had your annual eye exam, and we were looking at frames in the optometrist's showroom. Linda happened to walk in, and despite not having seen her in several years, you recognized her. As our brief catchup came to an end, I told her that you'd be moving full time into Northside Manor the following week. "Let me come to visit you," she said, reaching to hold your hand. "I can make time for that, no problem. Let's plan on it."

Linda enlisted Margo Parker, and almost as soon as you settled into Northside, they were alternating Tuesday and Thursday visits, which they kept up right to the end. A lot of empathy and compassion flowed to you from each of them, and I could see that Linda's allotment of both of those traits was plentiful. You knew it too.

My Friday evening email was sent hopefully. "If you're in something like the same situation I'm in," I wrote, "alone and watching movies streamed on your smart tv each weekend night, maybe you'd like to go with me to a real theater to see a film? Let me know." Since Linda rarely looked at email on weekends, by the time I had her reply the following Monday I'd started to think I wouldn't hear from her. She said yes, and one movie and dinner date led to another, and another, and quick hugs led to holding hands and a first kiss, and we gradually learned a lot about one another, discovered the many interests we shared and the unique obsessions we'd introduce one another to, found our lives intertwining, and saw that we'd fallen in love.

It seemed miraculous to me then, and in some ways it still does. To have had one soulmate with whom to share a full life would be anyone's reward. Unexpectedly, I'd found a second, albeit late in the race but with potentially many laps to go. I like to think that you were in that imaginary grandstand cheering us on, that your spirit blessed us when Jonathan pronounced us husband and wife, that your smile sent us on our way.

And I know now I'd wish this life for you, if you'd survived me.

AFTERWORD AND
ACKNOWLEDGMENTS

Each Alzheimer's journey is unique, complicated, and difficult. No one journey can be definitive, as the variables are too wide ranging. Age at onset, the physiology of the brain and the nuances of the diagnosis, the presence or absence of comorbidities, the personality and temperament of the patient and the patient's caregivers, patients' and their caregivers' social, financial, and racio-ethnic situations or conditions—all these and more are factors in how the disease and its trajectory impact those living it and their communities.

The account detailed herein is true to the best of this writer's recollection. It is faithful to Judy's and my lived experience, both during the period of her illness—from approximately 2007 when the first symptoms appeared, through to her death in 2015–and over the course of the thirty-five years of our marriage that preceded the disease's detectable onset. This memoir is an eyewitness narrative and retelling, scaffolded by notes, journal and calendar entries, medical records, letters to and from family and friends, professional caregiver observations, and photographs and recorded video documentation.

To the extent possible, I've adhered to the chronology of our personal experience while allowing myself some movement backward and forward in time when that seemed necessary for a fuller picture to coalesce. In some instances, I've merged features or details of related experiences or events when by doing so I could avoid either repetition or the "too much information" syndrome. My objective throughout was to document a personal experience of Alzheimer's from the inside out—how the disease showed up one fine day on our doorstep and took up permanent residence, how we adapted to living with and managing it, and what was learned, both by Judy and I and those around us.

I have changed the names and masked identifying details of most of the individuals who appear in this account, except for immediate family members and for several close friends including Judy's longtime business partner Kathy (Doyle) Davis, who always felt like family. All the professional and medical personnel who appear in this book are likewise disguised to respect their privacy and right to anonymity. I've done the same regarding the associations or organizations with which those individuals were affiliated. Similarly, I've changed the names of most businesses and agencies with which we interacted or that provided services, whether paid or unpaid, the sole exception being the Alzheimer's Association. Any resemblances to persons living or dead that may result from the changes I've incorporated are entirely coincidental and unintentional.

Options for in-home care, residential memory care, and hospice care are available in nearly all larger and many smaller communities. For those seeking such information, regional or local agencies providing general referral services to senior populations, or your regional or local chapter of the Alzheimer's Association are good places to start.

Not long after Judy started living full time in memory care, I began an almost daily accounting of the progress of her condition using the free online service provided by CaringBridge. This allowed me to share her condition with the many family members and friends who signed up to receive those online posts. I must start by thanking all of them for the support they offered us through their replies and reflections during those last months of Judy's life. It helped me to know that you shared my grief and had our backs.

While writing this memoir, there were numerous times when I asked myself, "How on earth did I manage all of this?" I'm the first to admit that it was not singlehandedly. In the context of my campus life at the time, I want to thank Marjorie Kostelnik,

Rosanne Samuelson, Sharon Reeder, and Leah Sorensen-Hayes, without whom my experience as a fully employed academic in a caregiving role would surely have been far more challenging.

I must once again thank "Judy's Angels" as I dubbed them, the group of women, unpaid friends as well as paid caregivers, who enriched Judith's life in her last few years, and especially in her last months. Lisa, Evelyn, Deborah, Pat, Maura, Margo—not your actual names, but I think you'll recognize yourselves in these pages—and Linda, the loving companionship you all gave to Judy and the encouragement and support you offered me are testaments to your generosity and compassion. My gratitude is ongoing.

Linda, I singled you out just above because you lived the journey of this book with me, not an easy thing for a new wife entering on a new life with a husband who, by virtue of the project he chose to bring to completion, has had a foot—and sometimes two feet—planted for over two years in his often sad recent past. Our many discussions about our respective lives helped me to frame a lot of this in what I believe is the right light. Your understanding of human nature and family dynamics, your capacity for deep empathy, and our common experience of loss and grief have helped me to see myself, both as a person and as a writer, more clearly and honestly. As my first reader, you raised important questions and caught some inaccuracies or inconsistencies that helped me bring greater exactness to the revision process. Above all, you agreed to join your life with mine and to share in making a home in which books and talk of books are central. I love you for all this and much more.

Sarah Disbrow kindly agreed to serve as second reader, bringing the rigorous eyes and ears of a professional editor to several thorough goings-over of this manuscript. Her questions and comments helped me to flesh out substance where it was lacking, to excise detail when it was unnecessary or redundant, and to reposition mislocated passages to stronger documentary or narrative effect. Encouragement from someone with Sarah's depth of literary experience would be gratifying for any writer, and it was invaluable to this one.

Our longtime Massachusetts friends Patricia Harris and David Lyon, successful professional writers both, kindly agreed to read my third draft. I asked for their candor and unvarnished perceptions, and their feedback prompted a major restructuring of the manuscript that strengthened it and made the narrative's logic and intimacy more convincing. They've always brought enormous integrity to their own work, and if my work can aspire to an equivalent integrity, it's in part due to their example and their generosity.

Incubating this manuscript with the guidance of Phil Whitmarsh and his team at Redbrush here in Lincoln has been both reassuring and affirming. The publishing experience and savvy that they brought to this project, from patient mentoring to careful editing, and through production to distribution, has provided this author much needed perspectives and the confidence necessary to make an independent go of birthing this book and putting it in readers' hands. My appreciation is sincere and deep.

Finally, I tip my hat in appreciation to the gents of the husband-caregivers group of which I am part—Brad, Wayne, Darwin, Ron, Mike, and Glenn—whose own dementia journeys overlapped this one. You tick off every box describing what good men and loyal, loving partners and primary caregivers are made of, and you're each part of the inspiration that incubated this book. What lingering grief I feel, I join to yours; what I've learned, I owe in part to you.

Michael James
Lincoln, Nebraska
September 2022

FURTHER READING

Over the course of, and since, our Alzheimer's journey, I found each of the following titles helpful in different ways at different times. There are hundreds of books about aging, about Alzheimer's and related dementias, and about death and dying. I read dozens. Some were worth my time and others weren't. The following books rewarded my investment in them. They may also be useful to you or to someone you know.

EARLY STAGE(S)

Forget Memory: Creating Better Lives for People with Dementia by Anne Davis Basting (The Johns Hopkins University Press, 2009). Alzheimer's and dementia care have improved in recent decades, if slowly. While some of the programs described in Davis Basting's book are not accessible to many Americans, they suggest ways to approach caregiving both in institutional as well as home settings. The final chapter, "Conclusion: How and Why to Move through Our Fears about Dementia" is particularly insightful.

Alzheimer's Early Stages: First Steps for Family, Friends and Caregivers by Daniel Kuhn, MSW (Hunter House, third edition October 2013) and *The Alzheimer's Action Plan* by P. Murali Doraiswamy, M.D. and Lisa P. Gwyther, M.S.W. with Tina Adler

(St. Martin's Press, April 2008). Both books contain essential information that's straightforward and practical, easy to understand and written in a clear style. Neither sentimentalizes the disease nor the conditions that patients and caregivers alike experience.

Never Say Die: The Myth and Marketing of the New Old Age by Susan Jacoby (Pantheon Books, 2011). Well-researched, smart, pragmatic. Boomers are a big demographic. We will all die. How we age and how we die are issues best paid attention to. Nothing short of cures–still remote–for Alzheimer's and other dementias is going to smooth the passage. So best to face it informed and without illusions. Jacoby details many of the social, economic and health care challenges faced by the aging and aged in the United States and does this realistically and factually.

In Love: A Memoir of Love and Loss, by Amy Bloom (Random House, 2022). Author Amy Bloom was challenged by her architect husband Brian Ameche to "Please write about this." "This" was his decision, in the face of a diagnosis of early onset Alzheimer's, to terminate his life with the assistance of the Swiss organization Dignitas. Bloom sensitively and at times painfully documents the process that led to his committed decision, and to his being approved for physician assisted end-of-life. In telling their story, Amy Bloom recalls the joys and satisfactions of their life together, the difficulties his diagnosis set before them, and she details the realities that condition the choices she and her husband made. In cases such as Ameche's, cognitive agency is necessary for the client to qualify for Dignitas' services, and therefore this option is available only in the earliest stages, when the patient can still be regarded as acting with full understanding and free will.

MIDDLE STAGE(S)

Strange Relation: A Memoir of Marriage, Dementia and Poetry, by Rachel Hadas (Paul Dry Books, 2011). A writer and academic struggles to understand the impact of the disease on her husband, the composer George Edwards, and on herself, using poetry–her own and others'–to try to make sense of her very complicated and conflicting emotions. Hadas has a gift for capturing with great nuance the inner turmoil that at times convulsed her as she worked to navigate the territory of her husband's disease. She sees that world through a poet's lens, and consequently her account is both moving and reassuring.

Beyond Forgetting: Poetry and Prose about Alzheimer's Disease, edited by Holly J. Hughes (Kent State University Press, 2008). This is an unusual collection in that the contents are consistently artful and intelligent, and avoid the clichés and mawkishness sometimes found in dementia-related writing. Most are written by offspring referencing an affected parent, and some by professionals caring for AD patients.

Can't We Talk About Something More Pleasant? by Roz Chast (Bloomsbury, 2014). Chast, the well-known New Yorker cartoonist, was a (sometimes absentee) caregiver for her aging parents, both eventually afflicted with cognitive impairment. She chronicles the challenges of trying to harmonize career, family, and caregiving responsibilities in a very humorous though unflinching survey of her parents' decline and her responses to it.

LATE STAGE(S)

Leaning into Sharp Points: Practical Guidance and Nurturing Support for Caregivers by Stan Goldberg, Ph.D. (New World Library, 2012). When this book came my way, it was overdue. My wife was in her last weeks of life. I wished I'd found it earlier, as it is so loving and level-headed, so grounded in the end-of-life experience with which Stan Goldberg is more than familiar, that it would have provided perspective when I needed it most. If I had only a single book to recommend to AD and other dementia caregivers, it would be this one.

Being Mortal: Medicine and What Matters in the End by Atul Gawande (Metropolitan Books, 2014) and *When Breath Becomes Air* by Paul Kalanithi (Random House, 2016). Two physicians look death squarely in the eye, and accept their own mortality, as we all must. If any books were to serve as prescriptions for how not to fear death, even how to manage to shake hands with it, it would be these two. No human has yet survived life. How we come to terms with that is, in the end, what *living* really means.

AFTERWORDS

The Light of the World: A Memoir by Elizabeth Alexander (Grand Central Publishing, 2015). Though her husband died suddenly and relatively young of a heart ailment, the author's work of coming to terms with grief and loss grabs hold of their universality and provides solace to anyone grieving the loss of a spouse or partner, regardless the age or the disease. "Flowers live,"

Alexander writes, "they are perfect and they affect us; they are God's glory, they make us know why we are alive and human, that we behold. They are beautiful, and then they die and rot and go back to the earth that gave birth to them."

The Best Day the Worst Day by Donald Hall (Houghton Mifflin Company, 2005). The late New Hampshire poet and author wrote extensively about the life and death of his wife, the poet Jane Kenyon, not least in his collection of poems titled *Without*, published after her death. Their experience of her leukemia was naturally different from a couple's experience of one or the other's dementia, but the post-mortem grief and loss are much the same. This very human account of their shared end-of-life journey and his survival is Donald Hall at his best, speaking to the reader on very personal terms.

The Art of Losing: Poems of Grief and Healing edited by Kevin Young (Bloomsbury, 2010). There are many experiences represented in this collection of poems, all addressing mourning – its diversity and its inevitability. While most of the works assume that the beloved is gone, many offer insights that are equally relevant to the kind of slow and extended "ambiguous grief" that qualifies dementia journeys.

FOOTNOTES

1 https://en.wikipedia.org/wiki/Whole_Earth_Catalog

2 https://www.nia.nih.gov/health/what-happens-brain-alzheimers-disease (retrieved 08.12.2020)

3 https://www.barrons.com/articles/women-make-great-financial-advisors-so-why-arent-there-more-51559952001

4 http://www.aricept.com/

5 Alastair Reid, *Whereabouts: Notes on Being a Foreigner*, Albany, CA: North Point Press, 1987, p. 24

6 https://www.webmd.com/drugs/2/drug-14335/aricept-oral/details (retrieved 10.06.2020)

7 https://pubmed.ncbi.nlm.nih.gov/19645027/

8 https://www.dementiacarecentral.com/aboutdementia/life-expectancy-calculator/

9 https://www.alzforum.org/news/research-news/gammagardtm-misses-endpoints-phase-3-trial

10 Stephen Sondheim, *Look I Made a Hat.* New York: Alfred A. Knopf, 2011, p. 7.

11 https://www.alz.org/alzheimers-dementia/what-is-alzheimers/younger-early-onset

12 https://www.census.gov/library/visualizations/interactive/2014-2018-median-household-income-by-county.html

13 https://www.alz.org/alzheimers-dementia/facts-figures

14 The author credits colleague and husband-caregiver Dr. Wayne Kaldahl, DDS, as the source of this aphorism reminding us that multiple factors condition each single case of Alzheimer's or related dementias, and that no two cases are entirely uniform nor predictable. Dr. Kaldahl in turn credits author Renée Harmon as his source; she in turn credits an internet search where she first encountered the phrase: https://www.reneeharmon.

com/2020/03/23/if-youve-seen-one-case/.

15 https://www.psychiatrictimes.com/view/finer-points-delusional-jealousy

16 https://www.agingcare.com/topics/295/anosognosia

17 J. Hollis, "Providing the Soundtrack for Life's Last Moments," *The New York Times* (August 1, 2020). https://www.nytimes.com/2015/08/02/jobs/providing-the-soundtrack-for-lifes-last-moments.html?smid=url-share.

18 https://en.wikipedia.org/wiki/Common_Burying_Ground_and_Island_Cemetery

19 See *Memorials for Children of Change: The Art of Early New England Stonecarving* by Dickran and Ann Tashjian. Middletown, CT: Wesleyan University Press, 1974.

PERMISSIONS CREDITS

I thank the copyright holders for permission to reprint excerpts from the following works.

Anonymous, excerpt from *Becoming Duchess Goldblatt* by Anonymous. Copyright © 2020 by Anonymous. Used by permission of HarperCollins Publishers.

Julian Barnes excerpt from *Levels of Life*, published by Alfred A. Knopf, copyright © 2013 by Julian Barnes. Reprinted by permission of Penguin Random House LLC (US).

Wendell Berry excerpt from *["Many with whom I mourned the dead"]* from *This Day: Collected and New Sabbath Poems 1979–2012*. Copyright © 2010 by Wendell Berry. Reprinted with the permission of The Permissions Company, LLC on behalf of Counterpoint Press, counterpointpress.com.

Louise Bogan excerpt from *Leave-Taking*, first published in *Poetry*, Volume XX No. 5, August 1922. https://www.poetry-foundation.org/poetrymagazine/poems/15668/leave-taking Work in the public domain.

Bono excerpt from *Surrender: 40 Songs, One Story*, copyright © 2022 by Bono. Used by permission of Bonanza Books, an imprint of Penguin Random House LLC. All rights reserved.

Pema Chödrön excerpt from *When Things Fall Apart: Heart Advice for Difficult Times*, published by Shambala Publications,

Inc. Copyright © 1997 by Pema Chödrön. Reprinted by arrangement with The Permissions Company, LLC on behalf of Shambhala Publications Inc., Boulder, CO, shambhala.com.

Baltasar Gracián excerpt from *The Art of Worldly Wisdom*, translated by Christopher Maurer, published by Doubleday, copyright © 1992 by Christopher Maurer. Reprinted by permission of Penguin Random House LLC (US).

Rachel Hadas excerpt from "Loneliness" from *Strange Relation: A Memoir of Marriage, Dementia and Poetry*, copyright © 2011 by Rachel Hadas, published by Paul Dry Books, Inc. Reprinted by permission of Paul Dry Books, Inc.

Donald Hall excerpt from "The Grandmother Poem" from *The Best Day the Worst Day* by Donald Hall. Copyright (©) 2005 by Donald Hall. Used by permission of HarperCollins Publishers.

Susan Jacoby excerpt from *Never Say Die: The Myth and Marketing of the New Old Age*, copyright © 2011 by Susan Jacoby, published by Pantheon Books. Reprinted by permission of Penguin Random House LLC (US).

Paul Kalanithi excerpt from *When Breath Becomes Air* by Paul Kalanithi, copyright © 2015 by Corcovado, Inc. Used by permission of Random House, an imprint and division of Penguin Random House LLC. All rights reserved.

Jane Kenyon excerpt from "Otherwise" from *Collected Poems*. Copyright ©2005 by The Estate of Jane Kenyon. Reprinted with the permission of The Permissions Company, LLC on behalf of Graywolf Press, graywolfpress.org. All rights reserved.

Diane Rehm excerpt from *On My Own*, copyright © 2016 by Diane Rehm, published by Vintage Books. Reprinted by permission of Penguin Random House LLC (US).

Trained as a visual artist, Michael James has had an unconventional career in both the private sector and academia. His textile art is included in numerous public and private collections, including those of the Smithsonian American Art Museum, the Museum of Arts and Design in New York City, the Museum of Fine Arts, Boston, the Baltimore Museum of Art, and many more. He joined the faculty of the Department of Textiles at the University of Nebraska–Lincoln in 2000, concluding that tenure twenty years later as Professor Emeritus and Chair Emeritus. He is the recipient of two Visual Artist Fellowships from the National Endowment for the Arts, and an NEA-sponsored USA–France Exchange Fellowship. He lives in Lincoln, Nebraska, where he continues studio and writing practices, and helps to sustain connections among a close-knit group of husband caregivers of dementia sufferers.

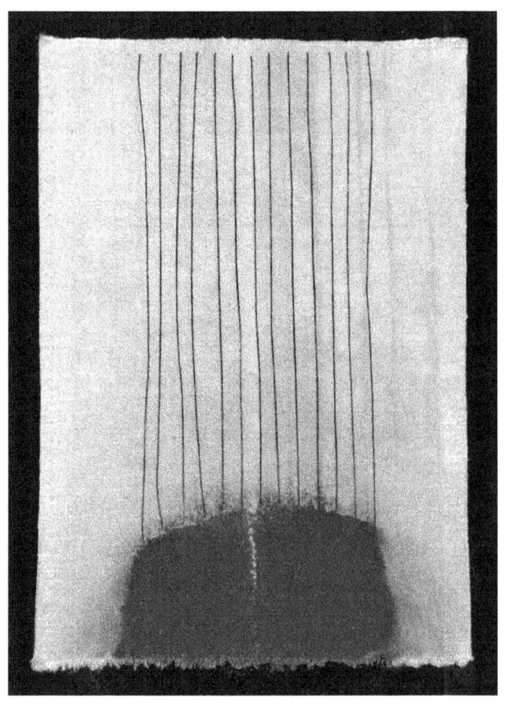

Artwork by Judith James can be viewed at this website:

www.judithjamestextileart.com